MURDER HE L

MURDER HE LIKED

A Half-Century of Tribulations and Trials

Nathan Cohn
with Rory McGahan

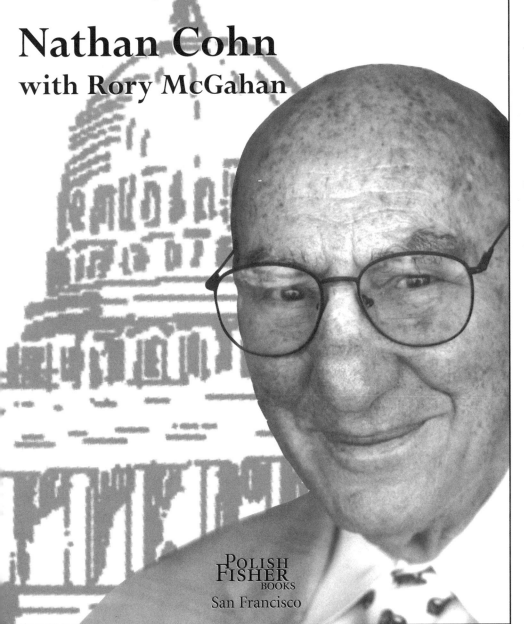

POLISH
FISHER
BOOKS

San Francisco

Murder He Liked

Published by Polish Fisher Books, San Francisco CA
San Francisco CA 94109

ISBN 1-59975-488-6

9 8 7 6 5 4 3 2 1

Printed and bound in the United States

Design: Lupe Edgar

PRINTED IN U.S.A.

Dedicated to my wife and partner, Carolyn Cohn

Acknowledgements

This book has been the fruit of many years of tales, tellings and torment putting a life in order, and I would like to thank some of those who made it possible, beginning with my fellow members of the Calamari Club, incomparable friends and companions. I would also like to thank my many friends in the American Board of Criminal Lawyers and my friends in the Irish-Israeli-Italian Society of San Francisco. I would like to thank Ivor Morris and Hank James for their many years of friendship; the officers and members of the American Board of Trial Advocates; Al Scoma, friend and fine *restauranteur* of many years; Jerry Flamm, for his unflagging encouragement of this book; Alexander and Yami Anolik; Michele Hays and Daniel Fiske, co-publishers of *Verdict* magazine and their fine organization, the National Coalition of Concerned Legal Professionals; Mary Ellen Flynn and Colleen Benson, for their many hours transcribing my sometimes prolix tales; U.S. District Court Judge Samuel Conti and Dolores Conti; Eddie Powell and the members of the Landsmen; John Shimmon, a good friend and Secretary of both the Calamari Club and the Irish-Israeli-Italian Society; Stephen Passalacqua, District Attorney of Sonoma County; Carolyn Carpeneti; Mayor Willie Brown; Mayor Gavin Newsom of San Francisco and his father Hon. William A. Newsom; my doctor, who kept me alive this long, Maury Kelisky, M.D.; Frances Morris; Tempest Storm; and Daniel P. Foster, for his care in reviewing and improving this book.

—Nate

Contents

Photo Credits

Cover Photo John Ravnik

p. 17 Bob Campbell

p. 28 Courtesy San Francisco Press Photographers Association and Nathan Cohn

p. 33 Frank Ortiz

p. 47 San Francisco Examiner

p. 48 Sid Tate

p. 53 San Francisco Chronicle (top); Emil Ederson (bottom)

p. 70 San Francisco Call-Bulletin

p. 71 Courtesy San Francisco Press Photographers Association and Nathan Cohn

p. 86 San Francisco Chronicle

p. 87 San Francisco Chronicle

p. 95 San Francisco Examiner

p. 111 San Francisco Chronicle

p. 112 Courtesy San Francisco Press Photographers Association and Nathan Cohn

p. 115 Courtesy San Francisco Press Photographers Association and Nathan Cohn

p. 117 Courtesy San Francisco Press Photographers Association and Nathan Cohn

p. 196 Moulin Studios

p. 289 Courtesy Nathan Cohn

p. 307 Courtesy Nathan Cohn

p. 345 Morton-Waters Co.

p. 356 Joe Rosenthal

p. 358 Courtesy Nathan Cohn

p. 365 Courtesy Nathan Cohn

p. 367 Courtesy Nathan Cohn

Preface

The first time I met Nate Cohn, he bade me sit in his office while he regaled me with tales of gubernatorial campaigns in which he participated, laws he had suggested, cases where he had beat the gas chamber, national professional organizations he had built, contributions he had made to the practice of law across the country. It was fascinating. Not only did he have a great record of wins in criminal cases in the United States (and could show the statistics to back it up, too)—but he had obviously foregone a career as a stand-up comedian.

As the hours passed, he told me of gypsies, bookies, movie stars, strippers, bankers, moguls, union bosses, and more. Through their lives, his eyes sparkling and the corners of his mouth smiling, he described the San Francisco that existed before Fisherman's Wharf was for tourists, when Pier 39 formed part of port teeming with ships from all over the world, when the days of the "Barbary Coast" were still a living memory for some, but where the Hobbesian hedonism of Gold Rush days had been tamed to a City where openness was a virtue—as long as nobody "got hurt".

This is the San Francisco of legend—every bit as much as in the novels of Dashiell Hammett; moreso, because it is built on the facts of the cases fought over a fifty-year period—where, in a bar lit by a single naked bulb, the City's cons, cops, judges and prosecutors and defense lawyers mixed business with pleasure. The bar closed when the owner got tired, took his coat from the rack and turned out the lights. Mail addressed to "North Beach, USA" somehow arrived.

San Francisco was home to America's most successful general strike; highly publicized newspaper wars and leaps from the Golden Gate Bridge. It was the City where a Police Chief was chosen by the Bishop and the Fire Chief by the Masons, and where unsavory-looking characters were turned away at the airport by a special police detail who gave them return tickets because, in San Francisco, the police ran the town.

On St. Patrick's day, a Jewish deputy grand marshal rode with the Irish Catholic grand marshal, driven by an Assyrian; where one of the semi-annual events politicians were best advised not to miss was the luncheon of the Irish-Israeli-Italian Society, whose letterhead declared it open to all races, colors and creeds, and which united them by a drinking song.

It was the City that famed columnist Herb Caen called "Baghdad by the Bay," with its most garishly pastel-painted stucco houses this side of Tijuana standing astride gingerbread Victorians; whose City Hall had been rebuilt to specifications by then-Mayor "Sunny Jim" Rolph, requiring its dome to be larger than the Capitol rotunda in Washington, D.C. It was a time when the word "dot" was part of the word "polka," before wine bars and condos and live-works and Vespa scooters, when it wasn't a source of embarrassment to work one's hands, whether building ships or handling the cards of a poker deck.

That openness spawned a breed of attorneys who fought with words and with fists, who made the courtroom—where the conflicts of this crazy-quilt world worked themselves out—into theater, where a trial could become *Guys and Dolls* and the jury laugh until they couldn't stop, or it could become *Les Miserables*, and the defendant Jean Valjean. When the City Attorney objected that the Plaintiff's attorney's closing was immaterial and irrelevant, the judge replied, "You're right, but I'd like to hear how the story ends…" There, the acquitted defendant (and victim—it WAS an unusual case!) invited everyone—judge, jury, bailiffs, defendants, defense counsel, prosecution, and witnesses—to a party hosted in his own bar to celebrate the conclusion.

There is no one better than Nate to tell the story. Everyone knew his Silver Cloud Rolls-Royce, which floated down the street at its casual pace with the license plate "Nate"—the first vanity plate issued, under a law he proposed—from the owner of the sky-scraping Transamerica Building to the impecunious plier of the street in front of Nate's office whose pocket held a donation of cigars from Nate.

Nate represents the spirit, now nearly lost, of the time, of the place, of the approach to life that Nate explains "I gross a lot of money, and I spend lot. I believe in keeping money in circulation. Give the other guy a shot at it."

Let the tales spin.

—Rory A. McGahan

Looking Backward

Cop-killer Harold Miller today
a strange bit of remorse over hi
of Police Inspector Denis Bradl
Miller says he's sorry it wasn't
Inspector ⬛ Girard, instead.
The string⬛aired ex-convict s⬛
Girard "bea⬛e up and was alwa
me."
"I'm sorr⬛⬛cop (Bradley) w⬛
killed," he declared at City Prison.
"If it had to be anyone, I wish it ⬛
have been Girard.

In over fifty years of practice as a lawyer I have represented people from all races and religions. I have represented Hollywood actors and musicians. I have handled both civil and criminal cases. But it has been murder cases that I enjoyed most.

I guess it has to do with my father.

I grew up in circuses and carnivals. My father loved to gamble and early became expert at pool, operating a poolroom in Baltimore which doubled as a gambling institution, later graduating from operating the privilege car of a circus, where members of the circus could play poker and other card games, to owning and operating carnivals and circuses. On occasion, he would take over an entire hotel suite for week-long, high-stakes poker games. While high-stakes poker was never to my taste, I found the same thrill in trying murder cases. Luckily, I never lost a client to the gas chamber—and I won more often than I lost.

My grandfather, Samuel Cohn, had brought his family to this country from Poland and was a tailor of great reputation in Baltimore. When my father was thirteen years old he was bar mitzvahed and, in the Jewish tradition, became a man and left school, taking a job in a pool hall racking balls and cleaning up. Over the next few years he became a proficient pool player. When he was twenty-one years old, he opened his own pool hall, which he named Kid Polish's.

My father was known as "Polish" because his family had come from Poland. He was also called "polish" because he was so smooth.

The pool hall had two floors, with pool tables on the lower and billiard tables on the upper. At one o'clock in the morning, my father would put a headboard at the top of one of the billiard tables and run a crap game. He never bet on the game, but he ran the table. Someone would put down a twenty-dollar bill and the gamblers would take any part of the twenty-dollar bill they wanted, or someone would put down a hundred-dollar bill, and six or seven people would take different denominations of that bill and cover it. The shooter would shoot, not against the house, but against the other participants, and on big pots my father would drag down small amounts of money to cover the costs of running the pool hall—and the crap game.

You could find the top gamblers in Baltimore at my father's pool hall shooting anywhere from twenty dollars to five hundred dollars—even a thousand dollars on some occasions.

In front of my father's pool hall, a newsboy named William sold the morning newspapers. William would work from nine o'clock at night through to the next morning. He also kept watch for the police sergeant who kept that beat.

The sergeant came into my father's pool hall quite often, but by the time the sergeant reached the second floor, the crap shooters, forewarned, would all be playing billiards and the sergeant would express his surprise that such well-dressed gentlemen would play billiards at two, three and four o'clock in the morning.

Every morning, my father would give William five dollars and buy all the papers William had left.

No one complained about the game. Everybody who played enjoyed it. But the sergeant kept coming and my father began to think about ways to allay the sergeant's suspicions—until William came to the rescue.

William considered himself a prizefighter, and he made my father a proposition. If my father would get him a fight, my father would get ten percent.

My father went to the gymnasium supply house and bought a punching bag, a heavy bag, a bicycle, a table and weights. He cleared away a place on the second floor and told William from then on he would pay William to come in and train there at night. William started training each night at midnight and trained until morning. When the sergeant came in, he found well-dressed gentlemen watching William train.

My father explained that since William was used to being awake during those hours and was more alert then, it was the best time for him to train.

"Somewhere along the line, this guy's got to fight. He can't just train!"

And William did fight. My father arranged a preliminary match. Even the sergeant came, and William won by a knockout. Of course, my father had fixed the fight, but it was a preliminary, and no one lost anything, and William kept fighting in preliminaries and knocking his opponents out.

My father was very happy. His friends were watching William train, and when the sergeant wasn't there, they would shoot dice—and my father would drag down his share.

However, every lucky streak breaks. After several months, William told my father a promoter had called from San Diego who wanted him to fight the champion there.

When William returned to Baltimore, he had beaten the top fighter in San Diego. He had also changed his name. He now called himself "Kid William."

William's victory had gone to his head and he wanted my father to change the name of the pool hall to "Kid William's and Kid Polish's." They argued. William kept coming at my father, pushing his finger at him and my father slapped him down—not a good showing for a fighter—and that was the end of "Kid William's."

My father continued to run the crap game, but the sergeant grew more suspicious; it was time to sell the pool hall and get a job.

As luck would have it, a circus was in town and they were looking for someone knowledgeable in gambling to run its "privilege car."

In those days, circuses traveled by railroad. Circus equipment was transported on railroad flatcars and the circus performers and hands rode in Pullman cars. Many of the performers and hands would sleep in the Pullman cars rather than pay for a hotel even when the circus was in town. The train also had a closed car, known as the "privilege car," which was exclusively for the entertainment of circus people themselves. Inside the privilege car there were tables for cards, poker, pinochle, blackjack and dice. The operator of the car was allowed to drag a little money from each pot and in this way he could make quite a bit of money.

When my father told the general manager of the circus about his credentials, the manager was impressed, but when the manager asked my father for his name, my father thought if something bad were to happen he didn't want it to reflect on his father in Baltimore. He recalled having passed a sign at the entrance of the circus for an aerial act, "The Flying Fishers."

"My name is Fisher."

"What is your first name?"

"Harry." (My father had a brother, Harry Cohn).

Thus, my father took the name "Harry Fisher," and because he was nicknamed "Polish," he became known in show business as "Harry Polish Fisher" and went on to become one of the top showmen in the country.

<hr />

In my many years in court I learned a lesson. Luck—or fate, if you prefer it—changes people's lives in so many ways we never can know, and this book is filled with examples of luck, or fate.

So it was when I was young I decided I wanted to become a lawyer after observing an attorney win the release of a young man in Florida held on false charges.

At the time, my father's circuses and carnivals traveled up and down the East Coast. At the end of October each year, he would put the show in winter quarters in Florida where we would repair it, repaint it and fix it up for the next year. My father, mother and I would then vacation in Florida for a month or two.

One year, when we went to Florida and checked into the hotel where we usually stayed winters, the clerk informed my father the rates had doubled.

"There is a boom going on here. When you go out, you will see real estate offices with long lines in front of them of people waiting to get in. People are buying land in Florida without even seeing it and, without knowing where it is. When they buy a piece of property, as they go down the line, they can sell the property for a good profit before they ever leave the real estate agent's premises!"

"They don't see the property?"

"No, they're buying property under water, they're just buying property. Everybody is buying property right and left."

When we went across the street for breakfast, the restaurant was packed. In those days, you could get bacon and eggs, coffee and toast, for a dollar, but when we looked at the menu, the eggs were a dollar an egg, and the toast was a dollar, and the bacon was a dollar. My father started talking to the owner, who informed him that people were coming to Florida in droves to buy property.

My father called all the employees of his carnival and gave them orders to take the show out of winter quarters; we were going to play throughout Florida that winter. Money was so fluid people would go to the carnivals and play the games as if they were throwing money away.

The way my father handled all that cash was somewhat unusual.

My father had a large wagon that he used for an office. Twenty feet away he placed a tent which was empty, except for two steamer trunks. Across these two trunks he laid a brand-new mattress. He would have someone stay in the tent with the two trunks at all times, and at night, when everyone turned in their receipts, he would have them throw all the paper money in one trunk and all the silver money in the other trunk. One fellow would sleep on top of the two trunks overnight, and the next day, when the banks opened, my father would put the two trunks on the back of a truck and drive them to the bank, and the bank would count the money.

On our way to Tampa that winter we saw a young man standing on the side of the road trying to hitch a ride. There were no other cars anywhere. My father stopped and asked the young man where he was going. He was trying to get to Tampa to look for a job.

My father offered him a ride with us and sat the young man in the back seat with me. He'd had been standing on the road in the heat for quite a while and his body odor was so bad I could hardly stand it even after I opened the car windows to try to get the smell out.

The young man introduced himself to us and told us his name was Johnny. My father looked him over and announced, "I'll tell you what. When we get into Tampa I'm going to give you some money. Go somewhere and take a bath, then buy some new clothes. The clothes you've got on, just throw them away. Then come out to the carnival." He gave Johnny a twenty-dollar bill—which would be like giving somebody a five-hundred dollar bill today.

Three hours later, Johnny showed up in red corduroy pants with shiny new shoes and a dark-colored shirt and windbreaker. He looked like a million bucks—considering what he looked like when I first saw him.

My father showed Johnny the two trunks that were being used to hold the money before taking it to the bank and my father showed Johnny the mattress that went on top. My father explained he would pay Johnny a good salary to watch the trunks. If he had to go to the men's room, all he had to do was to open the front flap and someone in the office would see him and go down and keep an eye on the tent for him. My father would have somebody from the cookhouse send him three meals a day.

It was a very easy job.

We were going to play Tampa for one week. However, the business was so good we decided to stay over another week. By Monday night, business had slowed down a bit, but we still had a big crowd.

I was out on the midway when I saw two policemen come on the lot with an older man and a younger man, both of whom were pointing and gesturing. I wanted to know what the policemen were doing on the lot. You very seldom saw any policemen on the lot unless there was some special reason for it.

I saw the two policemen go over to Johnny's tent and go inside. When they came out they had Johnny in handcuffs. I rushed to the office wagon and told my father what was happening.

The policemen explained that these two men were father and son. They drove a laundry route, and someone had held them up and taken $140 from them. The policemen said the men told them the robber wore red corduroy pants and that they had been to the show the week before and they had seen a young man with red corduroy pants and that they believed this was the same man.

My father was quite friendly with a feature writer for the Tampa newspaper and my father called him up. When the writer heard about what had happened he told my father to find out where the policemen were taking Johnny.

"I'll have a friend of mine come down there, a top-notch lawyer, and I'll meet you there."

My father took me with him in his car, and we drove downtown to police headquarters. Johnny was sitting in the cell and the two men were there, too, giving information to a police officer. When the columnist arrived, he brought a man who seemed to be the best-dressed man in Tampa, and my father explained to them what he knew of the story.

"Over the weekend there were thousands of dollars in those trunks, and we didn't even know how much money was there—we didn't count it. Johnny could have easily picked up a couple of hundred dollars and we would never have known it."

The attorney talked to the captain for ten minutes, then the captain told the two plainclothes policemen to take the father and son to opposite sides of the police station.

They took the father in one room and they told the father that the son had said the robber had a hat on down over his eyes so you could hardly see his face, and that he had on red corduroy pants and a black jacket, and that he had a shiny pistol that had six chambers with bullets in the chambers and that the robber had said: "This is a robbery, and this is a gun, and if you try to make any trouble you'll both be dead, so give me the money." The father confirmed it.

They went to the son and told him that the father had told them that the man had no hat on and that he had nothing on except a jacket and the red corduroy pants and he had a large .45 automatic in his hands and that he didn't say a word; he just motioned toward the money, then put his hand down and took the money from them and walked away without saying anything. When the son confirmed this story, the officers arrested the father and the son and let Johnny go.

The attorney laughed and patted the officers on the back.

My father asked the lawyer how much he owed him.

"Nothing. It was fun. I had more fun tonight than I've had in a long time. I just finished a long case (the columnist told us he had won it, too), and this really relaxed me. I had a ball."

"Do you have any children?" my father asked.

"Yes, I have three."

"I'll tell you what: whenever you want, you bring your three children and all their friends—all their friends—and I'll make sure they enjoy the carnival as no kid ever enjoyed a carnival before." My father also asked the columnist if he had children and invited him to bring his son and all his son's friends as well. All the kids could ride the carnival rides as long as they wished.

A few nights later, the attorney and the columnist came to the carnival lot with a car full of children. My father took them to every concession, and every child won the best prize in the concession. Whatever the concession had—novelties, stuffed animals, plaster of paris dolls, candy—they won. My father gave them each dimes and they'd put down a dime and the concessionaire who was running the wheel would stand by the wheel and when it came to their number he would take his hand

and stop the wheel and say they had just won a prize. The kids went wild. They rode all the rides and saw every show.

At the end, the attorney told my father, "You know, Mr. Fisher, I've got to tell you something. I've received a lot of large fees, I've been very fortunate, but this is the best fee I've ever received. I want to thank you."

I looked at this man and thought: "What a job this guy's got. He gets innocent people out, he makes money, and he's enjoying himself. You know, when I get old enough to go to work, I want to be a lawyer."

That's how the idea of becoming a lawyer came into my mind. When I entered myself into high school I told the counselor I wanted to be a lawyer, and she explained that I would have to learn Latin to become a lawyer.

The first semester I did well with Latin. Then I started going out for sports. I went out for basketball and track and baseball, and I was busy and I didn't study Latin. In the last semester, I failed Latin.

I thought I had better take another language, because I wanted to go to college. I knew a little Yiddish, because my grandmother spoke Yiddish, so I took German. It took the teacher a month and a half to wake up to the fact I wasn't talking German, I was talking Yiddish with what she thought was an accent. Then she gave me another incomplete.

Someone told me that Spanish was the easiest language, so I then took Spanish for two years and passed that.

And at that time, I gave up the idea of being a lawyer, because I didn't know Latin.

How to Get Your Picture in the Paper

2

It wasn't until many years later—1943, to be precise, when I was working in the shipyards—that I returned to the idea.

I was bored with working in the shipyards. Many of my colleagues there were sharecroppers from the South and until then had only worked on farms. Most of the young men who were educated had gone into the service. I'd been drafted several times, but I was working for a man who didn't know anything about building a ship but who'd been hired by Kaiser to do so. I was his assistant, and every time my name came up he would write to the service that I was essential.

My colleagues only talked about was how many acres of land it took to feed a cow, or what they had done the day before at the yard. I found it monotonous.

My father had always had great respect for the Masons and suggested I join them, and obtained an application for me from a friend. I put in an application to become a Mason at Paul Revere Lodge in San Francisco.

When you apply, the Masons investigate you thoroughly, and the last thing they do is to bring you before the officers of the lodge to be interviewed. They asked me to come over to one of the officer's homes.

I arrived early, and while I was sitting there waiting to be called, an energetic young man came in.

"How're you doing? My name is Andrew Bodisco. I'm an Assistant District Attorney in San Francisco and the reason I want to join Paul Revere Lodge..."—the words exploded with enthusiasm.

I threw up my hand. "I'm not one of the people interviewing you, I'm here to be interviewed, too." Just as suddenly—as if I had let the air out of a balloon—he said "Oh," and sat down.

We both passed the interview and were accepted, and we took the degrees, and we came to know each other quite well, because we would go on the same night to be coached on the Masonic rituals. The rituals were all oral and had be memorized. Andy had trouble memorizing them because he was working as a District Attorney. But I didn't have anything on my mind except working at the shipyard which didn't take any great intelligence. The coach would tell me the ritual one time, and I would know it. I'd then spend time with Andy coaching him.

Andy told me, "You know what? You've got a total-recall memory. With your memory you would be a great lawyer"

"But I don't know Latin!"

"You don't have to know Latin—maybe eight, ten phrases, and you can learn those in ten minutes. Nobody talks Latin, lawyers talk English. There's nothing to it." He suggested San Francisco Law School.

I went down to San Francisco Law School, which was a night school, and I saw the Dean, Packy McFarland. I told him what I'd been doing. and I explained I hadn't been to college.

"Well you've got a pretty rounded education in life. What we'll do is we'll let you in as a special student. That means if you get a B average or better through the whole four years, we'll give you a degree. If you don't get a B or better average and you get a C or better average, we'll give you a certificate of completion and you can take the Bar; you won't get a degree, but if you pass it you'll be able to practice law." That sounded fair to me.

Law school came easy to me because I had been working as a journalist and writing advertising copy, so I knew how to write and I knew how to see a story. I could look at the questions on the exams, take them apart, see what the elements were and answer them, and I did it very quickly. I would finish a three-hour exam in about an hour and a half.

One of the instructors in Contracts took me out for coffee after the first exam.

"You know, you're upsetting the other students. You're in for a three-hour session and you're walking out in one hour."

"Yeah, but I'm passing."

"Passing? You're getting A's! But you're making the other students nervous—and the fact that you're getting A's is making it worse. What you should do after this is stay in the room. Sit there and don't leave for at least two hours. If you're finished in an hour, just go over it and correct it or re-read it or pretend you're re-reading it—whatever you want to do. Just stay in there at least two hours."

After I graduated from law school, Andy told me the next thing that I should do was to get some group of people that might come to me as a lawyer. I had a ready clientele in the Show Folks of America.

My father had been working as general manager of Cole Brothers-Clyde Beatty Circus back east when World War II broke out in Europe and President Roosevelt began the lend-lease program. America was building ships and everyone was going to work, and it was getting too hard to get people to work at the smaller jobs in a circus such as putting up tents and taking them down.

So, my father decided he would hold on the circus business until the war was over, and he came back to San Francisco and rented a store at 28 Taylor Street where he sold novelties. What he stocked was determined by what people came into the store to sell. My father didn't care whether he needed it or whether he could sell it, he would buy it anyway.

He divided the store into two sections. In the front half was the cash register and all the merchandise that was on sale. In back, carnival and circus people would hang around and "cut up jackpots"—they'd tell war stories about their experiences in show business.

If someone came into the front of the store, one of the circus people would go into the front and make the sale. Each would make up his own price for what he thought the traffic would bear, then he would put the money in the cash register. Every day or two my father would go to the cash register, take the money out and put it in the bank, or he would use it to buy more stock. Sometimes my father and mother would take their car and visit other carnivals, leaving the store open, giving the key to someone who would hang out in the back and, if a customer came into the store, sell them merchandise and put the money in the cash register.

One of the carnival people who hung around in the back was Mary Ragan. It was Mary whose husband had obtained the application for the Masons for me. Mary decided the circus and carnival workers should form an organization.

She contacted Show Folks of America, and Show Folks of America issued Mary a charter. She knew a lawyer in town who put together a nonprofit corporation, and I asked some relations to be the incorporators.

We decided to have the first meeting across the street from my father's store in the lobby of a hotel because we couldn't get everyone in the back section of my father's little store.

Show Folks of America raised money by donations. In those days, $50 was a big donation, but we raised quite a few hundred dollars and moved over to Market Street, renting a huge loft several floors up, and members went there to fix it up. Jac Brown decorated the entire loft in a circus motif with clowns. Others donated rugs and chairs, and soon we had quite a nice club room on Market Street.

When the circuses and carnivals closed at the end of September and the show people came to San Francisco, they had nothing to do, and I would take them out canvassing door to door for politicians. The carnival people all knew how to make friends and get people on their side. I'm afraid some of them weren't as honest as they should have been—but that was politics.

Show Folks supported some of my candidates, and when the candidates were elected, they knew that part of their success was due to the carnival people who had gone door to door for them, so the candidates would come to the meetings of Show Folks of America, and make pledges as well. That was politics, too.

———— • ————

In 1947, when I took the bar at the Native Sons of the Golden West Auditorium, a very beautiful young blond girl came and sat next to me. I watched her and before the exam, her hand was shaking so badly she could hardly hold the pen; so I leaned over and said, "Do me a favor, miss. Either write big or wear short skirts." She started laughing, and it relaxed her completely.

Years later, when I was practicing law I needed something from the Corporations Commission and I sent one of my employees over there. When he came back, he announced, "Man, are you strong in the Corporation Commission! When I mentioned your name there the attorney in charge of the section dropped everything to take care of you. She said her name was Nancy Cannon and to give you her regards."

"Deathwatchers" by Bob Campbell. (l-r) Mr. Guzman, Mrs. Rhodes, Nathan Cohn.

I told the first person I saw there who looked as if he might have some authority that these were my clients and that I would like to ask some questions at the inquest, if this was possible. The gentleman checked with the Coroner and reported back that that would be fine, and I demonstrated for my clients my easy manner with a Coroner's office I had never seen.

In the meantime, Jerry Flamm, a reporter for the *Call-Bulletin*, was at the Coroner's office with a photographer. So were reporters and photographers from all the other newspapers. I knew Jerry and asked if his photographer could take a picture of Mrs. Rhodes and Mr. Guzman and me. When the other photographers saw us being photographed, they rushed over, too, and soon, the shutters were clicking away at myself and my clients. Maybe I would get in the newspapers after all...

At the inquest, the Coroner showed the film Guzman had taken while Dusty was preparing for the jump. The room was dark except for the screen. I was sitting next to Mrs. Rhodes and Mr. Guzman when I noticed Bob Campbell, one of the photographers for one of the larger papers, had moved down near us when it was dark and had turned around to to take a picture of Mrs. Rhodes and Mr. Guzman. I leaned over close to my clients.

The Coroner's inquest held the death of Dusty Rhodes was accident. My clients were very grateful.

When the newspaper came out the next day, there was Bob's photograph, over the caption: "Deathwatchers" and it won a photojournalistic prize. The picture that Jerry Flamm had his photographer take also ran in the *Call-Bulletin*, but his editors cut me out of the photograph.

It was time for Joe McNamara's comeuppance. I told Joe everything went precisely as I had predicted.

He never lived it down. Until the last day I knew him, Joe McNamara couldn't believe it. And he never understood that it was all an accident.

Getting Popular in Jail

3

A
s a result of my initial successes, I became very popular at the county jail. It would have been more effective for my career if I had become popular at the Pacific Union Club—the one thing all my prospective clients had in common was that they could not make bail—but so it was.

One of the first calls I received was from a Pentecostal Minister. I thought I was in luck—a respectable client with an income—but when I went to the jail to see him, I found I was not so fortunate. He worked at another job during the week and was only a minister on the weekend. He had a few dollars, and he would pay me if I represented him. Since I had no bankers waiting in the wings, I took his case.

He had a jury trial coming up. I had never even seen a jury trial, so I prepared everything I could think of—which was a great deal less than it is today. We had no discovery and no *Miranda* rights. A defense attorney had no idea what evidence the District Attorney had. However, the District Attorney was also in the dark as to what evidence the defense had.

The complainant was a 13-year-old girl who claimed the minister had sexually molested her. He was charged with "lewd and lascivious conduct with a minor," a felony, and "contributing to the delinquency of a minor," a misdemeanor. The distinction proved to have a very interesting significance in the case.

My client claimed the girl was trying to get back at him for not lying for her. She had asked him to say that she was working for him one evening when she actually planned to go out.

I was facing a serious opponent. The District Attorney assigned to the case, Tom Feeney, had just received a great deal of publicity for successfully prosecuting a fireman who had locked his children in a closet, and Feeney was a brilliant orator of the old-fashioned Irish type.

On the other hand, I was so inexperienced I couldn't even pronounce the charge against my client. The court reporter, Percy Gervin, corrected me during a recess: "Mr. Cohn, the word is 'lascivious'—not 'lass-vicious'."

But when I cross-examined the complainant on the stand her testimony began coming apart. She became angry, and the jury could see it. I could see in their faces that I had scored.

When the jury came in, they acquitted my client of the felony. But they convicted him of the misdemeanor of "contributing to the delinquency of a minor." I was stunned.

When I asked the foreman of the jury to explain their reasoning he said the judge had instructed them that if the defendant caused the youngster to commit a crime, that was contributing to the delinquency of a minor. He said they wanted the judge to know that they believed the girl had committed a crime by bringing false charges against my client!

Judge I. L. Harris gave my client a suspended sentence.

As for Tom Feeney, he became a Superior Court judge.

I was winning cases. Every time I won a case in criminal court there was some item about it in the newspapers, and I was building up a small reputation because I was lucky.

One case involved three Irishmen who had been drinking quite heavily. They walked out of a bar and found a man standing there. Two policemen, who were walking down the street, testified to what they saw happen next. One of the Irishmen became angry, started swinging at the man and knocked him down. The policemen claimed they saw the man give the Irishman his wallet and his watch while lying on the ground.

My defense was that the complainant had suggested something pornographic to my client, who reacted. In the excitement, the gentleman had lost his wallet and watch. My client had reached over to pick them up and give them back when he was arrested.

When the jury went out to deliberate I began walking back to my office, but by the time I reached it the verdict was in. The verdict acquitting my client had come back after only 10 minutes of deliberation.

The next week, I received a phone call from a friend of mine in the District Attorney's office. "I've got to talk to you, Nate. It's the funniest thing you've ever heard." He asked me to meet him at the courthouse for lunch.

"The D.A. called a meeting about you. He said you got a verdict in 10 minutes in a case that should have been won by the D.A. The D.A. says what happens is that in the preliminary hearing you ask questions that seemingly don't have anything to do with the case and then later you use them to blow these things up way out of proportion, so he told us: 'From now on, watch Nate in the preliminary. If he brings in something you don't think has anything to do with the case, go into that.'"

From then on, whenever I had a preliminary hearing I would bring in something that had nothing to do with the case, just to worry the D.A.

One of my clients had a little racket. It was legal, but it was a racket. What he would do is to go down to the wholesale jeweler and buy watches that had expensive names. He'd put them on his wrist and go into a bar. Then, he would pull up his sleeve and tell someone at the bar: "This is a top-notch watch. It's kind of hot, but I'll let you have it for almost nothing. "

He would sell for $20 what he had bought it for $5, and he would make a $15 profit on each watch. He sold hundreds of them in that way.

One day, my client was sitting in his convertible putting some of these watches on his wrist, when two policemen happened by and observed him. They assumed he was dealing in stolen goods and took him down to the Hall of Justice, where the police had a general work detail office. They told my client to put all his property on a shelf on the side of the office while they booked him. My client took everything out of his pockets and put it on the shelf. When the police officers turned back to him, he had a small package in his hand and they asked where he got it.

My client claimed he had found it on the floor and just picked it up to see what it was. It contained cocaine and the police charged him with possession.

Cecil Poole was the Assistant District Attorney assigned to the case. I'd been winning cases from Cecil, and any time I had a case, Cecil wanted to grab it to see if he could win one from me. Cecil went on to become United States Attorney for Northern California, a United States District Court judge and a distinguished judge of the Ninth Circuit Court of Appeals.

When the case came to trial I called the janitor at the Hall of Justice as a witness, and asked him at what time he had cleaned the office. He testified he had cleaned it early in the morning and that no one had cleaned it in between the morning and the time my client was arrested. The police officers admitted that they paid very little attention to the floor, and that they hadn't looked down, that there had been several people in the office who had been charged with narcotics offenses and that it was possible that one of them could have dropped it.

Cecil had the opportunity to cross-examine my client on the stand. At one point, I began to think my client was getting nervous, and I wanted to break up the rhythm, so when Cecil asked him his next question, I interrupted: "Your honor, I object."

Cecil asked the judge the basis of my objection, and the judge asked me the reason for it.

"It's not fair."

"That's not an objection," Poole interjected.

The judge agreed.

"Well, it ought to be…"

I saw the jury nodding their heads in agreement.

My client was acquitted.

I Sue
Sinatra

5

Because of my background with Show Folks of America, I came to represent many clients in the entertainment industry, including some of the best nightclubs in San Francisco. This brought me in contact with musicians such as Billie Holliday and Duke Ellington, comedians such as Jack Soo and Don Rickles, and Hollywood actors. The best known, however, was Frank Sinatra. My involvement with him came about through a lawsuit I brought to protect a friend of mine, the columnist Jack Rosenbaum.

On a Sunday morning in August of 1962, I was awakened early by a telephone call from a client, Jimmy Jaye Perini.

Jimmy went by the name of "Jimmy Jaye" and published a small weekly magazine called *Friday* which featured stories about the entertainment appearing that week in San Francisco's nightclubs.

Jimmy would go to the nightclubs and take pictures of the patrons and publish them in *Friday*, which was distributed free by the nightclubs.

Jimmy explained that he had been at New Facks nightclub the night before taking pictures of some of the patrons and was taking a picture of an attractive young couple who were very anxious to be in the magazine. Unfortunately, Jimmy had failed to notice that Frank Sinatra was at the next table.

When the flash went off, Sinatra went into a rage, grabbed Jimmy by the tie and started to choke him. Sinatra's two bodyguards, both well over six feet and 200 pounds, held Jimmy's arms while Sinatra choked him with his tie. Finally, a man came out of the crowd shouting, "You're choking him!" and Sinatra let go of Jimmy's tie.

George Andros, the owner of New Facks—and also a client of mine— came rushing over, demanding to know what the commotion was.

George told Jimmy to give him his camera, which he did, and Andros handed it to Sinatra who took it to the hatcheck room, took out all the film and tore it up, then threw the camera to the ground and stomped it to pieces.

Andros, according to Jimmy, then apologized to Sinatra and told Jimmy he would talk to Sinatra and buy Jimmy a new camera.

It was still early on a Sunday morning and I was wondering why Jimmy was telling me this whole story.

"Were you injured?"

Jimmy said it wasn't serious.

I asked what Andros said he would pay for camera.

Jimmy said $600.

I told Jimmy he could sue Sinatra if he wanted to, but that I didn't think he would get much. He might get some punitive damages, but that would be a long process, and he would make an enemy of Sinatra and probably George Andros, too.

The broken camera. Nate and Jimmy Jaye examine camera broken by Frank Sinatra.

He decided to let it ride and I went back to sleep.

The next morning was Monday and I had stopped for a donut and coffee at a cafeteria at Seventh and Market on my way from the federal court at Seventh and Mission, when I saw the front page of the *Examiner.*

Jack's column was on the front page. That was unusual, because Jack usually appeared on the front page of the second section. And it wasn't a column, it was a news story with Jack's byline.

It turned out to be word for word what Jimmy Jaye had told me the day before.

When I got to the office, my number one secretary told me that George Andros had called me and wanted me to listen to the radio because, he said, he was going to make me famous.

I tuned in, and George was being interviewed about Jack's story in the *Examiner.*

George said the incident never happened. Nothing even remotely like what Jack had written took place in his club. Listening to George, you would have thought Sinatra had been in a room at the Vatican at the time.

I don't know how he thought he was going to make me famous, but I was a little surprised at George because, as far as I knew, Jimmy's story was true; and as for Jack, he had always been helpful to George. I supposed George was afraid of losing his friendship with Sinatra.

Three hours later, it was Jack on the phone. Sinatra's lawyers had called his publisher and demanded a retraction. Otherwise, they claimed, they would sue the *Examiner* for defamation.

Jimmy's little dust-up was creating quite a wake. I told Jack not to worry and I told him to talk to his publisher and tell him to leave it to me. I would take care of it.

I immediately called Jimmy and told him to come over to my office—with what remained of his camera. When he arrived, I had a shorthand reporter and a photographer there.

I had Jimmy tell his story under oath, and it was exactly as he had told it when he ruined my Sunday morning, and exactly as it appeared in Jack Rosenbaum's story.

I put the pieces of Jimmy's camera on a little table on the side of my desk and had the photographer take pictures of it. I also had an investigator go out to New Facks and talk to George's employees, who corroborated Jimmy's story.

That afternoon, I drew up a complaint: *James J. Perini versus Frank Sinatra and John Does*, and filed it in the Superior Court as Case No. 524350. I then took the complaint to the press room at City Hall and left copies there for the reporters.

In the meantime, the *Chronicle* had published a front-page story claiming Jack and the *Examiner* had published a false story about Sinatra.

When the reporters from the *Chronicle* read the complaint I'd filed they were shocked.

"Nate, why didn't you tell us?"

"You wrote the story last night. If you had contacted me, I would have told you not to write that story."

I had nothing against Sinatra. I was doing it to help Jack.

At that time, I had an office in Beverly Hills which Ed Bardin ran for me, and I had my secretary send a copy down to Ed to see if he could serve Sinatra.

Ed Bardin called and said he had a young law student who served subpoenas for him. He asked if I would pay him $100 for serving Sinatra. I said, "Sure."

A week later, Ed Bardin called to say he was sending the proof of service.

It turned out the City of Hope was holding a dinner honoring Sinatra at one of the big hotels in Los Angeles. The young man borrowed a tuxedo from a friend of his and went down to the hotel.

In front of the room where the dinner was being served, there was a long table where people could go and pick up their table assignments. At the end of it were white ribbons saying "Committee." The young man went over and picked up one of the ribbons and pinned it to the lapel of his tuxedo, then walked into the dining area. When he saw Sinatra, he walked over to him.

"You're Frank Sinatra?"

"Yes."

"I've been told to deliver this to you."

He handed Sinatra the summons and complaint and walked out.

The next day, I received a call from a young attorney in the law office which represented Sinatra.

The young man had the theory that I was trying to shake Sinatra down.

He went on, telling me how important he was because he represented Sinatra and that he was going to prove the incident never happened.

I let him talk. After he finished, I suggested that he had accomplished a good deal for his client: now I would not settle cheaply.

I sent Sinatra interrogatories asking about his holdings. The lead attorney in the firm then called me and I explained why I had sent the interrogatories. I told him of the conversation I had had with his associate. He told me he was going to assign the case to his number one man and he was sure we would settle the case, but after my conversation with the young attorney in his office, I insisted I would have to have a good settlement.

In the end, we settled the case for much more than I would have requested if the young lawyer had been courteous, and Jimmy was able to pay a doctor's bill, buy a new camera, and receive money for the time he spent in my office. And Jack's reputation was safe.

I filed a request for entry of dismissal of the case with prejudice on March 13, 1964.

—————•—————

Some time later, I was representing a prizefighter by name of Thad Spencer. At one point in 1968, Thad was rated the number one heavyweight in the world. Thad was to fight Amos Lincoln on the same card as Muhammad Ali and Floyd Patterson in Las Vegas on November 22, 1965. Thad's trainer, Willie Ketchum, invited me to watch the fight.

I took some of my staff; my son, Norman, who was an attorney at that time, Ivor Morris, who was one of my close friends; Mike Berger, another close friend; and a client who at one time ran the entire state of California: Artie Samish, the lobbyist.

Artie knew everybody in Vegas. It was the night before the fight, Thad was with Willie and resting up for the fight. Artie said "Let's go out on the town."

After we saw the different shows, Artie said to all of us, "I'm going to give you a real treat. Do you like Chinese food?"

We did—and we piled in several cabs and proceeded to the Sands Hotel.

Artie told us about the cook at the Sands Hotel, Soey Fong. Soey had been the chef at Don the Beachcomber's in Palm Springs, and was the greatest Chinese chef in the United States.

Looking at Artie, one would guess that when it came to food he knew his subject well. Artie was some 100 pounds overweight.

The waiters set up a table for us at the Sands. We were about twelve people by that time, having picked up some other friends on the way. As we walked into the room, on our right was a table with some thirty people at it, including Dean Martin, Joey Bishop, Corbett Monica and, in the middle, Frank Sinatra.

Sinatra's table had not an item of food on it, and you could see they had been waiting for some time.

Artie told the waiter to tell Soey Fong that he was there.

The waiter came back with a Chinese chef in a white outfit and big hat. Soey ran over to Artie and vigorously shook Artie's hands.

"Artie! What do you want?"

"I want you to pick it out, just bring us some good food. "

Artie introduced Soey Fong to everyone at the table.

Sinatra saw us and he came over. "Hello, Artie. I just wanted to pay my respects to you."

Artie introduced Sinatra to everyone at the table, too. When Artie introduced me, Sinatra looked at me and gave a wry grin.

"Yes, I know Mr. Cohn. I've known Mr. Cohn for a while."

Sinatra talked to Artie for a few minutes and then went back to his table.

Jack Entratta, the General Manager of the Sands Hotel, hearing that Artie was there, also came over to our table to give his respects to Artie, and asked if there was anything he could do for Artie.

"You know I am the one who sent you Soey Fong. He's the greatest Chinese chef in the United States. You told me you wanted to open a Chinese restaurant in the Sands and I told you the best cook would be Soey Fong and you made an agreement with me that Soey would be the highest-paid chef in Las Vegas. I hope that you remember that."

"Don't worry. It's all been taken care of, Soey's happy and every-body's happy."

Then, all of a sudden, out came Soey Fong with a table on wheels, loaded with all kinds of food, and two or three waiters started splitting it up and putting it in front of us.

Sinatra's table looked over—they hadn't been served a thing and they had been sitting there before we'd even arrived. I felt a little embarrassed.

We were about halfway through the food when Artie told us not to get stuffed. He said there was going to be a lot more food coming.

In the meantime, Sinatra still had not been served. After twenty minutes more, Soey Fong came out with another table with wheels and was serving us again.

At that point, Frank Sinatra stood up, took the empty plate in front of him and threw it across the table, shouting "What do you have to do to get 85 cents worth of chop suey in this Goddamned joint?"

"Frankie, you're the king. You can have anything you want…" one of his entourage quipped.

Sinatra stomped out. When Sinatra walked out, Frank Sinatra Jr. went out after him and two of the four bodyguards Sinatra had posted around the table went out with them, but the rest of the ratpack remained seated, laughing.

We finished our meal and went on.

The next night, Thad Spencer fought Amos Lincoln, and lost on a split decision.

Nate counsels Thad Spencer, heavyweight contender, just before his fight with Brian London in Manchester, England, 1968.

After the fight, Artie asked Thad what he would like to eat—
"Chinese…"

Artie told Thad he would take him out for the best Chinese food in the country, and we ended up back at the Sands.

Frank Sinatra was there again, this time in front, while we had a table in back. All Sinatra's party were already eating when we arrived.

Jack Entratta spied Artie again and hurried up to him.

"You got me in a lot of trouble with Sinatra last night!"

"Fuck Sinatra!" Artie said, loud enough for everyone to hear.

Sinatra and his party went on eating. No one said a word.

"Nate, We Could Have Got Rich"

One of the first cases I handled proved to be the largest drug case on the West Coast until that time. It began in January of 1948, about six weeks after I started practicing law. By that point, I had handled several jury trials and had done quite well with them.

A young man called me from my most regular source of clientele, the county jail, and said he had been arrested for possession of a large amount of narcotics. Unlike our modern-day druglord defendants, however, he didn't have much money. The most he could raise was about $750.

This was how the case had come about.

He had been a sailor on a ship coming from Hong Kong. When the ship docked in Los Angeles, customs officials boarded the ship in large groups and searched the ship from stem to stern. They had a tip, the members of the crew told him, that a large shipment of heroin intended for delivery in San Francisco was coming into the United States on the ship. However, the customs officers came up empty-handed.

When the ship docked in San Francisco, customs officials again came on the ship and searched it thoroughly, but fruitlessly.

On the ship were square wooden bumpers used to prevent metal containers from striking the deck and giving off sparks which might ignite when loading and unloading.

After the customs officials had come and gone, the young man saw that one of the bumpers had some material showing, and with a chisel and hammer pulled up some of the wood. He found some packages buried in this large bumper. The wood in the middle of the bumper had been cut out and packages placed in there. My client told me he didn't know what the packages contained, so he closed up the bumper and the next day when he was leaving the ship, took the packages with him in his boots and tied around his waist.

Customs officials were waiting. They seized the packages and arrested my client. He told them he was taking the packages off the ship to see what they were. If they contained narcotics, he intended to turn them over to authorities, but if it contained something of value he would try to make a few dollars. The officials told him the packages contained heroin. In fact, it was the largest shipment they had ever had in San Francisco, and he was being charged with its possession for sale.

I explained to my client that I had only been practicing law a little over a month and a half and, although I had tried several cases before juries, I had never had a case in federal court. The young man didn't have much money with which to hire another lawyer and said he had been told that I had tried the Superior Court cases very well, so he hired me despite my limited qualifications.

I told him I would try and see what I could do for him, but from what he told me, I admitted, there did not seem too much I could do.

The case was assigned to Judge Goodman, who was very knowledgeable and tough. The prosecutor was the top Assistant U.S. Attorney in the office, Reynolds Colvin. Colvin had tried many, many cases, but this was my first federal case.

I used what I could find in the case. When I started to cross-examine the prosecution witnesses, I found that the customs officials claimed they had entered the ship in disguise. They had overalls on and were dressed as longshoremen, but for some reason they still wore their customs caps and I tried to ridicule the customs officials.

When I started to ask a question and the U.S. Attorney objected I would try to explain to the judge why the objection should not be sustained. Soon, Judge Goodman called me up to the bench with the U.S. Attorney.

"Mr. Cohn, I see what you're doing, and I don't allow that. From now on if you try to tell the jury what the law is, or try to tell the jury why you asked the question, I'm going to hold you in contempt."

This had worked well for me in state court, but, apparently, wouldn't pass in federal court, so I was learning.

Then my client took the stand.

He was a good-looking man in his early 20's and he told the jury exactly what he told me: he had discovered the packages and didn't know what they were. He thought the contents might be valuable and was taking it off the ship when he was arrested. If he found out they contained narcotics, he would have turned it over to Customs. That was his defense.

Colvin cross-examined my client pretty thoroughly, but the young man held to his story, and I could see the jury was very sympathetic. Several women on the jury had sons his age.

In the closing argument, I retold his story and reminded the jury that the U.S. Attorney had the obligation to prove his case beyond a reasonable doubt and, if they believed my client, there was a reasonable doubt. I also reminded them that my client was a young man with his whole life before him, facing a very severe sentence.

Everyone expected the jury to be back in an hour with a conviction, but they were out several hours. Finally, Judge Goodman called them back. They were deadlocked, and he was determined to break the deadlock.

"I'm going to give you another instruction. I'm instructing you that even if the Defendant did not know what the object was and it was heroin, he is guilty of possession of heroin for sale. I want you to take that instruction into consideration and come back with a verdict."

As soon as he excused the jury, I stood up.

"Your Honor, may I make a motion?"

"Yes, Mr. Cohn, go ahead."

"I make a motion for mistrial."

"On what grounds?"

"The instruction you gave is not according to law. In order for my client to be found guilty, he must have knowledge that he was committing a crime. Yet, under your instruction, if he didn't know what the substance was and the jury believes him, the jury must still find him guilty.

"I'm going to take your motion under submission and rule on it later."

Two hours later, the jury came back with a verdict of guilty. Several of women on the jury were crying, and I could see they had only reluctantly followed the court's instructions.

Judge Goodman excused the jury and directed Mr. Colvin and me to return in a week for sentencing.

At that time, federal judges were giving sentences for narcotics violations of up to thirty years.

The next week we came back before Judge Goodman and I reminded the judge that I had a motion before him.

"I'm going to do the sentencing first, and then I'll address your motion."

"Thank you, Your Honor."

Judge Goodman said he had thought about the case and gave my client a short sentence in an adult reformatory and five years probation after that.

I was shocked.

"Now, we'll proceed with your motion."

"Your Honor, I withdraw the motion."

"Thank you, Mr. Cohn."

When I sat down to talk to my client afterwards, he surprised me.

"Nate, we could have got rich."

"What?"

"We could have got rich. They were giving odds in jail that I would get a minimum of 20 years in the federal penitentiary. We could have bet and got good odds that I would have gotten less than twenty years and we would have gotten a lot of money."

Several years later my client called me and told me he had learned to be a shoemaker in the reformatory and had given up sailing. I never heard from him again.

Newspaper
Wars

Years ago, the most powerful of the newspapers in San Francisco was the *San Francisco Examiner*. The *Examiner* was the Hearst newspaper, and Bill Wren, its editor, was one of the most powerful men in town.

One of the *Examiner*'s columnists at the time was Bob Patterson, who wrote under the name "Freddie Francisco." However, Bob's way of getting a story was not always as jocose as his moniker.

One day, Patterson called up a well-known gambler in San Francisco—Bones Remmer—and asked him to drop by his office. When Remmer arrived, Patterson explained that someone had told him an embarrassing story which concerned Remmer, and he was going to have to write about it in his column. It wasn't a personal thing, Patterson explained, he hated to embarrass Remmer, but business was business, and this kind of thing was Patterson's business. Patterson said, however, that if Remmer were to give him $500, he might be persuaded not to put the story in his column.

The gambler thought about it but, being a gambler, five hundred dollars did not mean very much to him, and he pulled out his wallet and took out the money, then reached over to give it to Patterson. At that moment, the doors of Patterson's office burst open. Flash bulbs popped and camera shutters clicked in rapid succession. Photographers took pictures of the gambler giving Patterson $500 in cash.

The next day the pictures of Patterson and Remmer exchanging money appeared on the front page of the *Examiner* under a headline declaring Remmer had tried to bribe Patterson.

Remmer hired an attorney who gave a press conference at which he explained it wasn't bribery. "How do you bribe someone for not writing a story?"

But things didn't end there. The gambler hired an investigator to investigate Patterson—the sort that hire themselves out to look for lost heirs, not Sam Spade—and the investigator found that Patterson had a criminal record a mile long and had served time in prison.

The investigator gave the information to Remmer, who, in turn, offered it to the *Examiner's* competitors. The other newspapers didn't want it. Newspapers in San Francisco were friendly rivals.

Frustrated by his reception in San Francisco, Remmer tried Los Angeles. In Los Angeles he found a man named Jimmy Tarantino, who put out a magazine, *Hollywood Night Life*. Tarantino would go to different night clubs in Los Angeles and take pictures of the celebrities in the clubs, and the nightclubs would advertise in his magazine, which the nightclubs would, in turn, distribute.

Remmer went to see Tarantino and proceeded to make Tarantino an offer he could hardly refuse. He would give Tarantino the story about Patterson's penal background and Tarantino would put it on the front page. Remmer, in return, would buy all Tarantino's magazines and take them to San Francisco and distribute them.

Thus, one morning, all over San Francisco, there was Tarantino's magazine. Remmer had even hired people to go up and down the stairs at City Hall handing it out.

Bill Wren, the *Examiner's* editor, was upset. He had the *Examiner's* lawyers file an injunction to stop Tarantino's magazine from being distributed. The Hearst people back east, however, were more circumspect and they told the *Examiner's* lawyers to drop the case. Hearst's east coast lawyers didn't want to set a precedent for enjoining the distribution of news, because it could also be used against them.

San Francisco's mayor at the time was Elmer Robinson, a friendly Mayor who tried to make everyone happy. Robinson proceeded to try to bring Tarantino and Wren together. But when it came out that the *Examiner* had dropped its suit against Tarantino, Tarantino refused to meet. Tarantino thought he had made the *Examiner* back down. He thought he had beaten William Randolph Hearst, and he let it go to his head.

For several weeks, Tarantino printed more of the same about Patterson in his magazine, referring to Wren as "the secret boss of San Francisco." Wren grew angrier. Soon, Tarantino would learn how mistaken he was. Wren had two police inspectors installed in a hotel room next door to the Belvedere Hotel where Tarantino stayed. The inspectors bugged Tarantino's closet and recorded everything that went on in Tarantino's room.

Eventually, they put together a case and the District Attorney charged Tarantino with doing exactly what Patterson had done: when Tarantino was doing a story, the complaint alleged, he would call the subject up to his hotel room and offer not to run the story in return for money. Tarantino, however, didn't ask the subject to give him money directly. He would ask him to put a $500 ad in Tarantino's magazine. Often, the subject would point out that if they put an ad in Tarantino's magazine, it would have his name on it. Tarantino had a simple answer to that, too. He could have the ad simply say: "Anonymous." There was at least one ad in every issue which read: "Anonymous."

Tarantino came to me and asked me to represent him. I told him what my fee would be. When Tarantino told me he couldn't afford it, I told him he couldn't afford me.

Tarantino also had a man working for him selling ads named Al Siegle. The District Attorney wanted a more serious charge against Tarantino than extortion, so he charged Tarantino with conspiracy. Conspiracy required two conspirators, and the District Attorney called Al Siegle before the grand jury to be charged with the crime of conspiracy.

I agreed to represent Al. Al Siegle had no money at all, but Al was a friend; Tarantino wasn't.

Al called me and told me he had been subpoenaed to appear before the grand jury. I agreed to go with him to the grand jury, and I started to look up what to do. I had tried quite a few cases, and I had been very lucky and very successful, but I had not handled any cases before the grand jury.

When I started looking through the Penal Code, I found Section 1323.5, which stated that if you are being investigated by the state grand jury, and you are a possible subject of an indictment, you are not a competent witness to appear before the grand jury unless you request to do so. Until that time, no one had paid any attention to that section of the law. Some of the finest lawyers had missed that section entirely.

In those days, HUAC (the House Un-American Activities Committee) was holding its hearings on "communist influence" and the Kefauver Commission was holding its "rackets" hearings and everybody was "taking the Fifth," asserting the Fifth Amendment privilege against self-incrimination.

I didn't like the idea of a person taking the Fifth, because if someone refused to answer on the grounds he might incriminate himself, it sounded to the public as though he had done something wrong. Anyone who did "claim the Fifth" was sure to be convicted in the press before the trial even started.

Grand jury proceedings are secret, and I couldn't go into the grand jury room with Al, so I prepared a paper for him to read: "My name is Al Siegle, and I've been advised by my attorney, Nathan Cohn, that under Section 1323.5 of the Penal Code, I am not a competent witness to testify before the grand jury unless I request to testify, and at this time, I am not requesting to do so and I ask to be excused."

A few minutes after Al entered the grand jury room, the District Attorney came out, looking perturbed. Al Siegle came out of the grand jury room shortly thereafter. The District Attorney had left to look up the Penal Code and the grand jury had released Al.

A reporter from the *Examiner*, Ernie Lenn, was covering the grand jury, and Lenn walked up to Al and asked him if he had taken the Fifth. Al denied it and Lenn thought he was lying. He didn't understand how Al could have come out of the grand jury so fast.

"He didn't take it," I assured Lenn.

"What did he do, then?"

I said he had told the grand jury what the law was.

The grand jury indicted both Al Siegle and Jimmy Tarantino.

After the indictment came out I went down to the Hall of Justice to bail Siegle out. As I was walking over to the Hall of Justice, I thought to myself that I had been lucky with my cases, but few people had heard about them. Now, I finally had a case where there was some publicity, I was ready to go to trial, and if I took it to trial and won, everyone would know how good I was!

I entered the courtroom and told the judge I wanted to go to trial immediately. The case was before Judge Eustace Cullinan and Cecil Poole was prosecuting. I had been lucky on a few cases, and I was confident I could win at trial.

However, Tarantino did not have a lawyer. Tarantino told Judge Cullinan he had a lawyer in Los Angeles who was going to represent him and was coming up to San Francisco to tear up the town. I thought that would be good—Tarantino would have a good lawyer and that would mean more publicity.

But that lawyer did not come to represent Tarantino. Tarantino came back at the next hearing and said he had another lawyer instead who would represent him, a lawyer who had defended one of the members of the State Board of Equalization in Los Angeles. That lawyer also never appeared.

The next time the case was called, I announced again that I wanted to go to trial. I asked the judge to set a trial date. I could not understand how they could hope to show conspiracy, and I thought I could get my client off easily.

The next week, the grand jury was back in session, and another client of mine, Benny Barrish, called me. Benny was a bail bondsman and a former prize fighter. He was a character everyone liked.

Benny Barrish told me he had been handed a notice to appear before the grand jury, and I told Benny to come up to my office and I would give him a paper which would tell him what to say.

I went down to the grand jury again, this time with Benny Barrish. Benny read the same lines that I had had Al Siegle read, and a few minutes later, Benny Barrish came out of the grand jury room. A reporter, again, asked him if he had taken the Fifth, and Benny told him truthfully that he had not.

The Assistant District Attorney, by this time, had figured out what I was doing, and asked me how I had found that section of the Penal Code. I told him it had been in the Penal Code all the time.

Benny Barrish was indicted, and I went back before Judge Cullinan to set bail for Benny Barrish. I was back in the same courtroom, before the same judge and the same District Attorney, and, again, I announced I wanted to go to trial. Judge Cullinan reminded me my client was out on bail, and that the bail was quite low. If my client had had a high bail the situation would have been different, he opined, but it wasn't; and he continued the case. I declared again that I wanted to go to trial—I would go to trial on Al Siegle's case, I would go to trial on Benny Barrish's case, I would go to trial on both cases, but I wanted to go to trial.

Judge Cullinan assured me that since my clients were out on bail, I had no problems.

The next week, the grand jury was back in session again and they called another client of mine to testify, Jimmy Jaye. Jimmy Jaye was also a friend of mine. He also had no money.

The District Attorney claimed that Jimmy Jaye had gone to Sally Stanford and suggested that she put an ad in Tarantino's magazine and had told her that if she didn't, she would be sorry. Jimmy denied it. Sally was a well-known restaurant owner in Sausalito and later Mayor of Sausalito (thus, I reasoned, more publicity...). Sally told me Jimmy had gone to her place and asked her to take an ad in Tarantino's magazine, but that she had declined, and that was all.

When Jimmy was indicted, I went back to court to set bail for him. Same courtroom, same District Attorney. I told Judge Cullinan I wanted to go to trial on Jimmy Jaye's case. Judge Cullinan paid no attention. Cecil Poole paid no attention. No one paid any attention. Judge Cullinan assured me that my client was out on bail.

By this point, I was growing disturbed. I had Al Siegle, Benny Barrish, and now Jimmy Jaye, all cases with some publicity attached to them. I was confident I would win any or all of these three cases with little problem, but Judge Cullinan would not let me try them.

The District Attorney then indicted Rudy Eichenbaum for conspiracy with Tarantino. Rudy Eichenbaum had money, but Rudy Eichenbaum did not come to me for representation: the people with no money came to me. Eichenbaum hired Leo Friedman to represent Tarantino and another top-notch lawyer for himself. Now Tarantino had a lawyer, and his lawyer was one of the best trial lawyers in the United States, and Judge Cullinan set down a trial for the indictment against Tarantino and Eichenbaum—but not for Al Siegle or Benny Barrish or Jimmy Jaye!

I demanded a trial again. I told Judge Cullinan I demanded to go to trial and that he couldn't pass up my clients to try Eichenbaum and that the statute said so: the statute said a defendant had to be brought to trial in sixty days.

Nothing happened.

The sixty days passed. I went down to my office and worked all weekend researching the statute. On Monday, I went to the Hall of Justice and began going through their records. There was a big book there which showed what happened in every case. I made a list of the cases. I made a list of all the days there was no one trying cases and filed a writ of prohibition, demanding my clients' cases be dismissed on the grounds that none of them had been brought to trial within sixty days.

I filed the petition and waited to see what would happen. A couple of weeks later, a newspaperman called me and told me that the Court of Appeal was going to hear my petition. At the time, I was so naïve that I believed every case received a hearing at the Court of Appeal—you filed a petition, there was a hearing and you argued. The newspaperman had to explain to me that the Court of Appeal only heard cases they wanted to hear.

On the date of the hearing I went to Supreme Court building in San Francisco where the Court of Appeal was sitting and I asked the clerk what I should do. The clerk told me I should speak loudly, because the justice in the middle didn't hear well.

When the case was finally called, the justices asked me to tell them if I had anything new. I had nothing new, and they began to question me. They asked if I was saying that the state had to use all 24 departments of the Superior Court in San Francisco to make sure that all criminal actions were brought to trial in sixty days. I told them that was true, that the statute says a defendant has to be brought to trial in sixty days, there is only one Superior Court in San Francisco, and the Superior Court had to bring the defendant to trial in sixty days, and it would have to use all the departments to do so, if necessary.

Cecil Poole stood up. The justices peppered him with questions, and he sat down. Clarence Linn, with his long, flowing hair, was next to argue. He was a deputy attorney general, but he thought he was a Supreme Court justice. He imagined he was going to explain everything to the appellate justices, but they battered him with questions instead, and he sat down.

On my way into the courtroom, I had run into a deputy attorney general I knew, Bill Bennett, who later would become head of the State Board of Equalization. Bill Bennett asked me what I was doing there. I told him I didn't know, I was just a country boy, and it was not very familiar territory for me. When I came out of the courtroom, I saw Bill again. Bill told me I had done well, "for a country boy."

The Court of Appeal eventually ruled that all defendants had to be brought to trial within sixty days, or their cases would be dismissed for failure to prosecute. Now it is the rule, but that was the first time a court had so held.

The Court dismissed the case against all three of my clients and the District Attorney re-charged them. I waited sixty more days.

Meanwhile, Rudy Eichenbaum and Jimmy Tarantino were tried and convicted and sent to San Quentin.

The District Attorney offered me a deal for Al Siegle and Benny Barrish—Jimmy Jaye's case had already been dismissed by the District Attorney based on Sally Stanford's testimony to the grand jury. The District Attorney agreed to give Benny Barrish and Al Siegle a $50 fine each if they pled guilty to attempted petty theft, a misdemeanor.

They paid it, and I did not get to go to trial.

I was disappointed. I was trying all these cases, and winning them, but nobody was reading about them…

A Matter of Principle

One of the cases that stands out most in my career is the case of a young man the newspapers called "the smirking killer," a young ex-convict charged with killing a police inspector.

It all began one afternoon when a middle-aged woman walked into my office on Montgomery Street. She looked like she had had a hard life, and I had just settled a personal injury case that morning for an excellent fee and was feeling flush. I listened as she began to tell me the story of her son, Harold.

When Harold was about 13, some boys he knew asked him to join them for a ride. The car they were in was stopped by police, and it turned out to have been stolen.

Harold was in the back seat. He didn't even know how to drive a car, but the other boys in the car came from wealthy families who hired lawyers to represent them while Harold got the public defender, so the other boys went free while Harold was sentenced to a juvenile reformatory.

He was mistreated there and ran away, but the day after he escaped, the police picked him up and charged him with escape from a criminal institution. By this time, Harold was 16 and tried as an adult and Harold went to prison.

While serving his term in prison, Harold learned how to repair cars.

SMIRKING KILLER—Harold Miller, who slew a policeman and escaped the gas chamber, is pictured after he was sentenced to life imprisonment for his crime yesterday.

Cop Slayer Harold Miller Sentenced to Life Term

Harold Miller was sentenced...spector and other officers

When he got out, Harold got a job as a mechanic, but his employer knew that he was an ex-con and treated him like a second-class citizen. Harold made just enough money to support himself and to help support his mother, who was working as a housekeeper.

On Sundays, Harold would go to the aquarium at Golden Gate Park and watch the seals. Sometimes, he would go to the museum or listen to band concerts in the park. One day, while at the park, a fellow who had been in prison with him came over to him and told Harold he had a car parked over by the museum in the parking lot that wouldn't start and he asked Harold to take a look at it.

Harold walked over to the car, opened the hood and adjusted the carburetor. Then, Harold decided to try the car out so he could get the feel of it, so it wouldn't break down again.

As they exited Golden Gate Park, a police car noticed the license plate hanging down by a thread and the police turned on their siren to pull Harold over and tell him he was going to lose his license plate.

Harold, realizing he was one of two ex-cons in a car whose ownership he did not know, slammed on the accelerator. Harold drove into a nearby shopping center at 70 miles an hour, but a car backed out as he was passing and Harold smashed into it.

When the two cars struck, the trunk on Harold's car sprang open, revealing a set of luggage with someone else's name on it. It turned out to belong to a young couple who had

ENDLESS HOURS TO PONDER OVER HIS MISSPENT PAST
Harold (Smiley) Miller Sits With Chin On Clenched Fists In Jail Cell

'I DIDN'T SEEM TO GET ALONG'

Cop Killer Tells Life Story

been honeymooning in San Francisco and had gone to visit the museum and parked their car in the lot. When they returned to their car, their luggage was gone. They had reported the loss to the police, and here was the luggage.

When Harold gained consciousness, he found himself at San Francisco General Hospital. Figuring he was definitely in trouble, Harold tried to escape out the window. The police caught Harold crawling along the window ledge of the hospital, pulled him back in and charged Harold with burglary. They didn't bother to charge Harold with speeding or reckless driving because they already had a felony.

Harold's mother wanted to know if I would represent Harold. Since I was flush with dough and she seemed such an honest lady, I told her I would represent him. My minimum fee for a felony in those days was around $3,000, and she had less than a thousand, but I agreed to represent him for what she had.

The case went to trial at the old Hall of Justice before Judge Twain Michaelson. The other boy was represented by a public defender, William McDonald—everyone called him Billy. He was a very pleasant character. He also happened to own part of a mortuary, a fact which affected the proceedings in an unusual way.

We were selecting the jury, and had reached the point where there was one juror left in the jury pool as the lunch hour was approaching. The remaining juror looked as if he would be exactly the sort of juror I wanted, and I excused another juror to leave him on the jury. Things looked fine, the juror I wanted would be selected, Michaelson would hurry to end jury selection, and we'd proceed to trial after lunch.

Michaelson looked down from the bench. "I guess that's it. No more challenges, right?" Suddenly, Billy McDonald said "No."

"If we do that, we'll have to put it over until tomorrow to get some more jurors."

But Billy went ahead and challenged the juror I had worked hard to get on the jury. We were out of jurors, and the jury selection would have to continue the next morning.

After it was over, I asked Billy for an explanation.

"Well, Nate, I have a funeral at 1:00 o'clock and I wanted to be there because I own a piece of this mortuary..."

"Well, you are liable to go to a funeral you don't expect — you're lucky I didn't kill you!"

Billy just laughed. As I said, he was a pleasant character.

Fortunately, the next day, the first juror was someone I liked, so we added him to the jury and were able to proceed to try the case.

Billy put his client right on the stand, and the young man testified he didn't steal the bags. In fact, he testified he didn't know how the bags got into his car.

I had learned to make my closing last and waited through Billy's closing. Billy made a very short closing argument. In fact, he said practically nothing. Meanwhile, Billy's client was looking at me while Billy was talking: "Isn't he going to make a speech for me?"

I told the boy I would try to take care of him in my closing. I made a closing argument on behalf of Harold, and I also tried to say something nice about the other boy without involving him in my case, and without hurting Harold. When I sat down again, he whispered to me, "Thank you, Mr. Cohn."

The jury acquitted Harold, but convicted Billy's client.

Later, I was talking to another lawyer about Billy: "Nice guy," he said, "the nicest guy you could meet—friendly, courteous, but he just doesn't do a damn thing.

"Let me tell you something. In one case—he was busy, I think he wanted to go to a funeral or something—Billy's closing argument went: 'Ladies and gentlemen of the jury, you are now in a court of law in the State of California. The gentleman sitting up there is a judge, a Superior Court judge. The flag over there is a flag of California. The flag over there is a flag of the United States of America. This is an American court. Many things have not been brought up in this case. I ask you to acquit my client,' and Billy sat down."

"Did he get his client acquitted?"

"Of course not."

Harold, at least, was out of jail. His mother thanked me and Harold thanked me. But Harold had been in jail and his boss had fired him and Harold was out looking for another job.

I didn't hear from Harold for several months. Then I received a telephone call from Harold's mother telling me he had been arrested for robbery.

I told Harold's mother I would go down and talk with Harold, but I was going to have to charge my usual fee. I told her the last time I had represented Harold, I had felt for her and for Harold and let them get away with only paying a fifth of what I usually charge. I told her that this time they would have to pay my regular fee.

When I saw Harold at the jail, the left side of his face was swollen and greenish-blue.

"What the hell did you do? Did you take on the cops or something?"

"No, Nate, it wasn't like that."

It seemed a bar on Valencia Street owned by a gentleman by the name of Jack Lockhart, who had run for sheriff and lost, had just been held up. There had also been a police officer in uniform in the bar. Lockhart claimed Harold had gone into the bar with a gun, seized the police officer's gun, taken the money from the cash register, and sped away.

Inspectors in the robbery division of the San Francisco Police Department were assigned the case. One of the inspectors had the address where Harold lived, which was in a rooming house. After Harold let them in, the police put Harold up against the wall. Then they claimed that they found the policeman's gun under his pillow.

The police took Harold down to the to the robbery detail, and they brought in the policeman who had had his gun taken. They insisted Harold tell them who drove the car.

The officers handcuffed Harold and started beating the hell out of him. They hit him in his face and they kicked him to the ground and then they started kicking him while he was on the ground. Harold had handcuffs on during the entire beating. He showed me his wrists with the indentations from the handcuffs. His face had been kicked in, and was misshapen.

Harold's mother didn't have any money, and Harold told me the charge was phony; that the police put the gun under his pillow. So, I defended him anyway and I filed charges against the officers for the beating.

In the preliminary hearing I cross-examined the police inspector.

"Who beat up Harold?"

"Nobody beat him up."

I asked the inspector if he had been present at the questioning. "Oh, yes."

"Did you see him after the questioning?"

"Yes."

"Didn't you notice that his whole face was bluish-green?" I had pictures of it.

"Oh, you know how Harold is. He can't look you in the eye. I didn't see anything like that."

The inspector gave the same testimony at trial. He denied the beating, but the pictures showed otherwise.

I also asked him if the police had fingerprinted the gun or the bullets. They hadn't. It was a policeman's gun, and he had put the bullets in, so the police had never fingerprinted it.

The jury went out and were out for two days. The judge sent them home and brought them back. In the end, they hung nine to three for conviction.

The case was reassigned to another judge for a new trial. The jury hung again, this time ten to two for acquittal. Harold had been in jail through both trials.

The judge called me and the prosecutor in.

"Nate is gaining. He's gone from nine to three against him to ten to two for him. In another trial, he'll probably win it. Why don't we work out something? Harold's been in jail for months. Why don't you plead him to a second-degree robbery? I'll give him a sentence for the time served and he'll be out tomorrow morning. He's already got a record, so it's not going to make that much difference." (There was no three-strikes law in those days).

I told Harold, and he was pleased.

But what was Harold going to do? In those days, when prisoners were released from county jail they received 15 cents—a nickel and a dime. The nickel and the dime was car fare back to San Francisco from San Bruno where the county jail was. When they reached San Francisco, they had no job. They had no money. They had nothing to eat. They had no place to sleep. They usually got involved in crime again.

Harold met a Chinese man who hired Harold to deliver packages, for which Harold was paid several hundred dollars apiece. They were later found to contain heroin.

Another thing about Harold was that Harold was kind of a nut about guns. He liked guns. Harold had a lot of guns, and he kept them in his room.

Harold jumped over the fence. On the other side, he saw two college kids sitting in a car and he put his gun on them. He told them to drive to Los Angeles.

In Los Angeles, he ran into a theater. The college kids told the police and pointed out the theater Harold had gone into, and the police arrested him inside. They weren't sure it was Harold. If they had been, Harold would probably never have left the theater alive. The Los Angeles police would have taken care of that.

The next morning was a Saturday and Harold was arraigned in a special session. I had a sport outfit on. In those days, one never went to court in anything less than a suit, and I ended up spending more time apologizing to the judge for my dress than I did anything else.

I didn't want to leave Harold out on a limb, so I told the judge I was not sure whether I was going to represent Harold, and that I was only appearing specially for the time being, but had to talk to Harold and make arrangements if I was going to represent him, although I told the judge that I doubted I would represent Harold in the case.

After, I went over to Vanessi's for lunch. There, a police captain I knew well saw me.

"Nate, I understand you arraigned Harold Miller this morning. I thought you were a friend of the police department."

I said I thought I still was a friend of the police department, and I reminded him I had represented quite a few policemen successfully.

"We don't want you representing Harold Miller."

I explained someone had to represent him.

"Yes, but we don't want *you* to represent him."

I wasn't going to have the police department tell me who I could represent.

"Nate, if you represent him, you'll be the sorriest lawyer in San Francisco."

After lunch I drove all the way down the beach to where I could park and look at the ocean, and I looked at the ocean for two hours, thinking about what the hell I was going to do.

I decided to take the case.

Harold had no money, but he had a little car that he drove around which Harold offered to me. In the end, I sold it for $500, and that was used for costs.

When I appeared in Superior Court and announced I would represent Miller, Jake Ehrlich, who was a very good friend of mine and one
of the top lawyers in town called me. "Nate," he said, "you've got a great
reputation, but don't take this case. You've got nothing to gain and you
can really hurt yourself badly."

I told Jake I couldn't have the police department telling me what to do.

"Who knows it?" Jake asked.

"The captain knows it and I know it, and I'm sure a lot of other
policemen would know it if I didn't take the case."

"If I can be of any help to you in any way, let me know—but I tell
you, don't take the case. I'm just telling you. I mean this as a friend."

The captain's wasn't the only or the strongest threat I received.

My son, Norman, was young then. Norman used to send in boxtops
from cereals for whistles and gadgets, which came in the mail. One day
an envelope arrived at my house addressed to "N. Cohn." It felt like it had
one of those whistles, so my son opened it, thinking it was for Norman.
In the envelope was a piece of torn cardboard, and a .38 caliber police
bullet. On one side of the cardboard it said, "Drop Miller case or else."
On the other side, it said, "For your head. Same as Bradley got."

I called the San Francisco Police Department station close to my
home. I told them I had received a death threat through the mail.

"Who is this?"

"Nathan Cohn. Let me talk to the captain." I told the captain I was
representing Harold Miller in the Bradley case and I read him the note.

"You know, we're very busy out here and we don't have too many
men. We can't protect you. All we can do is have a car drop by your
house a couple of times a day."

"Well, suppose somebody comes up and shoots me? Suppose some
policeman shoots me? It looks like a police bullet."

"Oh, the police don't do that."

I called up the FBI.

I told them I had received a death threat through the mail. "That's a
federal offense, isn't it?"

"Yeah."

"Can you send an agent out to my house to look at this? I won't let
anybody touch it. Maybe we can get some fingerprints off of it."

I would have an agent at my house the next morning.

Next, I called my friend, Jerry Flamm, at the *Call-Bulletin*.

"Jerry, I got something that might be a story for you."

"What's that?"

"I got a death threat through the mail. The FBI is coming out to see me tomorrow morning. Why don't you come out here with a cameraman. You might get a good story out of this."

The FBI agent came out there the next morning. So did Jerry and his cameraman. Jerry sat there while I explained the situation to the agent.

"Well, we don't do any protection," the agent explained. "We only investigate, and we ask the local authorities to do the protection. We can't protect you, but we can investigate."

The agent took the card and the bullet for investigation. Meanwhile, Jerry took photos of the bullet and the card. He had been listening to the story and taking it all down.

"We'll let you know if we can get anything off the cardboard or off the bullet," the agent concluded.

The next day was Saturday, and a friend of mine had given me two tickets to the Cal game over in Berkeley. Walking out of the Cal game Hank James and I saw the *Call-Bulletin* headline: "Threat to Kill SF Lawyer." I smiled. I thought the cops would not be too happy with that...

I defended Harold on a self-defense theory. In putting together the theory of the case, I had run across an old decision. A rustler was branding cattle out in the wilderness, and a sheriff came up to him and caught him re-branding the cattle.

The sheriff put his gun on him. "You son of a gun. In the old days, if we'd caught you like this, we'd hang you right on the spot. But nowadays you get a lawyer and go to court. Some sharp lawyer confuses a jury and you get off. I'm going to go back to the old days. I'm going to take care of you right now." As the sheriff cocked his gun, the rustler pulled his gun and killed the sheriff.

The court held the shooting was self-defense because the rustler thought his life was in danger and the officer was going to fire.

My theory was that Harold thought they were flushing him out to kill him and he returned fire. I told Judge Cullinan it was self-defense and gave him a copy of the case about the sheriff.

I took a friend, Hank James, who was chief building inspector for the City, with me to look over the scene of the shooting. The lady that owned the building took us through it. I had her take us through it so that no one could say that we had changed anything.

She showed us the room where Harold had lived and where they found the package of heroin. She showed us where they found the guns lying on the ground. She took us out to the stairs going down to the backyard. When I looked down, I saw she had all these beautiful flowers, but the police had pulled down the flowers to take the bullets out of the fence Harold had fired into.

"Oh, my God, who did that to your beautiful flowers?"

"The police did." I let her know I completely sympathized with her.

As Hank and I walked further down the street, I saw a big house with shingles. In one of the shingles we noticed three little holes. They could have been from police bullets fired at Harold, so I took a piece of chalk and I put circles around the three holes, and I took several pictures of Hank pointing to the holes.

But how was I going to use them?

When we started to get ready for trial, I heard a rumor that Cecil Poole, who was the District Attorney on the case, was going to bring in Dr. Kirk, a top criminalist at U.C. Berkeley.

I called Dr. Kirk. "Doctor, I'm the attorney on the Miller case, and I'd like to talk about retaining you."

"Mr. Cohn, I can't do it for you."

He didn't tell me why he couldn't, but he gave me the name of a criminalist down in San Jose that might help me. That gave me a pretty good idea what was happening.

The District Attorney had charged Harold with possession of narcotics, a big bag of heroin; possession of guns by an ex-felon; first-degree murder; assault with intent to commit murder; assault with intent to do great bodily harm and a few other things—such as kidnaping.

I went to Cecil Poole, and I told Cecil, "Look, I will plead him guilty to first-degree murder if he does not get the death penalty. I'll plead him guilty to everything if he doesn't get the death penalty."

"No way. The police won't stand for it."

"Look," I said, "why try the case? We'll plead him guilty. You've got him in there. He'll stay there in jail on first-degree murder. He's been in prison before and you'd accomplish what you wanted to."

I'd just won two cases in a row from Poole, and Poole said no, he wouldn't do it—and we went to trial instead.

The courtroom was full of police. There were more police in that courtroom than I had ever seen in such a confined space. In the front row at the corner was Chief English, who was chief of inspectors. English was in full uniform. He was completely bald and looked tough as hell.

Every newspaper was covering the case. A lot of lawyers were there, and a lot of reporters. Jack Rosenbaum, the *Examiner* columnist and close friend of mine, was also covering the case.

Jack came over to me. "Nate, be very careful."

"What do you mean?"

"Well, I talked to the policemen over there, and I said, 'You know, I'm kind of curious. This man has been charged with murdering a policeman and you are asking the death penalty. Now, he's sitting there with no shackles on and five feet in back of him is a door. Aren't you afraid he'll run out the door?'

"'We wish he'd run out the door. He would be hit by at least 10 bullets at the same time.'"

I got the message. I told Harold, "If you drop anything, don't make any sudden moves. I'll pick it up. If you make a move, they will start shooting. They're liable to hit me, too, you know?"

We began trying the case. I kept showing the pictures of the three holes to all the police witnesses and asking them if they had looked at the bullet holes. And I kept calling them bullet holes. Cecil objected over and over again on grounds there was no evidence that these were bullet holes, but I kept saying it.

I hired the expert in San Jose, but I told him not to do anything until I called him. And every day I would go out to look at the holes. After a couple of weeks, I went out there and someone had dug out the holes. Then I told the expert to go down there and look at the bullet holes.

He went down there and reported to me someone had dug out whatever was in there. He couldn't say whether there had been any bullets in there or not.

Poole then put Kirk on the stand, who testified he dug out the holes and there were no bullets in there. Kirk testified it looked like somebody had thrown something against the wall and made these holes.

"You know, I tried to hire you to go look at those holes."

"Yes, you did."

"You told me you wouldn't do it for me."

"Yes, I did."

"You recommended a person down on the Peninsula."

"Yes, I did."

"Why wouldn't you do it for me?"

"Well, I'd already been hired by the DA."

"You didn't tell me that."

"No, I didn't."

I put on my expert who testified he couldn't tell whether they were bullet holes, because Kirk had dug out the shingle.

Finally, I put Harold on the stand. He told the jury his life story and that he thought the police were flushing him out to kill him, and he just reacted. He took pains to point out he didn't hurt the students who drove him to Los Angeles. Harold explained he simply wanted to get away because he didn't want to get killed. He figured the police weren't going to arrest him; they were going to kill him.

In his cross, Cecil even allowed Harold an opening he had not anticipated. "When you were in your apartment and the cops came, you looked out, you saw they were policemen: is that right?" he asked.

"Yes."

"Well, if you didn't have any problems, why did you run out with the guns and shoot them? Why didn't you go and answer the door when you saw the policemen?"

"Last time I did that they took me downtown and beat me to a pulp."

The two college kids whose car Harold had commandeered also supported Harold. They testified that Harold never harmed them.

I also made a motion for the jury to go out and view the premises where it all happened, and the judge granted my motion and provided an insight into his integrity.

A big bus came and took the jurors. The policemen all got in police cars and went out there, too.

Judge Cullinan asked me to stay with him.

"Would you like to get a drink before we go out there?"

"I don't need a drink. I don't drink when I'm trying a case."

But the judge wanted a drink. We went into Cookie's bar, and he ordered a drink. Then the judge called a cab to take us out to the site after he had given everyone else a chance to get there.

But as we were riding in the cab, I commented to the judge, "It doesn't look good for the jury to see me coming there with you because they'll figure that you are prejudiced in my favor. I don't want to do anything to embarrass you."

"No, Nate. Nothing happens if I'm late. But if I get there and you are not there, then it looks like you are holding things up. You take the cab and go there and I'll walk the last couple of blocks."

So the judge got out of the cab two blocks away.

When I arrived, I asked "Is everybody ready?"

"The judge isn't here."

"He'll be here in a minute."

Then the judge came waltzing in. Nobody knew we had driven out together.

For my closing argument, I went to a sign painter, and I had a folding sign made. Each section was a yard wide and it was four feet high and each of the three sections folded together. On the first panel, I had the definition of murder. On the second one, I had the definition of excusable homicide. On the third one, I had the definition of self-defense.

When I made my closing argument, I unfolded it. It went all the way across the courtroom. The jury could see it, and I explained to the jury that I had done this deliberately because I wanted to impress them with the elements of self-defense and I wanted to impress them with the elements of excusable homicide.

I also reminded the jury that while Poole was a brilliant attorney who had graduated from Cal *summa cum laude*, and had gone on to Harvard Law School, I had gone to night law school. The argument they had heard by Poole was brilliant and beautifully spoken, but I told them to remember one thing. When he choked up and he asked the judge for a recess at the end of his argument, I looked at the clock. It was exactly 12:00 o'clock. "...that's all I'm going to say," I concluded.

The judge instructed the jury, and at my request, he gave self-defense instructions.

Cecil was asking for the death penalty, and I was asking that Harold be found not guilty on grounds of self-defense or excusable homicide. I admitted everything else. I admitted to the jury Harold did the shooting. I admitted that Harold was guilty of the possession of the heroin, and of the possession of the guns, and of making the college kids drive to Los Angeles, but I asked the jury not to give Harold the death penalty and not to convict him of homicide.

At about 10:00 that night, the jury sent a note to the judge and the judge called the jury in and read the note. In the note the jury said they wanted the judge to give them the self-defense instruction again.

"Well," the judge responded, "you have worked hard today. I'm going to send you to the hotel. You come back tomorrow morning and we'll complete this and I'll take your note under advisement."

As things were breaking up, one of the press photographers came over to me. "Nate, will you give me a ride home?" I said, "Sure."

The two of us walked out of the Hall of Justice and over to my car. I asked him where he wanted to go.

"I don't need a ride home. I just wanted to walk you over to make sure you got safely to your car because the place was full of policemen. I didn't want to see anything happen to you." The atmosphere was that tense.

The next morning, I arrived at the courtroom 9:00 o'clock, but I didn't see Cecil and I didn't see the judge. I asked the bailiff. "Did you see Mr. Poole?"

"He's in with the judge."

"He's what?"

"He's in with the judge."

"I'm going in, too."

"No, the judge said not to let you in."

"What do you mean? He can't be there without my being there."

"Well, that's what I have been told."

After ten minutes, Cecil came out of the judge's chambers. Although Cecil and I were friends, this was the courtroom and we were each fighting for our own side.

"What the hell is going on here? You're not allowed to see the judge without my being present."

"Don't give me a bad time; I'll punch you out."

"You'll have to do it from a sitting position because I'm going to knock you on your ass if you make one move."

The bailiff had to separate us, and the headline soon hit the papers:

"Lawyers Fight in Courtroom."

Finally, the judge called in the jury. When he instructed them, I was furious.

"I'm withdrawing all the self-defense instructions, and I'm going to give you a new instruction. That instruction is: at the time of the shooting, the defendant, Harold Miller, was a fleeing felon and the police had a right to shoot at him. That's all I'm going to tell you."

I rose and made a motion for a mistrial. The judge denied it.

"I'll make a motion for new trial."

"I'll take that under submission. Why don't you and Mr. Poole come into my chambers."

When we took our seats in chambers, the judge looked at me and announced, "Nate, take it easy. You'll win your case."

I didn't know what he was talking about. "How can I win my case, Judge," I said, "you just took it away?"

"You have your motion, right?"

"Yes."

"We'll decide that later."

In the meantime the jury went out, and they stayed out quite a while. When they came back—we had already stipulated to the verdicts on all the other charges—they found Harold guilty of first-degree murder, but did not give him the death penalty.

In those days there was no separate penalty trial in death penalty cases. There was one verdict, and in a murder case, they either gave the death penalty or not.

This time, they didn't.

When that came out, Harold broke out in a big smile.

The judge called me up to the bench. "Mr. Cohn, you'll have sentencing in ten days. I'm going to get a pre-sentencing report and then we'll have the sentencing hearing. "

I told Harold to relax. The jury had brought their verdict. They couldn't change their verdict now. The judge could have reduced it if they had given the death penalty, but he couldn't increase it if it was life.

I also told Harold I had another little kicker that nobody seemed to realize and told him to hold tight.

We were back in the courtroom ten days later. The judge had the lawyers and the reporters in chambers to discuss the sentence.

Cecil Poole was in there along with Norman Elkington, who was Chief Assistant District Attorney. Abe Dressow, a Public Defender, was also there. There was a bevy of newspapermen in the chambers as well, ready for a story. I gave them one.

"You know," Cullinan intoned, "I've seen a lot of cases, and I think Nate did one of the best jobs I've ever seen done by a lawyer. But, Nate, your client is going to go to jail for a long time. I'm going to run everything consecutively. Consecutively. He won't come up for parole until he's 150 years old."

"You can't do that, judge," I interjected.

"I can't?"

"No, Your Honor. My client was found guilty of first-degree murder. Under the Penal Code, all other charges that he's found guilty of merge and become part of the murder conviction. You can only sentence him on the murder charge."

One of the reporters asked Elkington: "Is that true?" Elkington shot back, "Nate is talking through his hat." But Abe Dressow ran to get the Penal Code and came back. "What section, Nate?"

"Nate's right," he announced. "You can't run them consecutively. They all merge if it's first-degree murder and he will become eligible for parole in seven years!"

One of the reporters looked at Elkington. "How is it Nate knew that and you didn't know it?"

"I have no comment."

The reporter then looked at Cecil.

"No comment."

"Have you got anything to say, Nate?"

"Yeah, you don't have to pass any test to be a D.A. Anybody can be a D.A., I'm telling you."

Now we entered into the courtroom and I could tell Harold what had happened. We held the formal sentencing, with Harold smiling. The newspapers called him "the smirking killer"—and Harold was sent to Folsom Prison.

Some time after, a young man came into my office and said he was bringing me a watch from Harold. Harold had read in the papers that the police officers had gotten together and presented Cecil Poole with a watch for his work on the case, and Harold was giving me his watch because I had won the case.

The two young men whose car Harold commandeered to take to Los Angeles became well-known politicians. John Foran went on to become State Senator and Leo McCarthy, Lieutenant Governor. Cecil Poole became United States Attorney for the Northern District of California and Norman Elkington became a judge.

It was several years later, though, when a police inspector explained to me why Judge Cullinan was so confident in telling me I had won the case when he reinstructed the jury.

It turned out that the night before, when the jury was sent to the hotel, a police inspector sneaked into the jury room and looked at the ballots. There were three ballots for death. There were five ballots for life. And the rest were ballots for acquittal.

Someone had tipped the judge off. The judge knew that a jury with four votes for acquittal and three votes for death would not give the death penalty. That's what he had meant when he said, "Don't worry about it. You've won your case."

I did see Jake Ehrlich many times, and he told me his advice had been wrong. "You know, Nate, you were smart not taking my advice. That case did more for you than any case you ever had. You did a hell of a job."

But the stress in that case was amazing. When I went to the bar, I drank soda water with bicarbonate. You couldn't have given me coffee.

In a trial like that, it's like throwing the dice. When you finish the trial, whatever comes up comes up.

And even the police warmed after a while. The next time that a police officer needed a criminal defense attorney, he came to me.

After the Miller case, I represented policemen in several cases.

One became known as the "flying carpet" case.

I received a phone call one day from a policeman who wanted to see me in my office. He said that he had been out with a friend of his who was in plainclothes. They'd had quite enough to drink and they were driving in his friend's pickup truck. On the way, his friend said, "I have to stop to pick up something."

They went to a garage and his friend opened the garage door. Inside was a large rolled-up carpet. His friend asked him to help load it into the truck. While they were loading the carpet, a police car driving by saw them and one of the officers went to them and asked them what they were doing. The policeman grew suspicious.

"Where do you live?"

The man showed him his driver's license.

The police officer said, "You don't live here."

"No, I don't."

"Whose rug is this?'

"I just picked it up for a friend."

"What friend?"

"I can't remember his name."

"What's the name of the man who lives here?"

"I don't know."

The policeman went to the front door and asked whether the owner had given authority to remove a rug from the garage. He hadn't.

The officer arrested my client and his friend for burglary and took them down to the nearest police station.

My client insisted he didn't know the rug was someone else's, but admitted he had helped his friend load the rug into the truck. He was intoxicated and hadn't known what was going on.

When the lieutenant at the station recognized my client, he called the captain down to the station. I knew the captain to be a very honest person. I went to talk to him.

My investigator had already gone out to the police station and had talked to the lieutenant, who insisted my client was stone cold sober.

The captain disagreed. He told me my client was obviously under the influence of alcohol at the time of the arrest, but he could neither testify that he was drunk nor that he was sober.

I contacted the Police Commission and suggested that they remove my client from the force but not go after him for drinking. I told them I had two different stories, one that he was under the influence and one that he was not.

They had accepted the lieutenant's word and they did not remove my client from the force. Instead, they took him off duty and held up his salary.

When I took the burglary case to trial, I defended it on the grounds that my client was intoxicated and didn't know what he was doing. I called the captain as a witness and he testified that my client had been drinking, and that it was very possible that he was under the influence and didn't know what he was doing.

The jury acquitted my client. In the meantime, the Police Commission had suspended him from duty and suspended his salary. I went back to the Police Commission and asked they reinstate my client as a police officer, as he had been acquitted of the criminal charge. The Police Commission reinstated him but they would not authorize the payment of backpay for the period of time he was suspended from the force.

I filed a lawsuit against the City, and a jury gave me a verdict for the full salary.

My client was reinstated to his job and received his full salary, less, of course, my fee, and the flying carpet was laid to rest.

The Ding Dong Daddy of the D Line

9

Because of my background in circuses and carnivals I became West Coast Counsel to the American Guild of Variety Artists, the union of entertainers, as well as Show Folks of America. That brought me into association with a certainly more colorful clientele than the Pacific Union Club and their morning suits. Some were well-known, such as the stripper Tempest Storm, Jack Soo, the comic actor, and Duke Ellington, but some of the most colorful were not so well-known.

Peter DeCenzie owned the El Rey Theater in Oakland, a burlesque house and Tempest appeared there quite often.

One time when Peter had a show that wasn't drawing people, he came up with an idea how to increase his audience. There was a gentleman who had been a conductor on a streetcar in San Francisco who had been arrested for bigamy. They called him the "Ding Dong Daddy of the D Line." The man had gotten out of jail for bigamy and was on probation in Los Angeles and Peter hired him to come up and stand on the stage in a conductor's uniform while the strippers danced. Peter thought that would attract some publicity.

The new act opened, but it didn't draw too many people. The second day after the "Ding Dong Daddy" opened, Peter DeCenzie asked me to come over. He said he had a problem at his theater. When I arrived, there were two police inspectors from Los Angeles in his lobby and a prominent lawyer and his wife. The lawyer had obviously had a few drinks and he was giving these two inspectors a difficult time.

"What's going on?" I asked Peter.

"These policemen came up to arrest the Ding Dong Daddy and my manager called a friend of his who's a lawyer to come over, but this man is causing more trouble than I had to begin with! He's arguing with the police. They're going to come to blows in my lobby. Get rid of that lawyer and handle it!"

Daddy Jailed In Bigamy

Francis Van Wie (center), Ding Dong Daddy of the D Line, is shown as he was arrested on bigamy charges last night in the Oakland burlesque house where he was working. Others (from left): Chester Sharp, L. A. County officer; Ivan Sperbeck, Van Wie's lawyer; Nate Cohn, theater attorney, and Oakland Inspector James Mangini.

In Oakland jail, Van Wie, former S. F. street car conductor, waved goodby, and soon was peacefully asleep. He is accused of having married wives Nos. 15 and 16 without having divorced No. 14, Mrs. Martha Moyer (No. 15)

I knew the attorney and he knew me, and I explained, "I'm Peter's lawyer, I'm going to handle it."

"Well, the manager called me."

"I know. But Peter owns the place and he doesn't want anybody but me to handle it."

In the meantime, the detective had grown red-faced and furious. He was ready to slug the lawyer.

I saw this, and stepped between this detective and the lawyer and I pushed the other lawyer away.

"Look, you don't want to go back to L.A. and have someone complain you hit a lawyer up here. I know he's arguing with you and I know you think he deserves to be slugged, but if you do, you'll regret

Ding Dong: (l-r) Nate, several performers from the El Rey Theater, Francis Von Wie, the "Ding Dong Daddy of the D Line" and photographer James Leterer.

it. I'll take care of this whole thing."

Finally, the other lawyer left, and I turned to the detective.

"What's the problem?"

"We got a tip that the star performer, the Ding Dong Daddy, has been married again against the orders of the court, and we checked it out and it's true. We've been told to pick him up and take him to Los Angeles."

"Relax. Let me take care of this."

I went over to Pete DeCenzie. "Where is the Ding Dong Daddy?"

"I've got him sitting in the audience."

I went back to the detective.

"The next show goes on in about thirty minutes. Let him do the next show and then I'll deliver him to you and everyone will be okay. All you have to do is wait 40 minutes."

"Thank you very much. You know, I really lost my temper with that man."

"I don't blame you. I understand you thoroughly. I might have felt the same way, but you're a detective and you don't want to go back to L.A. and have people say that you got in a fight with a lawyer up here over foolishness."

"You're right, you're right, you're right. The man had too much to drink."

"I understand. Relax, and I'll take care of it. Have a seat in the theater. The show goes on in about fifteen minutes. As soon as the show is over, I will personally bring the man to you and you can take custody."

"That would be very nice."

The show went on and the Ding Dong Daddy got out of the audience, put on a conductor's cap, put a moneychanger on his belt and he punched the moneychanger while the girls danced. When it was all over—there weren't very many in the audience, anyway—I went up to him and I told him what the situation was. "I have to turn you over to them because they have orders to pick you up."

"Okay."

I introduced the Ding Dong Daddy to the detective and I told him to go with the detective and Peter would probably get someone in Los Angeles to represent him there.

Jimmy Leterer was from the newsreels and had been taking pictures of the argument, and I asked the lieutenant if he could get a picture of the Ding Dong Daddy.

"Sure. Take a picture, do whatever you want."

Later on, I received a phone call from the L.A. detective at my office.

"I want to thank you very much. I was so angry. I appreciate what you did. I sent you a pair of cufflinks with the Los Angeles Police Department emblem on it. If you have any problems down in Los Angeles with the police, just show them the emblem and they'll know you're a friend of ours."

"Thank you very much, I appreciate it." I received a pair of cufflinks with the Los Angeles Police Department emblem.

Some time later, a client who had been a paratrooper in the service came up to see me. He told me that he understood that a warrant had been issued for his arrest in Los Angeles for giving out checks that bounced.

"What about these checks?"

"I made a mistake in my accounting, and I thought I had more in the bank, but I'll be glad to put money in the place of the checks. There's only one problem I have."

"What's that?"

"I had a sex-change operation. I'm now a woman. I dress like a man because that makes it easier, but if I get arrested and put in jail, they'll put me in with the men and I'm a woman and I'm scared to death to go in the men's jail. I could have all kinds of problems. Would you go with me down to Los Angeles and see if we can straighten this out?"

"Sure."

We flew down to Los Angeles. When we arrived in Los Angeles, he told me he had to go somewhere first. We got in cab and we went to Wilshire Boulevard to Jerry Geisler's office. Jerry Geisler was probably the best criminal lawyer in Southern California. He had been the lawyer for Errol Flynn and won an acquittal for him. Jerry was also a friend of mine. I had tried several cases following Jerry and several court attachés told me I tried a case just like Jerry Geisler, which I thought was very complimentary.

In any event, my client and I went in to see Jerry.

"I want to hire you to help Mr. Cohn because he's a San Francisco lawyer."

"You don't need me. Mr. Cohn's perfectly competent to handle anything down here. He's had several cases down here and he's done very well. I tell you what I'll do. I have a young attorney in my office, and I'll have him help Mr. Cohn in any way he can."

He introduced this young lawyer and the lawyer asked if we wanted him to go with us. I said, "If you want to, it's all right, if this man wants to pay you for it, but I don't need it. Let me just see what I can do."

"Here's my number. I'll be here. If you need me for anything, call me and I'll come down."

We went down to the police station and we ran into the same

detective. The detective saw me and he shook hands with me. He was very friendly and I told him the situation.

"Your client shouldn't have been giving bum checks!"

"Look, he's had a sex-change operation and he's now really a woman and you know how women are with their checking accounts... There's a story about this lady who went to the bank and said, 'You bounced my checks.' 'Yes, you don't have any funds in your account.' She said, 'That's silly. I still have a lot of checks...'

"He wants to pay for all the checks."

The detective introduced me to the inspector who was handling the case: "This is a friend of mine. Do whatever you have to do, but I want you to be courteous to him."

I told the inspector my client wanted to pay for the checks and we made arrangements to pay all the checks and the inspector dismissed the charges.

My client was pleased. "Mr. Geisler was right. You're a good lawyer."

"Well, thanks for telling me."

There was one thing about Jerry Geisler's office. I had never been in a law office before where all the secretaries looked like movie stars. I asked Jerry about it.

"It's very easy for me. Most of these young ladies who want to break into movies hear that a lot of producers and movie stars come to my office; so they're anxious to work for me, thinking they might meet someone who might think them a good prospect for the movies."

They Called Him the King of the Gypsies

He wasn't really the king of the gypsies, but that was what they called him on a television program in Sacramento which led to his becoming my client. My client knew someone working for a television station in Sacramento who was curious about gypsy life and my client told him stories of the way gypsies live. The result was a show setting forth the romantic lives of gypsies, featuring my client.

Actually, he was a concessionaire with a carnival that played throughout the State of California and he also had a concession at the Sacramento State Fair each year and was part of a group of gypsy families that had concessions with carnivals. One of the families had a daughter, however, who, instead of following gypsy traditions, ran away with a soldier.

She became pregnant. She also became involved with drugs, and the family disowned their daughter and advised her never to come back.

The daughter saw the television show featuring my client as "the king of the gypsies," and one afternoon she went over to my client's house with her little daughter who was four years old.

She told my client that her husband had deserted her, and that she had no money and no place to live. She said that she wanted to leave her daughter with him, so that the daughter would have a place to live, food to eat and someone to watch over her.

My client told her he had no room in his house for another child. He said he would be happy to have her and her daughter have dinner with them at nights, but he had no room for them to stay.

She repeated that she was out of money and that she had no place to live. After thinking about it, he recalled a gypsy couple in Auburn, a short distance from Sacramento, who couldn't have children and who had adopted a five year old girl. He called the couple and they were interested in helping.

The gentleman in Auburn told my client to give the young woman some money to pay for a motel for the night, and he would come down to Sacramento the next morning and would pay my client back.

The next day, the gentleman from Auburn, with his wife and adopted daughter, came to my client's house, and the young lady and her daughter returned.

The couple wanted to take in the child, and the gentleman from Auburn told the child's mother he had called a lawyer in Sacramento who was preparing guardianship papers and he would have the lawyer bring them to my client's house the next day for her to sign to document that he had the permission of the child's mother.

They all agreed that the couple in Auburn would take over the guardianship of the daughter and in return would send her mother some money to take care of herself.

The gentleman from Auburn gave my client back the money he had advanced for the young lady and her daughter the previous night, then he gave the mother some money for that night and told her to come over the next day.

The next day, the guardianship papers were signed and the couple went back to Auburn with the daughter.

The man in Auburn was so happy about having another little girl to be with his adopted daughter that he told my client, "Give the young lady a thousand dollars which will help her get on her feet and will keep her from being hungry. And tell her also that any time that she wants to visit her daughter, she can come up to Auburn and I'm happy to have her visit."

My client did so, but he wanted to make sure that he got the thousand dollars back that he was advancing, so he took a piece of paper and told the mother, "Put down something to show you got my thousand dollars."

The mother of the child was half-high on dope during the entire proceeding and he wanted to make sure she knew what she had done, so he told her to write everything in her own words. She put down on the piece of paper, "For my daughter, I received $1,000," and signed it.

My client gave her $1,000 and told her that if she did get into any trouble or have any problems to give him a ring. He also told her that he couldn't guarantee that he would be able to do anything because he didn't have much money—all the money he did have was needed to support his family during the season before the carnivals went out on the road again.

The little girl went to Auburn and she lived with the couple there who took good care of her.

The couple in Auburn had been operating a fortune telling business for some time and were well-established, but an Assistant District Attorney in Auburn named Shelley had the idea that this Auburn gypsy and his wife were living better than he thought a fortune teller should live, and he prepared a declaration with a police officer that they believed there was evidence in the gypsies' home that would indicate they were involved in money laundering and they obtained a warrant from a Municipal Court judge in Auburn to search the gypsies' home.

They searched the entire house and found no evidence of money laundering or any other illegal activity, but in the desk they found the piece of paper that said, "For my daughter, I received $1,000." And then Shelley commenced a prosecution against the couple for buying the child. My client was also named in the complaint.

The authorities found the mother in Sacramento and brought her to Auburn. The mother was stoned from narcotics and drunk. They threatened her with jail for selling her child.

The mother was scared to death. She didn't know what to do. The authorities told her they would take care of her while the prosecution was going on, and they got her to sign a statement that she had sold her child to the Auburn couple.

Shelley wanted my client to appear in Auburn on the charges, so I called Shelley and he seemed a reasonable enough person.

I found out they had already arrested the husband and wife in Auburn and the Auburn couple had retained lawyers who were representing them, so I told Shelley that I would bring my client to Auburn and we would place bail and see what we were going to do.

My client was scared to death. He had never been involved with the police in his entire life, so I picked him up in Sacramento and I drove him up to Auburn. I used my car phone and called Shelley to ask him where he wanted me to meet him. He told me to meet him in front of the courthouse.

When we arrived, we were greeted by more television cameras than I had seen at one place in my life. There was Shelley amidst the cameras, and I was an unwitting actor in a colossal television show, with Shelley arresting my client and giving him the *Miranda* warning, then announcing to the cameras there was a $100,000 bail on my client.

I had been set up.

The reporters asked me for a statement. I told them I was not making any statements, but that this was just a show for the District Attorney's publicity department and the case would be dismissed as soon as it got in front of a judge. There was nothing else to say.

I knew the $100,000 bail was outrageous and began to reverse that. There was a Superior Court judge in that county

I knew, Judge William A. Newsom, (his son is now Mayor of San Francisco) and I sought him out. I was told that Judge Newsom was sitting in Yreka, California for the next several weeks, so I went to Judge Newsom's courtroom and I found out from the clerk where he was and I called him. Judge Newsom said to tell the D. A. to reduce the bail to $3,000 or he would order it himself. Shelley acquiesced.

I had a bail bondsman ready who posted the bail, my client was arraigned, we set a date for a preliminary hearing and I got out of Auburn as quickly as I could.

Then Shelley called me to tell me he had charged my client's wife as well and he didn't want to have to go in and arrest her in Sacramento and incarcerate her until she could be brought to Auburn, so would I bring her in. I agreed and made arrangements for a similar bail for my client's wife.

However, when I brought my client's wife to the courthouse to surrender, again there were the television cameras. I made arrangements for a $3,000 bail, and set a preliminary hearing for both my clients in four weeks, so I could prepare.

I told Shelley it was fine for him to play it for all it was worth, but he could never prove his charges. "Yes," he said, "but these people are gypsies!" He thought that was all it would take for an Auburn jury to convict.

He asked me if I would stipulate to waive the preliminary hearing and take the case directly to Superior Court as the attorneys for Auburn couple had done. I refused. Then he asked if I was willing to plea bargain. He said he would offer to break the charge down to a misdemeanor and he would give my clients a fine and probation.

I told him I didn't think it was a very good offer, but I would talk to my clients.

My clients felt differently. They were scared to death of the American jury system and convinced that American juries were against gypsies. Their first question was: "Do we go to jail?"

I explained that they wouldn't have to go to jail, but they would be on probation and would have a criminal record.

They insisted that I plead them out, so I called Shelley that afternoon and advised him that, against my advice, my clients wished to plead out and would plead guilty to the misdemeanor in return for a suspended sentence and probation.

The reply took me by surprise: "I've changed my mind. We're not going to give them a misdemeanor. They're going to have to go to jail."

At any rate, he had solved my dilemma for me.

In the meantime, I had all the information I wanted. I found out where the mother of the child was—she had been picked up—and I received copies of her statements to the police and copies of quite a bit of information that I was fortunate to get in those days. I also went to the D. A. and made copies of his information. I was fortunate to get that, too. He wasn't a bad man, but he thought he had a thing going, and that he was going to get a lot of publicity which would make him well-known—a hero, in fact.

On the night before the preliminary I drove up to Sacramento and I saw my clients.

My clients were scared to death. They were scared of the law, they were scared of judges, they were just scared.

The next morning, we drove up to Auburn and went to the court house. The judge had the reputation of being a tough judge, but he was fair—and that was all I wanted.

Shelley was smiling and friendly. He knew the judge, too—or thought he did.

He put on the police who had taken the statement from the mother of the child, and I cross-examined them, lightly—mainly to show that everything they testified to had happened in Sacramento.

Then Shelley called the child's mother to the stand. You could see she was high on dope and her testimony reflected it. It was, to put it mildly, off-the-wall, and her condition was evident to all. By this time the judge understood where I was coming from.

I had established that all the events in question had happened in Sacramento, and that the child's mother had never been in Auburn at any time. I also established that she had been arrested and had pled guilty and had been given probation on condition that she cooperate with the police.

Halfway through her cross-examination, the judge looked at me and said, "Mr. Cohn, you don't have to go any further. I understand your position."

"Your Honor, with all due respect, I would like to finish the cross-examination of this young lady. I appreciate what you're saying, but I think for my benefit and for the protection of my clients, I should continue and finish it."

She was high on dope and I wanted to show for the record that she did not know what she was saying.

When I finished cross-examination, I moved to dismiss the prosecution against my clients on the grounds of lack of jurisdiction. My clients were never in Placer County, and nothing that happened involving the child in Auburn involved my clients.

The judge looked at Shelley. "What have you got to say about this? Mr. Cohn has just presented me with some cases which say that you're in the wrong county. "

"Well, we've got the other defendants here."

"These defendants are in Sacramento County, and everything you claim against these defendants happened in Sacramento County, and you have no jurisdiction to try someone in this county for something that happened in another county, and you haven't charged them with conspiracy, you charged them with selling a child. They didn't sell a child in this county. In fact, probably, from the evidence I see here, it doesn't look like they sold a child at all, but nothing happened in this county, so I'm going to dismiss the case."

"What do you think, Mr. Cohn?"

"Mr. Shelley has been very courteous to me. I'm willing to be courteous to him. I have no objection if Your Honor wants to postpone this for thirty minutes to give him a chance to look up some of these cases. Obviously he didn't look up the cases I gave him."

"That's very nice of you Mr. Cohn. Mr. Shelley, you'll have thirty minutes..."

Shelley said he couldn't do it in thirty minutes.

"Your Honor, why don't we give him forty minutes."

"Okay, we'll give you forty minutes, Mr. Shelley, and you come back in forty minutes and tell me why I shouldn't dismiss the case.

Forty minutes later, Shelley came back in, sweating. "Your Honor, I checked Mr. Cohn's cases and what he says is correct, but I'd like to put this over for a week so I can look up something."

"Mr. Cohn was courteous enough to give you forty minutes to look at those cases. Mr. Cohn served you with a brief. If you had read the brief you would probably have understood where Mr. Cohn was going. He didn't say exactly what he was doing in the brief but still, the law is the law, so I'm dismissing the case."

Now I also had the record of the mother under oath on the stand high as a kite. She had impeached herself and her testimony was not only contradictory, it was irrational. The District Attorney in Sacramento was not going to proceed against my clients with her testimony, because it made the Sacramento Police and the Sacramento District Attorney's office look very bad.

I explained to my clients with some difficulty, but to their ultimate relief, that the case against them was all over.

A week later, the attorney for the couple in Auburn called. They had replaced their initial attorneys. Apparently, the first attorneys were more concerned about their fee than defending their clients and had waived the preliminary hearing. Their new counsel wanted to know how to proceed since the former attorneys had waived the preliminary. I suggested he get a copy of the record of the preliminary hearing for my clients and bring a motion before the Superior Court in Auburn stating that the Sacramento defendants had been dismissed and not recharged, showing no crime had been committed. How could the D.A. prove the sale of the child if the Sacramento defendants were not involved?

A few weeks later I received a note from him saying that the case against his clients had also been dismissed.

Thus ended the case of the King of the Gypsies.

I had another case involving a gypsy and a gift.

One gypsy in Los Banos, California made her living telling fortunes. She had become very friendly with a customer who had given her a substantial sum of money. When the customer's relations heard she had given the gypsy the money, they went to the police and complained the gypsy had taken money by theft.

The fortune teller's husband came to see me in San Francisco and asked me to represent his wife.

Los Banos was quite a distance from my office, and I told him that I wanted a retainer up front which would be substantial. He paid it and I went down to Los Banos for the preliminary hearing.

The District Attorney introduced evidence that my client was a gypsy, that the alleged victim had given my client a substantial sum of money and that when the family wanted the money back, my client would not give it back.

Then, the woman who had given the money to my client took the stand. She was honest.

I asked her, "Did you give my client the money?"

"Sure, I did."

"Did you intend it to be a gift to her?"

"Yes."

"Did you expect her to give it back to you?"

"No."

"Did you expect her to do anything for this?"

"No."

"Did she tell you that something was going to happen in your favor because you gave her this money?"

"No."

"So you just made a gift to her."

"Yes."

By that time it was noon and the judge recessed for lunch.

We came back at 1:30 and the judge announced, "You heard the testimony of the complaining witness. I wanted to give you some time to prepare yourself. Under the circumstances, from the testimony Mr. Cohn has elicited, there's no crime here."

The D.A. admitted that, from the testimony elicited, there was no crime committed. It was a gift, and—even though he might believe it was wrongfully obtained—with the testimony of the complaining witness, there could be no other conclusion.

And the case was promptly dismissed.

I told my client, "It's all over. You're dismissed. There's nothing else."

The drive to Los Banos took longer than the entire case.

The Cash or Clobber Collection Caper

In my most unusual case, my client faced a death penalty charge—kidnaping—but it was humor that saved the day.

One morning, *the San Francisco Chronicle* featured an article written in comic style announcing an arrest in a case involving a bookmaker and a gentleman who went by the name "Madman" Marcus.

The story said the bookmaker had hired Marcus to collect an obligation owed him by one Walter Barkett, a layoff bookmaker in the East Bay. Barkett was alleged to have taken bets on behalf of Paul "Bouquet" Cohn (no relation to me).

"Bouquet" Cohn was a well-known bookmaker in San Francisco who owned several cigar stores, several bars, and restaurants. The cigar stores had a sign in front with the legend "Bouquet Cohn," which told people it was a bookie corner.

The newspaper said Walter Barkett owed Cohn $12,000.

Marcus—who had adopted the moniker "Madman" in the style of "Madman" Muntz, and later "Crazy Eddie," because all three sold household appliances—allegedly had with him one Grant Butcher, a heavyweight prizefighter who had boxed in the Olympics; Grant's brother, Terrell Butcher; and another friend by the name of James Eberhardt.

According to the story, the four had followed Walter Barkett from the Bay Meadows Race Track to his house and accosted Barkett when he got out of his car to lift his garage door; whereupon they all proceeded to a bar owned by "Bouquet" Cohn on Geary Street.

The story went on to say that they entered the bar and went upstairs to a big office where, after a time, Barkett signed two checks for $6000 each and they placed a call to "Bouquet" Cohn. Marcus was said to have been holding the two checks when Cohn arrived, at which time Marcus gave one check over to Cohn for the money Barkett owed to him and kept the other as his collection fee.

On Witness Stand—Paul "Bouquet" Cohn, on trial with four others on charges of kidnapping, extortion and conspiracy, is pictured on the witness stand yesterday. *(San Francisco Examiner photo and caption.)*

Acquitted—Paul "Bouquet" Cohn shows visible relief after his acquittal in the "snatch and squeeze" kidnap-extortion trial yeesterday. *(San Francisco Examiner photo and caption.)*

By the time they took Barkett back to his house, Barkett's wife, worried that he may have been picked up by some Nevada gamblers, had called the police. Barkett had a big black eye. He tried to tell the police that nothing had happened, but they leaned on him. Based on Barkett's statement, the police arrested "Madman" Marcus, along with the Butchers and Eberhardt for kidnaping, robbery, assault and other crimes. Then the police arrested "Bouquet" Cohn for conspiring to strong-arm Barkett for the money.

Courtroom Gag—Defense Attorney James M. MacInnis stands before a poem he wrote on the courtroom blackboard at the trial of his client, Paul "Bouquet" Coh. *(San Francisco Examiner photo and caption.)*

The *Chronicle* called it the "Cash or Clobber Collection Caper," and it made quite an amusing story.

When I arrived at the office, my secretary told me that a gentleman wanted to see me—a gentleman by the name of Marcus. Marcus told me that he had been arrested, but that all he and the Butchers and Eberhardt had done was to walk across the street to Barkett when he got home and tell him "Bouquet" wanted to talk to him. Marcus said Barkett had gone with them voluntarily.

I told Marcus I wanted a fee up front before I got involved with him.

According to the newspapers, Marcus and his friends then went to Cohn to get money for attorney's fees. Cohn told them that he had put up the bail for them but he wasn't going to give them any money.

Allegedly dissatisfied, "Madman" Marcus and his cohorts grabbed Cohn and threw him in the back of a sedan with Eberhardt on one side and Grant Butcher on the other side, while Marcus drove the car to Marin County where they checked into a motel. They told the manager that they had a relation who was having a nervous breakdown and needed a quiet place where he could rest for three or four days without anyone bothering him, and they rented a room.

According to the newspapers, they took Cohn into the room, gagged him and put adhesive tape around his arms on a chair and told him they would not let him go until he signed some checks. After a long night, Cohn signed two checks for $6000 each. Marcus and his friends had breakfast in the motel and then they brought Cohn back to San Francisco.

The story went that Marcus drove to 333 Montgomery Street where the Pacific Bank was located, in which "Bouquet" Cohn kept his funds. 333 Montgomery was also the location of attorney Jake Ehrlich's office.

Ehrlich was Cohn's attorney. Ehrlich was just walking to his office when Marcus arrived there early in the morning. Marcus called out to Ehrlich, "Hiyah Jake. How are you doing? Look, there's Paul Cohn. We're going to go somewhere. We'll be using these checks. Will you okay them for me?" Erlich looked into the sedan and saw Cohn signaling to him, but thought Cohn was telling him it was okay. Erlich went into the bank and okayed the checks and Marcus left with the $12,000, drove four or five blocks and let "Bouquet" Cohn out of the car.

"Bouquet" Cohn, from what I read, went up to Jake Ehrlich's office, where he fired Jake, then walked over to James Martin MacInnis' office and hired MacInnis. All I knew was that Marcus came up to my office and gave me a retainer of $6000. I read everything in the newspaper the next morning.

When I heard that MacInnis was Cohn's new lawyer, I called him and told him I'd like to come over and see him. He had also read what I had read in the newspapers, and that was about all either of us knew about the case.

I reminded Jim the first article had been written in a humorous style, and I had always had it in the back of my mind that if you had a serious case which could be made humorous, you might be able to laugh the jury to an acquittal. We had one defendant who was a heavyweight prizefighter, spoke with a lisp and wore little bow ties. We had another defendant who was a bookmaker. Then we had my client, "Madman" Marcus. So, I suggested to Jim that we try the case as *Guys and Dolls*. Our clients were charged with kidnaping—a charge which carried the death penalty. How could a jury laugh at our clients and send them to prison, much less the gas chamber? He agreed I had a point.

When I arrived back at my office I learned the police had arrested Marcus and the Butchers and Eberhardt again, this time for kidnaping "Bouquet" Cohn and forcing him to sign the checks.

Marcus had taken the second $6000 and given it to his wife. After he paid my retainer, Marcus had gone to his wife to get the $6000, but his wife refused to give it to him. She told Marcus she wanted a separation, and she wouldn't even let him in the house.

According to the newspapers, a couple of days later when Marcus' wife drove their kids to school, Marcus grabbed his wife, threw her in his car and drove out to the beach at Fleishacker Point. Marcus' wife alleged he hit her several times, until she agreed to give him the money. Then she went to the police.

The police arrested Marcus again—this time, for assaulting his wife. I hadn't known any of this was going on, but now I had a client with three separate sets of charges against him.

The first thing I had to deal with was a preliminary hearing on the assault in municipal court. Marcus had already been charged with major felonies, so I went to the judge and the district attorney and suggested we ought to continue the hearing until after those cases were tried—

why waste time over this when he was facing more serious charges? They agreed. One prosecution was halted.

I tried to prepare for trial on the other charges, but my client wouldn't talk to me. No sooner had I walked into court for a hearing to set the date for a trial, which was to be in a week or so, than Marcus announced he wanted to speak to the judge. He wanted to fire me because I had had lunch with Jim MacInnis. However, Judge Cullinan explained to him that he had a fine criminal lawyer and that he would not permit it, so Marcus agreed to go ahead with me as his counsel.

At the trial, I took Walter Barkett apart, piece by piece. I established that Barkett was just a bookmaker who wouldn't pay his bills.

MacInnis put on a several minor witnesses from a restaurant "Bouquet" owned called the Bonanza Bar: "A nice little place run by a wonderful man, Mr. 'Bouquet' Cohn."

MacInnis also caught on to the *Guys and Dolls* idea. Jim had a woman dressed up in a Salvation Army uniform sit in the front row. In the middle of the trial, Jim stood up and asked, "Is Sarah Brown here?" (Sarah Brown had been the female lead character in *Guys and Dolls*, a Salvation Army worker). Judge Cullinan announced, "I'd like to see the lawyers in chambers."

He was not amused.

Jim was an excellent lawyer and a wonderful man, and we were good friends. We tried cases together and won them all. We had a good style together: while Jim was intellectual, I was down to earth. But the prosecution started pounding us, and Jim began to think that the atmosphere of the trial would hurt his client.

The way Jim saw the case, there was a rope coming from the ceiling. There was a knot on the top of the rope and that was where his client was holding on. Under that knot were knots for my client, Marcus, for the Butchers and for Eberhardt. To save his client, Jim would have to cut the rope beneath where his client was holding on and sacrifice the other defendants.

Emmett Haggerty (a fine Irish tenor)represented the Butchers and Richard Shortall (from a fine old San Francisco family and a staid law office) represented Eberhardt. We all sat with our clients around one table, facing the jury. But now Jim was sitting at a little table next to the clerk, so it would appear that his client was not connected with ours.

I put Marcus on the stand and the District Attorney, Walter Giubbini did his best to impeach him. Although Walter was a fine attorney, he had little success; but Jim decided to play it safe and put "Bouquet" Cohn in a sanitarium where he was safe from testifying, claiming he'd had a nervous breakdown.

When Jim launched his cross-examination of Marcus, he gave worse than the District Attorney, so I started barging in and objecting. In the middle of the cross-examination, Jim realized I was making him look like the heavy, and he agreed to a truce.

"But," Jim asked, "how do I get out of it? I've got your man on cross-examination."

"After everyone is seated, stand up and tell the judge, 'I think this poor man has had enough of this. I'm not going to ask him any more questions.' The district attorney won't know what to do. He won't expect it."

It worked.

But, after we finished our case, the prosecutor brought in an elderly lady on rebuttal. She lived across the street from Barkett's home. She claimed to have been sitting by her window and seen Marcus, the Butchers, and Eberhardt get out of a car, walk over, grab Barkett, physically take him to their car, and drive away.

Jim began to get nervous again, I assured him here was an old woman who stays at home and looks out the window. She reads about it in the newspaper, she doesn't even tell the police about it for weeks. This was her way of becoming somebody. I told him there was nothing to worry about. However, as events showed, I was less than successful in convincing him.

After the District Attorney's closing argument, Jim was next. I thought I was fortunate to have Jim ahead of me. He was a good-looking man, and a court reporter once told me that you could take a transcript of his closing argument, take it down word for word, and it would come out in perfect English. Very few lawyers can do that. Jim would quote Archibald MacLeish, he would quote from *The Rubaiyat of Omar Khayyam*. It made an excellent contrast to our clients' backgrounds.

But when I heard Jim's opening, my heart sank.

"I want to apologize to my client and to this jury. I've been taking this not very seriously. With Mr. Cohn, Mr. Haggerty and Mr. Shortall, I made it all a funny joke. But when I heard what this woman said I realized how serious this all was. I'd been making comedy out of this trial when I should have been very serious. It was a terrible thing that those four evil men did."

While I was listening to Jim, sitting at the table with Haggerty and Shortall, I thought to myself: how could I answer this? What was a good approach to someone so intellectual? We had a jury of normal, ordinary people. None of them knew anything about poetry. I asked myself where was his point of weakness?

I had to ridicule the poems. The jury didn't identify with intellectual poems—but how could I do it?

"I knew 'Mary Had a Little Lamb...' Then, all of a sudden, I wrote down four lines, without any changes—a poem.

I showed the poem to Haggerty. Haggerty had been listening to MacInnis, too. Haggerty looked at my poem and started laughing. I showed the poem to Shortall. He looked at the poem and he smiled, too.

When MacInnis finished, I stood up. I knew what I had to do.

I told the jurors, "You know, Mr. MacInnis is very well educated. He's a highly intellectual man and he makes a eloquent argument. He speaks beautifully. I'm a night law school person. He knows all those poems and I don't know who J. Archibald MacLeish is. Omar Khayyam? I couldn't tell you what he said. But, you're not here for that. I figure I'm going to be kind of embarrassed if I can't do something for the jury, but the only poem I know is 'Mary Had a Little Lamb' and I didn't know how to work it into this case. So, I wrote my own poem. I'll tell you about it later, so that you'll feel better about my not having a poem to quote."

I went on: "This case reminds me of a story. There were these Russians aboard a sled: a general, a lieutenant, a sergeant and a private. They have very important papers to deliver to Moscow. They're in a wilderness in Siberia. All of a sudden, they see wolves catching up with the sled, and the sled dogs are tired. The general says, 'You must go ahead. The message must go through. I'll stop the wolves.' The general jumps off the sled, starts fighting the wolves, and the wolves eat him.

"Soon, the wolves are catch up again. The lieutenant says, 'You must go ahead. The message must go through. I'll stop the wolves.' The lieutenant jumps off the sled and the wolves eat him. Now, there is only the sergeant and the private on the sled. They're not far from Moscow, but the wolves are right on them. The sergeant says, 'Those wolves are right on us. The message must go through,' and the sergeant throws the private off the sled…"

I did a whole day as a stand-up comic, interweaving Barkett's admissions into it. I told the jury they could not believe anything Cohn said because he was incompetent and in a mental asylum.

When I came in the next morning I could see that the jurors had loosened up. The judge was relieved, too. In chambers he admitted, "At least Nate got the smell of gas out of my courtroom."

When I continued my closing, I reminded the jurors, "I promised you a poem. It's one I made up myself:"

"MacInnis had a little Cohn
Who was a client all his own
If the DA starts to knock us,
We will blame it all on Marcus."

The jury laughed like hell. Judge Cullinan called a recess and ran into his chambers he was laughing so hard.

After lunch, when the jury was back, Jim walked over to me and presented me with a butcher knife. I felt my back—"Isn't your knife still in my back?" We were on the same team again. I had the jury laughing.

It was Friday afternoon, and I told Haggerty, "I want you to talk to that jury all day. I don't care if you have to sing a song, if you have to read them the whole Bible or the Constitution of the United States of America. I don't want the District Attorney getting back to that jury today. Let Richard go on as long as he can and then you finish it up so that you go to at least 4:30, so there will be no way the District Attorney can get to the jury until Monday."

Haggerty agreed. Shortall summed up in about 40 minutes, and Haggerty talked for three hours about everything he could think of. Finally, at 4:30, Judge Cullinan announced, "I think the jury has had enough today. We'll recess until Monday."

The newspapers called it the "Laughing Jury." Every one of the jurors had been laughing.

When we came back on Monday, Jim MacInnis was back in the ball game. When I arrived in the courtroom, MacInnis had written a poem on the blackboard, and all the jurors were reading it as they walked in.

"I gave my all for old St. Paul
Upon this field of battle
But Nate does not appreciate
My poems nor my prattle.

"Says he: 'My Madman's pure as snow
He wasn't there at all;
But if you find he struck a blow
Please also tie in Paul!'

"Since misery loves company
Our standards he must whittle
But in the end, I'll still contend
For all—a fast acquittal."

The bailiff came out. "Mr. MacInnis and Mr. Cohn, the judge wants you in chambers."

Judge Cullinan was furious. "I want you to go right out there and erase that. I don't want the jury seeing that."

The District Attorney added, "The jury has already seen that, your Honor."

I want that erased and I want Mr. MacInnis to let them know it shouldn't have been there." Jim had to go out and erase the whole poem.

Judge Cullinan also informed us that one of the jurors had taken sick and was being replaced by another gentleman, an alternate who had laughed the hardest of all at my verse.

I felt wonderful. The District Attorney had tried to get the jury thinking hard, but he couldn't do it. And in order for the jurors to have an alternative in case they felt they had to convict someone of something, I gave them one. Barkett claimed that my client Marcus hit him in the eye to make him sign the checks. Barkett had had a black eye. They could find Marcus guilty of simple assault.

A little over a day later, the jury came back with an acquittal on all charges.

All the newspapers in town were there. All of the attorneys were standing with their clients getting their pictures taken for the front page. I looked for my client so I could get my picture taken with him for

Tear-dimmed Marcus thanks his attorney, Nate Cohn.

the publicity. I couldn't see him. Then, I saw he had walked over to Walter Giubbini, the District Attorney, and put out his hand, and Walter was shaking Marcus' hand! My client was shaking hands with the District Attorney, so I grabbed Marcus and finally had his picture taken with me.

That was the big trial. Over in Municipal Court, due to the fact the charges had been brought by his wife and she had second thoughts about proceeding against him, the assault charges there were dropped.

After it was all over, I had an idea. We would have a party for everyone involved in the case. We would invite the jurors, all the court attachés. "Bouquet" Cohn's bar, the Bonanza, was six or seven doors from my office. I asked Jim if Cohn would let us use the Bonanza for the party. Jim told me he would even furnish the liquor and the *hors d'oeuvres*.

I had a big sign printed, "New Headquarters: Cash or Clobber Collection Agency." I had a card printed up, "Property of James Martin MacInnis" and I put it on the cash register. I sent myself wires saying there were different types of evidence in there.

The judge didn't come but a lot of other people did. A few of the jurors came. Unfortunately, "Bouquet" couldn't come because Jim was still having trouble getting him out of the institution, but it was a memorable occasion.

Not too long after, I was playing golf and I sprained my ankle, and had to walk with a cane. I went to the Bonanza for lunch. The waitress who had been a character witness for her boss (and I hadn't treated her too kindly), saw me limping, and smiled: "I see one of the witnesses got to you!"

It was my turn to laugh…

Making Law
on Making Book

I had quite a few clients who were bookmakers, or alleged to be bookmakers. While their cases were not nearly as serious, they had their own excitement.

One day a well-known bookmaker in San Francisco came to my office and announced he had been arrested.

He explained that the police had broken into his office. They had come right in through his door and found all his betting slips. Worse, the phone had kept ringing, and the police kept answering the phone and taking down bets.

"They've got me cold. Do you think you can do anything for me?"

"Well, I might, but I don't guarantee anything. All I'm going to do is go into court, and if I can get you out of it, I will."

He asked what I would charge. I told him that would be $3,500.

"That's enormous! You haven't have a snowball's chance of winning this case, you know."

"Look, you can't tell. I could win the case, or I could lose the case, but if you want me to do it, it's $3,500 bucks. I want it now. On the table."

He asked if I could get him a better sentence, and would that lower the fee.

"I'm not going to try to get you a better sentence. I'm going to try to get you out of it. $3,500."

He came back over with $3,500 and put it down on my desk.

At the trial, the prosecutor put on the police officers who had broken in. My cross-examination was brief.

"By the way, is it true that you didn't have a search warrant?"

"Yes, it's true."

"Is it true that you didn't have a warrant for my client's arrest?"

"Yes, that's true."

"Is it true that you broke in the door and went in without his permission?"

"Yes."

"No more questions."

And I asked the same questions to each of the police officers.

When the prosecution finished with their case, the judge asked, "Do you have any motions?"

"Yes, Your Honor, but I think that we should take these motions in chambers, not in front of the jury."

In chambers, I explained why I did not want to make my motion in front of the jury: "If the Court grants my motion," I said, "the District Attorney will be in a bad position because the jury would still have not heard my arguments and will have them on their mind."

A case had come down from the Supreme Court several weeks earlier ruling evidence from an illegal search and seizure could not be introduced, and I made a motion to exclude all the evidence the officers had seized.

The judge had seen the case, and the District Attorney realized that the evidence was the fruit of an illegal search and seizure. The law said that the evidence could not be introduced, but he had already introduced the evidence. There was no procedure for a motion to suppress in those days. "Nate, what do you suggest we do?"

I pointed out that panels of jurors sit for three months, and the same juror might sit on two or three cases during that time. I told the District Attorney this was an opportunity to impress the jurors with his honesty. I suggested that when we returned to the courtroom, he should say that we had gone through the evidence in chambers and that, under the evidence before the court right now, the court should dismiss this case against the defendant, because it is his duty not only to prosecute, but to make sure that everyone gets a fair trial, and he should ask for the case to be dismissed with prejudice. "That way," I pointed out, "the next time this jury heard him argue, they would think: 'There is an honest man.'

So he did, and all the jurors smiled.

My client, however, was not so sanguine. "What happened?"

"You're dismissed. Not guilty."

"Dismissed?"

"Yes."

"You mean it's all over?"

"I mean it's all over."

"Well, you didn't ask but three or four questions in the whole trial!"

"Of course. I didn't want to open any doors to anything else."

"You didn't ask many questions. Do I get some of my money back?"

"Look, you got acquitted. You didn't think you were going to have a snowball's chance in hell of getting acquitted, and I got you acquitted. Now you want money back? You've got to be the biggest idiot that ever came down the pike! Would you rather have me make a long speech and get you convicted and sent to San Quentin? Or would you rather have me keep my mouth shut so you can walk out with no record?"

"Well, you know, it didn't seem like you did much."

"I got you acquitted."

Four months later the bookmaker returned.

"I got arrested again."

"You did?"

"Last time it cost you $3,500 and you wanted some of it back, and I got you out of it. Now I want $4,500 and you're not going to get anything back—whatever happens."

"Well, you didn't ask many questions..."

"It's $4,500 if you want me to do it again, and I can't guarantee it. The chances of you being acquitted this time are ten times worse than they were last time."

"Well, I've got to use you because you got me out of it."

"Fine."

"Bring me up the $4,500 and you've got a deal."

He never returned.

Several weeks later, he called me again.

"Nate, I got a lawyer who offered to do it for me for $2,500, but he got me convicted. I'm going to have to go to jail. Would you have gotten me acquitted?"

"I don't know. I doubt it very much. You hired a good lawyer. So, you can always look at it from the standpoint that you saved $2,000."

"Can you tell me whether you would have had me found not guilty?"

"That's just like coming up to me and asking, 'Will I win the lottery?' or 'Will my horse win the Kentucky Derby?' Nobody knows that—only when the race is run."

Several days later, one of my client's friends called me up and told me, "He's going around asking everybody, 'Do you think Nate would have gotten me acquitted, or do you think Nate would have gotten me convicted?'"

People have funny ideas.

Another bookmaking case involved the brother of a very prominent man in San Francisco. The brother had a bar and also made book.

A young police officer went into the bar in full uniform and saw a patron give a piece of paper to the bartender. The bartender took the paper and, without even looking at it, threw it in a box. With that, the officer jumped over the counter, pulled his gun, told the bartender he was under arrest and gave him the *Miranda* warning.

"What are you arresting me for?"

"Bookmaking."

"What bookmaking are you claiming I've done?"

"You've got that paper in there."

The officer unfolded the paper and on the paper there was a name and address. In the box there were some things which could have been betting markers, and the officer arrested him.

The officer was assigned to the gambling squad. The head of the gambling squad was an Irish inspector named Murphy. I had run into Murphy at the Cow Palace where the college basketball finals were being played. We were both basketball enthusiasts and we had talked about basketball, and when we got to court that morning, I was talking to Murphy about the basketball tournaments. We had a very friendly conversation, then we went into the courtroom.

In court, I brought out the fact that the officer had jumped over the bar without a warrant and without probable cause. The judge, naturally, threw the case out.

I had also cross-examined the policeman at great length. He was young, and had only been on this detail for several months.

After the judge dismissed my client, I saw the young officer run over to Murphy shouting, "How can you do that? How can you stand there and talk to that Cohn so friendly? Did you see what he did to me in that courtroom? Did you see what he did to our squad in that courtroom?"

Murphy looked sternly at the young man. "Officer, he just did you a great favor."

"What? What kind of favor?"

"He gave you a lesson that you probably need and probably never would have gotten. He showed you what you did wrong, and how to do it right. Now, if you're smart, you'll learn from that. And don't get mad at him, because he's just doing his job. It's like a game. He plays to win, we play to win."

The Coup de Grace

13

One of my most difficult cases concerned a woman who had shot her husband, an abusive Highway Patrol officer. This was long before the "battered woman" defense was recognized. It was in December, 1956 that a highway patrol officer called me at home and asked if I would do him a favor and represent a lady by the name of Rose L. who had shot her husband several times. Her husband was dead and Rose was being charged with first-degree murder.

He told me that Mrs. L. didn't have a lot of money, and asked me to try and handle her case for as little as I could.

Thirty minutes later, Mrs. L. called me from the Hall of Justice and I agreed to go down and talk to her there.

There, I met Mrs. L.'s daughter and her two sons who were visiting her. Her daughter was a beautiful young lady and pregnant with a child. Mrs. L.'s two sons were good looking boys, bright and intelligent. The three of them told me that they wanted me to represent their mother and that they thought that what had happened was not her fault; but their father had abused her.

In the interview room, Mrs. L. told me that her husband, a highway patrolman, had been beating her up for many years. Also, she had the feeling he was looking for a way to kill her if he could get away with it.

That night, he had come home and had gone into the living room where he sat in a chair, drinking beer, reading the newspaper and smoking a cigarette.

She tried to talk to him, but he wouldn't talk to her and he threatened her. Afraid, she went to the other end of the house and found his revolver. She opened it and saw that the chambers were empty. She looked through the drawer for bullets and was able to find five bullets. She took the five bullets, put them in his gun and put the hammer on the empty chamber.

She then walked the length of the house to the living room and stood in the hallway outside the front room with the pistol in her hand and told her husband, "I want to talk to you. I don't want you to beat me. I just want to talk to you."

He jumped out of the chair and came toward her in a rage. She started pulling the trigger and he went down at her feet, dead. She stood there, then called the police and an ambulance. When the police arrived, they arrested her for murder.

She told them she thought that when her husband came at her he was going to kill her, so she kept pulling the trigger until he stopped.

Mrs. L. told me she had an insurance policy on her husband for $10,000. If she was found guilty of murder, she couldn't collect the $10,000. However, her insurance man had told her that if she was found guilty of manslaughter, she could still collect the $10,000. Mrs. L. also told me they owned a home in the Geneva Avenue district of San Francisco which was not worth a lot of money, and that they had some belongings, but not too much in the way of funds or savings. However, she said she would pay me $10,000 either from the insurance or from their savings, where they had almost $10,000.

At that time I was charging much more than $10,000 for this type of case, but I felt badly for Mrs. L. and I had told the highway patrolman who had called me that I would attempt to try the case for as little as possible. And she seemed nice enough.

We went before the Municipal Court for the arraignment. The District Attorney's office had assigned a top misdemeanor D. A. to represent them in the preliminary matters. The judge we appeared before was an excellent judge, but one who always proceeded on the theory that he was closer to the District Attorney than to the defense—so much so that he would allow the District Attorney to advise him on what he should do.

I had found that the law in California had been quite a bit misapplied in murder cases. Judges were under the misapprehension that no bail could be allowed on a first-degree murder charge. However, I looked into the law applying the Constitution of the State of California and the Constitution of the United States, and all of the laws applying to bail in California; and I put together a brief that said, in effect, that the District Attorney must make a presentation to the judge to convince the judge that the case would more likely end in a first-degree murder charge than anything else, or the judge must set bail.

I found other authorities that said if the judge granted bail, the judge must grant bail in an amount that could be deposited by the defendant.

I tried to explain this to the Municipal Court judge. He was nice enough. I had tried several cases before him successfully, and we were very good friends, but he simply repeated what the District Attorney said. I pointed out that I believed I had tried many, many more cases than the D. A. who was assigned to the case had at that time, and that I had won many, many more cases than the District Attorney, even though D.A.'s should win over 80% of their cases because they have the full force of the law behind them; but the judge was adamant and would not set bail.

A preliminary hearing was scheduled, but it wasn't held because the District Attorney obtained a grand jury indictment. I immediately asked the court to send the case to Superior Court so that I could attempt to set bail in the Superior Court.

In the Superior Court, the case was assigned to Judge Walter Carpeneti. I knew Judge Carpeneti very well. He was a brilliant student of the law, and as honest as one could possibly be. If he liked you, or you were a friend of his, you had to work harder because, in the back of his mind, he wanted to make sure he wasn't favoring any party in the litigation.

The Assistant District Attorney was Jack Berman, who was one of the brightest lawyers in the District Attorney's office. He was a brilliant young man who graduated from college very young and also graduated from law school quite young—and in some ways he was an excellent opponent for me.

I had previously been successful with two or three cases against Jack. Jack's brilliance was his undoing. When I would throw a curve in a case in which Jack was the D. A., he would know exactly what I was doing. Many times, the judge or the jury didn't know what I was doing, but Jack was so bright he knew exactly what I was doing and why I was doing it. But if no one else caught on, it would upset him. He would get angry. I would keep throwing curves and he would keep trying to knock them out of the park, to little avail.

Here, Jack thought he had the perfect first-degree murder case—Mrs. L. had shot her husband five times, and she was claiming self-defense when it was she who had a gun—and Jack wanted a little retribution for the cases I had won against him in the past.

I made my motion for bail before Judge Carpeneti. No one expected the judge to grant bail—it wasn't done and it hadn't been done. But when I presented my brief to Judge Carpeneti, who read it, understood it and followed it, he realized that the only way the court could refuse to grant bail was if the District Attorney were to produce witnesses who would testify to facts which would show that the charge of first-degree murder could be proven—not second-degree, not manslaughter. It had to be proven that the evidence would show first-degree murder.

The grand jury had returned an indictment, and cross-examination by a defense attorney is not allowed in the grand jury proceedings. I argued to Judge Carpeneti that Mr. Berman would have to put on witnesses to show that this was a first-degree murder charge, and that I would have the opportunity to cross-examine those witnesses thoroughly.

I believed there was no way Jack was going to let me cross-examine his witnesses before trial. And, as it turned out, Jack refused to put anyone on the witness stand and Judge Carpeneti decided to grant my client bail.

I then proceeded to the second step of my argument. I explained to the judge that since he was going to grant bail, he had to grant bail in an amount that my client could actually meet, otherwise it was not bail. Jack was talking about bail in the amount of $700,000. I was talking about bail of $10,000. The judge granted bail of $20,000.

Before I went into court to ask for bail, I had talked to the bail bondsman, Boyd Puccinelli, and I sold him on the idea that if I could get the court to grant bail on a first-degree murder charge, it would be a great advantage for every bail bondsman because now they would have a completely new category of potential clients. Boyd agreed if I could get a judge to allow bail on a first-degree murder charge he would give my client a break on the bail.

When I went to Boyd to set arrangements for the bail for Mrs. L., however, he was so impressed with what I had accomplished, he put up the bail without charging my client anything.

Judge Carpeneti received phone calls and letters from judges all throughout California complaining he had set a bad precedent, but Judge Carpeneti was a brilliant student of the law and would not be intimidated by other judges or by politicians. He would only do what he believed was the correct thing to do, and he had done so.

Thus, Mrs. L. was out on bail throughout the whole proceeding, including after conviction, on appeal.

In preparation for trial, I retained Dr. Paul Kirk, head of the criminology department at the University of California, as forensic expert. The prosecution's theory was that Mrs. L. shot her husband with four bullets as he came toward her. Then, after he fell to the ground with his head on the floor, she shot him in the head as he lay on the floor completely helpless. Jack called it the *coup de grace*.

However, the police could only find four bullets. Jack argued that the fifth bullet, because it was shot down into her husband's head, bounced around, becoming little pieces which disintegrated.

I brought Dr. Kirk over to the scene of the shooting, and he used strings to follow the path of the bullets from where Mrs. L. was standing at the time she fired the shots. He could do that with four bullets, but not the missing fifth bullet.

The trial began, and Jack went to town. One of the pieces of evidence was the bloody uniform that Officer L. had been wearing when he was shot. The shirt was full of blood and Berman waved it around during the trial like a battle flag. He described how Mrs. L. coolly loaded the bullets into the revolver. Meanwhile, I attempted to establish that Mr. L. was a brute, the sort of man who would beat up his wife and threaten to kill her.

The case generated a great deal of publicity, and, as a result, I received a phone call from someone who told me that Mr. L. had been having an affair with a telephone operator at a hotel. He thought it could help my case and suggested I talk to the lady.

The catering manager at the hotel was a friend of mine, and it was very simple for me to go to the hotel and talk to the young lady because she knew that her employer would be cooperative if she was willing to testify.

I explained to the young lady the position Mrs. L. was in. My client was facing the death penalty; and she would be doing Mrs. L. a great service if she would testify. I also informed her I would only call her to the stand if she agreed to testify.

She agreed to testify and told me Mr. L. had actually told her that he was thinking of killing his wife.

I kept all details about her quiet and arranged with her to appear in court on a certain date at a certain time. I then told several members of the press to appear at the courtroom at that date and time.

I didn't tell the press what she was going to say. I told them I had a witness who was going to be quite interesting, and I left it at that.

One other problem I had to face was Mrs. L.'s appearance. Mrs. L. had very thin and harsh lips, making her look severe, even though she was a slight lady with nice children. I took her to a cosmetologist to try to soften her lips and her face and give her a friendlier, softer look, but we couldn't do anything for her.

One Saturday, while I was sitting at home going over the case, I had the big break. All of a sudden I remembered something that Dr. Kirk had said to me: there has to be a reason for everything that happens, and if you look at evidence, you can figure out what actually happened. If someone you have confidence in states that something happened in a certain way, then you should look it over because, most likely, it did happen in that way.

Dr. Kirk called this deductive reasoning, and he explained it in this way: if you see a car that has a dent on the hood, you know that something hit the hood to cause the dent.

I was sitting there that Saturday thinking about the fifth bullet. I got in my car and drove over to the L. home. No one was there, but I had a key, and there were no more police ribbons to stop anyone from going inside. I went into the house and stood where Mrs. L. said she had stood, and I did what Mrs. L. said she had done. I held an imaginary gun pointing toward the back wall, and as I started to imagine her pulling the trigger and Mr. L. start to fall forward, I turned slightly to my right and fired the last bullet.

When I did that, I saw that my imaginary gun was pointed at a spot where there was a chair with a slipcover on it. I thought, if what she said was true, the bullet would have to go through that slipcover. I examined that slipcover from every angle. I got down on the floor and examined it. Then, without touching the slipcover, I took a pencil, and I moved a little bit of the slipcover around and saw what appeared to be a hole in the slipcover. Something had gone through there and it had closed up again.

I moved the chair and I took the pencil and pointed it toward the floor as if it were a bullet going into the floor. I got down on the floor and examined the carpet in that spot very closely, but without touching anything. I could see there was something in the floor, but I didn't want to touch it and have prosecution claim I had tampered with the evidence, so I called Dr. Kirk and asked him to come over right away.

Dr. Kirk came flying over to the house. I went through the same steps I had gone through with Dr. Kirk. I stood where Mrs. L. stood, holding an imaginary gun, and I explained to him what Mrs. L. said had happened and how she said it had happened. Then, I turned the gun to the place where the gun would go off when Mr. L. was falling down but did not yet have his head on the ground.

"Deductive reasoning, Dr. Kirk."

Dr. Kirk went through the same steps I had gone through, and lo and behold, he found the bullet in the floor. Dr. Kirk was excited, and he took detailed notes and photographs of the scene and the bullet.

On Monday, we exhibited the photos and notes to the jury. I introduced into evidence the testimony of Dr. Kirk and his photographs, which showed that Jack's theory of the *coup de grace* was completely wrong—Mrs. L. was telling the truth when she said she kept firing when Mr. L. went down.

That killed Berman's idea that the fifth bullet was fired when Mr. L. was on the floor. In fact, the fifth bullet had been fired while Mr. L. was falling.

With Jack's theory "shot," if you will pardon the expression, he tried to strengthen his case in other ways—chiefly by trying to impeach my witnesses, and I fought back, interrupting him. I got Jack to the point that he was arguing with my witnesses and the witnesses were convinced he was trying to call them liars.

While Jack was going full blast, Judge Carpeneti halted everything. "Gentlemen! Stop this!"

"Mr. Berman, if you do that one more time, I'm going to hold you in contempt."

Then Judge Carpeneti looked over at me and said, "I'm going to hold you in contempt too, Mr. Cohn."

"Me?"

"Do you want me to explain why?"

"No, Your Honor. I'll take your word for it."

The next day it was a front-page story in all the newspapers, and that evening, my phone rang. It was Lou Lurie.

Louis Lurie was one of the wealthiest men in San Francisco. Every year he would have a birthday party at his hotel at the Top of the Mark (the world famous cocktail lounge atop the Mark Hopkins Hotel on Nob Hill in San Francisco) with Maurice Chevalier, who had the same birthday. Lou invited me every year.

"What is it, Lou?"

"I saw in the paper where Judge Carpeneti is threatening to hold you in contempt. You tell Judge Carpeneti that if he holds you in contempt, I'll put up $50,000 bail for you and I'll get Jake Ehrlich to represent you."

I laughed. "Lou, he's not going to hold me in contempt. He's just suggesting that if I cause him any trouble, he might hold me in contempt. Don't worry about it."

When we went back to court, Jack made his passionate closing argument and asked for a verdict of first-degree murder. You'd think from his argument that he was going to be there to personally execute Mrs. L. if she got the death penalty.

Unfortunately, the fifth bullet had driven a hole into his case and the jury returned a verdict of manslaughter.

When the verdict came in, Mrs. L.'s son was sitting in the front row with a young man from my office, Larry Shostak. Her son asked Larry, "Can they do any more to my mother?"

"No," Larry explained. "When they bring in a manslaughter verdict, that is also a verdict of not guilty of murder, so they can never try your mother for murder again."

"There's nothing more they can do to my mother now?"

"No, they can't."

I was up at the front rail with Mrs. L., talking to Judge Carpeneti, when, all of a sudden, I heard a commotion.

I turned around and saw two police inspectors holding onto Mrs. L.'s son and running him up the aisle. I ran up the aisle trying to stop them.

"He just slugged the D. A.," one of the inspectors said.

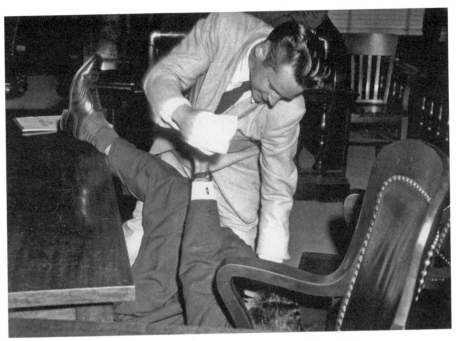

Decked. Prosecutor Jack Berman's feet in the air as the son of a disgruntled defendant gets his revenge.

When I looked back, I could see that Jack had been knocked over the table. His feet were still up in the air and he was just pulling himself together.

The bailiff announced, "The judge wants to see Mr. Berman and Mr. Cohn in Chambers."

I went into Chambers with Jack and Judge Carpeneti directed his remarks to him.

"Mr. Berman, I saw everything that happened. That young man came through the rail, grabbed you by the tie when you were looking toward the bench, hit you in the face and knocked you over that table. I saw the whole thing. If you want, I'll have him thrown right in jail for contempt. And I'll issue a complaint against him for assault and battery."

Jack brushed it off. "Judge, forget it. I can understand it. Forget it. No problem."

From that moment on, I thought Jack was one of the finest people I've ever known. It took a lot of class to do what he did. We were close friends from that day until his death.

An interesting sidenote: during the L. trial, Jack was married to a young lady, Dianne Berman. She was pregnant and sat through the trial to watch Jack perform.

Dianne Berman later divorced Jack and is now Dianne Feinstein, United States Senator from California. The child she was pregnant with is now a Superior Court judge in San Francisco. Jack himself was also appointed a Superior Court judge.

In addition to Dianne Feinstein, Mrs. L.'s daughter was also carrying a baby during the trial. Mrs. L.' daughter's baby was also born after the trial. In honor of the job I did for her mother, she named the baby 'Natalie,' after me.

After the case was completed, Larry Shostak asked me if I would mind if he appealed the case. I allowed him to do it. The appellate decision characterized the conduct of the trial in a unique way, declaring that both counsel had "frequently reverted to the ancient form of trial by champion." It was truly a battle of skill, but one in which the facts carried the day.

The appellate court held that under the evidence, Mrs. L. could not have received an acquittal or any verdict lower than manslaughter.

A young Dianne Feinstein, George Reilly and Nate.

Stormy Weather

14

Another high-profile client (if you will excuse the pun) was the legendary stripper, Tempest Storm, for whom I helped arrange the first million-dollar contract in the field.

The first time I met Tempest Storm she was facing contempt charges. Peter DeCenzie, who ran the El Rey Theater in Oakland, had booked Tempest a few months earlier. While she was there, an advertising man for the theater put an ad in the newspaper which used the expression: "Tempest Storm and her Treasure Chest."

Another stripper, Evelyn West, filed a lawsuit against the El Rey Theater and Tempest Storm claiming infringement of Evelyn West's trademark: "Treasure Chest."

A friend of Tempest's referred her to a very well-known and highly publicized lawyer in San Francisco and she hired him to represent her. While the Court found that Ms. West had not been damaged by the use of her trademark in the advertisement, the court enjoined Tempest from using the phrase in the future. Tempest was not very satisfied with the result.

Tempest went back east and played different clubs and theaters there, but when she returned to San Francisco, she was served with papers claiming that an advertisement had appeared in a newspaper back east using words "Treasure Chest." Ms. West's attorneys sought contempt against Tempest and wanted her jailed for violating the injunction. Tempest was predictably upset and Peter suggested she come see me.

After I looked through all the papers, I told her everything would be all right.

We set a date for a hearing and we went to court. While walking toward City Hall where the courts were held, Ed Devere, Tempest's publicity agent made a suggestion. Ed was one of those old-time publicity agents who thought anything you did for publicity was okay.

"Tempest, you know, we're missing an opportunity here."

"What do you mean?"

"Well, if the judge finds you guilty and sentences you to jail, just think of the pictures we would have!"

"I don't think Miss Storm really appreciates that kind of humor." I didn't think it was really humor with Ed, but, I took it as if it was humor, just black humor.

I argued that the advertisement was placed by the theater back east without Tempest's knowledge. After a two-hour hearing, the judge held for Tempest.

A few days later, Peter DeCenzie called me and told me that Miss Storm had another problem she would like me to handle. She had married a young man she had met down in Los Angeles, and the young man was living high off the hog on her money, spending it like there was no tomorrow. She had just bought a new Cadillac—she was staying in a suite at the St. Francis Hotel and she had been driving back and forth to Oakland—and he had that, too.

I drew up a complaint for divorce and I gave the papers to Larry Shostak. I told him to find her husband, show him the papers and retrieve the car for Tempest.

Larry retrieved her car and called me back: "I'm here with Ms. Storm at the St. Francis Hotel. She's not working today and she wants to talk to you."

When I arrived at Tempest's suite, Larry was seated in front a bottle of great Scotch surrounded by all manner of *hors d'oeuvres*.

"Miss Storm said that she would like to buy me a drink and she wanted to know if you drank. I told her you have a drink once in a while, so she ordered up a good bottle of Scotch and some *hors d'oeuvres* for us."

"Did you serve the husband?"

"Yes, I served the husband, I retrieved the car and everything's under control."

Tempest interjected, "When can we finish this up?"

I set the dissolution for Valentine's Day. The press got a big kick out that. It didn't take more than ten minutes for the judge to issue the dissolution. Tempest wore an expensive full-length mink coat and a suit. The press photographed her continuously after we emerged from the courtroom.

Tempest Storm with Nate.

Tempest wanted to take me to lunch, but I had a table at The Palace Hotel reserved for me. George Christopher had been elected Mayor and there was a big luncheon to honor him there.

I asked her whether she had ever attended a political luncheon.

"No."

"Well, would you like to go to one?"

"I guess."

"Come on. I'll take you over there."

As we walked to the table—I had a table for my office and Tempest at the front next to the head table—Tempest smiled at everyone. With her flashy red hair and long mink coat, and her figure, every eye in the room was on Tempest. The whole luncheon Tempest attracted more attention than the Mayor, and she enjoyed it thoroughly, and people kept coming over to meet her.

When we took her back to the office she thanked me: "I never realized how interesting politics could be!"

The next time I saw Tempest and Ed proved a historical occasion.

Tempest explained that a chain of burlesque theaters in the East had offered her a ten-year contract. She would perform at their theaters for ten years, he would only have to work ten weeks a year, and they would pay $100,000 a year for ten years."

The proverbial light bulb went off.

"Ed, don't you realize what you have here?"

"What do you mean?"

"That's a million-dollar contract. I don't know of any stripper in the world who has ever signed a million-dollar contract to appear in any theaters exclusively for ten years. I've never heard of it before. Tempest is now a million-dollar performer."

In those days, a million dollars was a lot of money.

I asked to see the contract. It had been drawn up by a big firm in Florida.

It was three hours later in Florida and it was around one o'clock California time. I called the attorney in Florida who had drafted the contract. He assured me that it was completely legitimate. They wanted her to sign it, but she wouldn't sign the contract unless I had seen it and approved it.

I had a talk with the attorney in Florida.

"Do you mind if Tempest publicizes this? It will be very good for your chain and it would also be fantastic for Tempest to have signed a million-dollar contract."

"No, go right ahead. You can refer anybody to my office and we'll confirm."

"Thank you very much. I'll go over the contract and as soon as I go through it I'll have her sign it and send it back to you."

"Fine, I appreciate it."

Ed asked to use my phone and he called the city editors of the four daily newspapers in San Francisco: the *News,* the *Call-Bulletin,* the *Examiner* and the *Chronicle.* The *News* and the *Call-Bulletin* were the afternoon papers and The *Examiner* and The *Chronicle* were morning papers. He called up the city editor of The *Chronicle* first and told him what they had.

"Can you confirm this?"

"I'm in Nate Cohn's office. You can talk to him."

The city editor asked me what the situation was, and I told him it was true: a strip-tease artist signs a contract for a million dollars to play burlesque chains back east for ten years.

I gave him the names of the attorneys in Florida to confirm it. The

Tempest Storm poses with the San Francisco press photographers.

city editor asked to interview Tempest Storm, and I referred him to Ed.

All the city editors reacted the same way. Then Ed contacted the newsreels and the TV stations and the radio stations and set up a press conference in my office for the next morning.

"There's one thing you have to do," I warned him. "I don't want my picture in my office. If we were in the courtroom, or if we were in City Hall, I'd love my picture with Tempest. But, I don't want my picture taken in my office with Tempest. Some lawyers are quite jealous and they will think I set this up so I could get publicity. So, keep me out of it. I don't need the publicity but Tempest can use my offices for the interview."

That afternoon, as Tempest was leaving, she said, "We'll also order some drinks and some *hors d'oeuvres* for the press." I told her it was fine for her to use my office for a press conference, because she was a client, as long as my office was not identified in the stories or any photographs, but I could not have the press drinking and eating *hors d'oeuvres* there, too.

The next morning we had photographers and people with recording machines for the radio stations in my office. We had reporters and press photographers. It seemed everything and everybody was loaded into my office to interview Tempest.

I placed myself far in the back, so no one could bother me; I sat behind my desk watching it all, and I kept out of the view of the cameras.

The press photographers wanted to take pictures of the contract and they wanted to take pictures of Tempest. Finally, one of them came up with an idea. He said to Tempest, "If you could go in Nate's closet and take off your clothes and put the two contracts, one across your bosom and one across your lower part of your body, it would completely cover you, but you'd be nude holding these two contracts. It'd be a fantastic picture."

Tempest refused.

Jimmy Leterer, who was a newsreel photographer, was there with his wife, who came because she wanted to meet Tempest. Mrs. Leterer told Tempest she had an idea.

"Mr. Cohn's associate has an office right next door. If he could get out of that office for a few minutes, you could go in there and take off your clothes and put on your mink coat. You'd be fully covered. You could come in here and then you could go in Nate's closet and take your coat off. I could hold your coat up in front of you so nobody could see in there until you covered yourself up with the two contracts. Then, I could back away and let the photographers take your picture. When they're through, I'll come back with the coat and cover you up and then you can go back in the other room and put your clothes back on. That way the photographers would have the pictures of you basically in the nude, holding these two contracts to cover you and it'd be a fantastic picture."

"I guess it's okay, Mrs. Leterer."

Tempest came back in in the full-length mink coat. Mrs. Leterer held the coat up before her so she could get herself set with these two contracts covering her, with her back to the back of the closet, with the two contracts over the front of her. Mrs. Leterer backed away and everyone started taking pictures. Finally, when they had finished, Mrs. Leterer came back and put the coat up again. Tempest was able then to put down the contracts and cover herself with the coat. She went in the other room and put on her clothes and came back in.

One of the photographers asked Tempest Storm what her measurements were.

"My measurements are 39, 32, 34."

Mrs. Leterer added, "Well, those are my measurements, only not in the same order!"

While this was going on, a friend of mine called me on my private line. "Hi Nate. What are you doing?"

"If I told you what I was doing there is no way you would believe me!"

To this day he doesn't know what I was talking about.

When Tempest finished the press interviews and the pictures, all of the photographers and reporters expected they would be offered a drink, but I had to decline.

Finally, Tempest came over and thanked me. "You know, I feel bad. I've never seen so many reporters and photographers and cameramen. It was unbelievable. I'd like to do something for them."

I had a suggestion.

"What's that?"

"You're playing at the El Rey Theater tonight. Is that right?"

"Yes, I have to go over there after this for a show tonight."

"How long are you going to be there?"

"I am going to finish out this week and that'll be the end of it."

"Well, why don't you do this? If you want to do something to show your appreciation to the press, what you could do is to throw a press cocktail party at the St. Francis Hotel where you're staying. Rent a large suite, order drinks and *hors d'oeuvres*. Invite all the press to come to this party to show your appreciation. You do that after you've finished at the El Rey Theater so they'll realize that you're not doing it to get publicity because you're not showing anymore. You're only doing it to show your appreciation."

"That's a wonderful idea."

"It might cost you a couple of thousand dollars."

"I don't care, Nate. That's a wonderful idea."

"I have to come over and see Peter DeCenzie who runs the El Rey Theater on another matter. I think I'll be there on Thursday night; if you have any questions or anything you want to say, you can talk to me then."

Tempest called the management at the St. Francis and rented a large suite. She had them set up a bar in there and she ordered hot and cold *hors d'oeuvres*. I assigned Larry Shostak to her and he ordered all the liquor he thought she might need.

When I went over to see Peter DeCenzie, Peter told me that Tempest wanted to talk to me, so after I finished with Peter, Tempest and I went next door to a bar to have a cup of coffee and talk. She wanted to update me on the arrangements for the party and make sure that everything was all right.

Standing at the bar was a man dressed exactly like Elvis Presley. He even looked like Elvis Presley. I asked Tempest if she would excuse me.

"Excuse me, are you an Elvis impersonator?"

"Yes."

"Have you ever worked as a bartender?"

"Yes, I have."

"Well, after Miss Tempest Storm closes here, she is going to have a cocktail party at the St. Francis Hotel on Monday afternoon from five p.m. to eight p.m. If you come over and work as a bartender, she will pay you one hundred dollars.

"You be there at five o'clock and dressed as Elvis Presley. You be the bartender."

"Wonderful. Would you introduce me to Miss Storm?"

"Of course, come on over."

When I told Tempest what I had done, she thought it would be cute.

On Monday at five o'clock I had my whole staff go over to the St. Francis Hotel to the suite where Tempest was throwing the party. Her publicity man had sent out letters to all of the newspapers inviting the publishers, editors, reporters, and staffs to come over to the St. Francis for a cocktail party. He did the same thing with the television and radio stations. Tempest had rented a very large suite for the party and I sent my secretaries and other lawyers to the St. Francis to be there with Tempest.

I had one matter which I had to finish before walking over. When I was through, at about five-thirty, I walked into the party.

The room was completely full. I had never seen so many press people in my life. I saw all of the reporters that I knew. I saw the editors that I knew. One of the editors introduced me to his publisher, and to the publisher's wife who had come.

It seemed everybody wanted to meet Tempest Storm. One of the reporters told me that he had covered a cocktail party honoring the President of the United States, and that party had not had the representation of editors and editor's wives, publishers and publisher's wives that this party had.

At the bar, serving drinks, was the gentleman dressed as Elvis Presley. Everyone got a big charge out of that, too.

Larry Shostak had selected all of the best whiskeys and ordered them from the hotel. Waiters were passing out hot *hors d'oeuvres*, and there was a table of cold *hors d'oeuvres*.

And Tempest, dressed elegantly, was walking around talking to everyone.

At eight o'clock, they ran out of *hors d'oeuvres*. Larry ordered some more. Whenever we ran out of hot *hors d'oeuvres*, more *hors d'oeuvres* came in. Tempest kept telling Larry, "Go ahead and do it."

It was one of the finest parties you could ever see. A few photographers took pictures of Tempest, but it was primarily a party to thank the press for being so nice to Tempest in San Francisco. That was how she put it. She was not showing anywhere in the vicinity and the press knew she had not given this party for the purpose of publicity. It really was a thank you to them.

About eight-thirty—there were still a lot of people there—she closed up and paid the bartender and thanked him for his services. He had had a ball.

A friend of mine came over and told me that four reporters from the downtown newspapers—a couple from the *Examiner*, one from the *Chronicle* and one from somewhere else—had gotten a hold of the bartender and they had grabbed a full bottle of bourbon, taken it with them and left.

"Let it go. No big thing," I assured him.

After she had stopped the liquor and stopped everything and everyone left, I took Tempest and my whole office along with Ed Devere to Ernie's for dinner. When it was over, Larry and Ed Devere took Tempest back to the St. Francis where she was staying, and I went home.

When I arrived at my office the next morning, one of my secretaries said that a woman had been calling me and that she sounded hysterical. Since I did a lot of criminal work, I was used to having people who were hysterical calling me, and my secretary gave me her number and I returned the call.

"This is Nate Cohn. What can I do for you?"

"Mr. Cohn, what did you do with my husband? That Tempest Storm has got my husband."

"What are you talking about?"

"He went to that party last night and he's disappeared. I know he likes Tempest Storm and she's got him."

"When the party was over last night at about eight-thirty, I took Miss Storm and her publicist and my whole office out to dinner. We were all out to dinner, and after dinner Miss Storm was taken home. There was nobody with her except her publicist when she went to her room. I don't know what you're talking about."

"Did you have a fellow there who was a bartender who looked like Elvis Presley?"

"She hired him to be a bartender. He came over there but he left at eight-thirty."

"He hasn't come home all night."

"She hired him and paid him for his services. I don't think Miss Storm said four words to him all evening. She's not interested in an Elvis Presley imitator."

"He didn't come home."

"Call the police, I don't know where he is. Miss Storm doesn't have him."

About an hour later she called me back and told me what had happened. The four reporters from the newspapers had taken the bottle of bourbon and her husband and gone to all of the different nightclubs and bars in San Francisco. With four of the top reporters with him, everyone thought they knew who they were, and the reporters told everyone that her husband was really Elvis Presley. All of the owners of the restaurants and bars bought them drinks and treating them royally until around one o'clock in the morning when they ended up at a very famous bar in Chinatown. When the owner came over to see them and discovered that this was not Elvis Presley, he threw them out of his bar. They were all smashed and decided to go home, but they then concluded they were all too smashed to drive and slept in the car. Her husband had just gotten in a few minutes ago, ending the story of Elvis Presley, the Bartender.

Some time later, Tempest came into my office in San Francisco with her publicity man, Ed Devere, and said she would like some way to change her name legally to Tempest Storm. I told her that wouldn't be tough, she could file a motion to change her name legally before the court, and unless somebody had some reasons why she couldn't, it was usually automatic.

She said, "Could you do it?"

I said, "Where are you living?"

"In Los Angeles."

"I would have to make the motion in Los Angeles. "

"You set it up and I'd be happy to pay for your time and the trip to Los Angeles."

"Okay, I'll set it up."

I drew up a petition for change of name and filed it in Los Angeles. They were having a jury trial in Los Angeles for invasion of privacy or defamation against a magazine called *Confidential*, and this attracted all the newspapers. I set it for the morning when this trial was being held and I told Tempest to meet me at the courtroom at 9:00 on that morning and she should tell Ed Devere that she was going to change her name, and she might get some publicity out it.

When I arrived in court at 9:00, the courthouse was packed with photographers wanting to take our pictures, which they did. After we changed her name legally to Tempest Storm, the press took her and started taking pictures of her, and I stood around watching it for a while. When they were finished, Tempest told Ed, "Why don't you go ahead, I want to talk to Nate."

She asked me to give her a ride home.

After she got in the car, I asked: "What do you want to know?"

"Is this legal?"

"Of course it's legal."

"Well, it was awfully simple."

"It's no big thing. Any lawyer can do it."

"I want you to come into my apartment for a minute. I want to talk to you."

When we got into her apartment, she asked if I would take her out to lunch.

"Sure."

"I just have to make a phone call..."

She made a phone call to Michael Wilding, who had been married to Elizabeth Taylor: "I want you to come over to my apartment right now. Look, I'm telling you to come to my apartment right now. It's very important. I don't care what you have to do, come over to my apartment."

About fifteen minutes later, in walked Wilding.

"Michael, this is my lawyer, Nathan Cohn."

"Very pleased to meet you."

"I'm happy to meet you."

"Nate, give him your card."

"Pardon?"

"Give him one of your cards."

I gave him a card, he took it and studied it.

"He's always getting in trouble," she explained to me. "Now you have Nate's card. He's the best lawyer I know. If you get into any kind of trouble and you need a lawyer, call Nate."

"Okay, Tempest."

"Okay, you can go now."

"That's all?"

"That's all. I'll talk to you later."

"What was that all about?"

"Well, he's been married to Elizabeth Taylor and he gets into trouble at times and I wanted him to know you. He wants to marry me."

"What?"

"He wants to marry me. What do you think?"

"What do you mean, what do I think? Are you in love with him?"

"No, I like him, but I'm not really in love with him."

"You can't marry someone you're not really in love with!"

"He's a nice man—and just think of the publicity."

"You can't marry someone for publicity. That's ridiculous, Tempest."

"You don't think I should?"

"Of course not."

"Well, you're going to take to take me to lunch. I'll be right back."

She went to her bedroom. In the meantime, she asked me if I wanted anything. She made me a cup of coffee.

When she comes out, she was wearing elastic pants that fit her as if she was without clothes and she was braless.

"Tempest, I'm not going to walk into a restaurant with you looking like that."

"What are you talking about? That's the way people down here in Hollywood dress."

"I'm not going to walk in like that."

"These pants cost $300. They're the best pants you can get. This is the style."

"I'm not going to do it."

"You told me you would take me to lunch and this is the way I'm going to lunch. You're a man of your word and I know you're going to do that."

"Okay, come on."

We went out and got in the car and I drove to a drive-in. The waitress put a tray on the side of the car I asked, "What do you want, Tempest?"

"I want to go to a restaurant."

"No, I told you I'd take you to lunch, this is lunch. Pick out what you want. I'm going to have a hamburger and a coke."

"I'll have a hamburger and a coke. That's a fine thing. I'm dressed like people dress down here."

"You're dressed like someone I'm not going to walk into a good restaurant with."

"What do you think of my marrying that man?"

"I told you. Unless you're in love with somebody, you shouldn't marry them. Publicity doesn't mean that much. You've got all the publicity you need."

"Well, I guess you're right. He's a nice man and I like him, but I don't love him."

"Then, don't get married."

"Okay, you're right."

She started telling me about a booking she had and how much money she was making.

I told her, "Tempest, what you've got to do is you've got to save your money. Your career will end before you know it. Time goes by fast. Put your money in the bank or put it in stocks—good stocks, blue chip stocks—or invest it in property, but invest it."

"Oh, I'm not worried about it. I buy a lot of jewelry."

I drove her home and she invited me in. She said she wanted to show me something.

She had a closet full of shoes. It was like a shoe store.

"What in the world are you doing with all those shoes? You can't wear all those shoes."

"I'm in a funny position. A man wants to date me. He's got one thing in mind, and I don't want to go out with a guy who's got one thing in mind so I don't date very much. Once in a while I go out with a young man because I know he's not interested in me that way."

"What have the shoes got to do with it?"

"I feel low, so I go into a store and I buy several thousand dollars worth of shoes. One day I went into a store and I bought a couple of thousand dollars worth of gloves. I can't wear them, but it gives me something to make me feel I can do what I want to do."

"Tempest, put your money in blue chip stocks, or property, or even in the bank. But don't go around throwing it away like that."

"Well, it makes me feel good."

I understand Tempest has now been elected to the Entertainer's Hall of Fame.

He Drank Too Much

15

I read in the paper one day there had been a shooting in North Beach and the police had arrested a certain Ballestreri for murder. The next day, a gentleman by the name of Tom Ballestreri came into my office and told me that his brother had been charged with murder. He asked me to represent his brother and get him bailed out.

I told him I would try.

I contacted the District Attorney's Office and the District Attorney who was handling the case preliminarily told me that Mr. Ballestreri was in the city prison and the District Attorney agreed to bail. I called Tom and told him that the D.A. agreed he could bail his brother out, and to bring his brother up to my office.

His brother was a short, heavyset Italian man in his sixties who had been working in a brewery for many years.

The story he told me was this:

He was not married and had no children, but he had a friend of his who had a daughter, a very pretty Italian girl, and the girl would bring her friends over to his house in North Beach and he would cook a beautiful Italian dinner for them. This had been going on for several years. On this occasion, she had called him and told him she was going to bring over her new boyfriend and she arrived with a young man. Her boyfriend was over six feet and weighed over 200 pounds. The dinner was very friendly. They drank wine with dinner. They drank brandy after dinner and music was playing on the radio. After dinner, Mr. Ballestreri started washing the dishes—they were all half-loaded by this time— and the girl came over to the sink to help him wash the dishes. The girl's boyfriend insisted she dance with him.

"No, I've got to help him with the dishes."

"What? You have something going with this old guy?"

She had been drinking pretty heavily, too.

"No, no, no. He's a *finocchio*!"

Ballestreri became very upset and slapped her on the face. "You ought to be ashamed of yourself!" *Finocchio*, in Italian, means a homosexual.

With that, the boyfriend jumped over the counter and grabbed Ballestreri, threw him to floor, sat astride him with one leg on each side, and started punching him with both hands.

The girl tried to pull her boyfriend off of Ballestreri.

"Leave him alone, he's an old man."

Finally, the girl pulled him off and Ballestreri lay on the floor, pretty well beaten.

Ballestreri pulled himself up, went to his bedroom where he had a gun under his mattress, pulled the gun out and came back into the kitchen. Ballestreri fired a bullet into the floor to show the boyfriend that the gun was loaded.

The boyfriend ran out the back door and started running down the stairs. Ballestreri ran to the head of the stairs and shot five bullets into him. The boyfriend went down and Ballestreri, who was very intoxicated, came back in, laid the gun down and called the police and an ambulance.

The police arrested him for first-degree murder when they arrived.

The case was assigned for trial to Judge Donald Constine, whom I knew quite well. He had been a U.S. Attorney and I had had cases against him; then he became U.S. Commissioner, then a Municipal Court judge, then a Superior Court judge. We respected each other very much, but not so that he would do anything more for me than he would do for anyone else.

The D.A. was one of the top trial lawyers in the office, Ernest Goldsmith, a real gentleman who came across well to juries.

My client had made a statement, and in his statement he said that the reason this all happened was that he had drunk too much, so I defended on the grounds that it was not murder but manslaughter: my client had no intent to kill the young man because he was drunk at the time. I also argued that it was self-defense. The jury found my client guilty of manslaughter after a several-day trial.

Based on my client's testimony and his obvious remorse over the shooting, I made a motion for probation, which Judge Constine granted, and my client returned to work.

A short time later, my client called to tell me he had been sued by the wife of the young man who had been there that night with this young girl. It turned out he had not been single at all. So, I told Mr. Ballestreri to come to my office the next day so I could see the complaint. Mr. Ballestreri had homeowner's insurance. I called his insurance company and informed them that, due to the fact that the incident happened in his home and he'd been found guilty of manslaughter, and thus lacked intent, it could have been negligence and they would have to cover him. He had a $25,000 policy.

I called the attorney who had filed the lawsuit and told him he should contact the insurance company. They settled the case for the insurance money and Mr. Ballestreri was very happy.

Every year after that he would come to my office and bring me a bottle of good brandy and a box of good cigars, and my wife an Italian art object. I kept telling him that I had received my fee and that I was perfectly satisfied, but he continued to do so every year. Finally, he developed a form of Alzheimer's. I didn't want him buying anything for me in that condition, so I asked his brother to tell him to stop, and he did.

The funny part about it was when he first came to me his brother wanted to make sure that I did not let it be known that he was a cousin of the Mayor, Joseph Alioto, because it could possibly hurt their cousin. No one ever found out.

Ernest Goldsmith was appointed a Superior Court judge and is stll serving in that position.

Cop-killer Harold Miller today
a strange bit of remorse over hi
of Police Inspector Denis Bradl
Miller says he's sorry it wasn't
Inspector Max Girard, instead.
The dingy-haired ex-convict s;
Girard beat me up and was alwa
me."
"I'm glad that cop (Bradley) w;
killed," he declared at City Prison.
"If it had to be anyone, I wish it v
have been Girard.

16

One for One

Because I was counsel for Show Folks of America, I continued to represent carnival and circus workers throughout my career. One case I managed to solve in an amusing way.

My client was a concessionaire for a carnival at a small fair in Northern California who had been arrested for operating a concession with a hidden mechanical device or defect which lowers the patron's chances of winning.

The charge was based on an obscure law lobbied for by an equally obscure opponent of carnivals, so obscure that neither the owners of carnivals nor the concessionaires themselves had opposed it. Before they knew it, the bill had passed.

This particular concession featured a large, 50-gallon metal milk container with a large mouth at the top. It stood four feet high, and it tapered into a neck and had an opening at the top where milk was poured in. What the manufacturers of the concession had done was to weld a very large rim inside the opening with a hole through the ring large enough for a softball to go through the hole. If the softball was tossed into the can and didn't hit the hole exactly correctly, it would hit the ring and bounce out.

The ring could be seen by the patrons from where they stood. On this occasion, the concessionaire found that the ground that the can sat on was slanted, so he had built a small platform on which he put the can, which made it difficult to see the ring from where you threw the ball if you were under five feet in height. It was simple to see if you looked for it, and once you threw the ball and saw it bounce out, you would know the ring was there.

Unfortunately for my client the gentleman who had lobbied this particular bill through, had gone out the carnival grounds, seen my client's concession and gone to the police in that town, asking them to make an arrest. The police went to the carnival and saw the concession, but didn't think it violated the law.

Unsatisfied, the man went to the Sheriff's office and threatened to contact the Attorney General and a few other things. In order to placate the man, the Sheriff's officers arrested the concessionaire, charging him with conspiracy to operate a concession with a hidden mechanical device.

My client had never been arrested or charged with a crime before. In fact, one of the large publicity firms down South had featured his concession on newspaper front pages in publicizing the fair. It was obvious even on the front-page photograph how it was manufactured and operated.

The District Attorney who was handling the matter offered very little in the way of discovery, and he offered my client a chance to plead guilty to a misdemeanor and pay a small fine. But if he did he would be admitting the concession was illegal and could not reopen his concession, so we decided to fight the charge. The District Attorney talked to his superiors, then called me, and told me that they weren't going to proceed with the preliminary hearing, but were going to reduce it to a misdemeanor, which would be heard in the Municipal Court. We continued the matter; several times the trial date was set and then changed because my client was operating concessions around the state and the District Attorney had other cases which had preference over this case.

Finally, a trial date was scheduled and agreed upon. I requested time and again to view the milk can and the ball that the District Attorney had taken into evidence. The District Attorney told me that the Sheriff's Office had it in their storeroom. Every time he could make them available, I was tied up in San Francisco. Every time I was available, the Sheriff was tied up. Still, I wanted to see if there was something different about this can and ball from the others.

The morning of the trial, my client and I arrived at the courthouse ready for the jury. I again asked the District Attorney to allow me to examine the can. He replied, "Of course," and took me to the parking lot in back of the courthouse where a Deputy Sheriff had the can in the trunk of his automobile.

The Deputy lifted the can out of the trunk of his automobile. I asked for the ball. The ball was inside the can. He turned the can upside down, and the ball fell out through the hole.

"Well," I announced, "there goes your case. If the ball can come out of the hole, it can go into the hole."

"You take the ball and throw it," I continued. "There is no mechanical device." I was standing eight feet from the can and tossed the ball. The ball arched itself and went through the hole without a quiver into the can.

The Deputy and the District Attorney were startled. I was surprised. Looking at the size of the hole, I did not believe I could do it again in ten thousand tries.

The Deputy asked me to try again.

"No way. I'm one for one. Why should I be one for two? Both of you saw me do it on the first toss. How can you go into court and charge this man with running a fraudulent concession when the first time I ever saw the ball or the can, I stood as far away from the can as a patron would and threw the ball right into the can?"

The District Attorney admitted there was no way he could try the case. I had sunk the ball the first time I had seen the can or the ball, and from as far away as a customer would be at the concession, and hadn't even aimed. The District Attorney had to admit that both he and the Deputy Sheriff had seen it, and if they were called as witnesses, they would have to so testify.

"Let's go see the judge," he said.

The District Attorney told the judge he wanted to dismiss the case.

"What do you mean you want to dismiss the case? We've got a jury here and we're ready to go."

"Well, we're charging this concessionaire with running a fraudulent concession and Mr. Cohn threw the ball into the can with one toss—one for one."

The Judge turned to me. "Maybe Mr. Cohn has practiced and maybe Mr. Cohn knows how to do it."

"Judge, you take one look at the can and you take one look at the ball, and you can realize that all the practice in the world is not going to do it..."

The judge started to smile.

"... this is the first time I ever saw the can, the first time I ever saw the ball, and I think this is the first time I've ever played the concession.

"I want to explain this to you, Your Honor."

I explained to him that the complainant had an obsession against carnivals.

The Judge turned to the District Attorney.

"That's terrible. What I think you ought to do is to find out who that man is and arrest him for obstructing justice and for filing a false report and bring him before me."

"Well, Your Honor, it's going to be a lot of trouble. We'll check it out, but it's going to be a lot of trouble."

"That's okay, we don't need any more trouble. Case dismissed."

And I kept my perfect record.

—————— ● ——————

In another instance, a gypsy friend of mine called me to represent someone who was running a concession at a carnival. The concession was a simple one: it consisted of tossing dimes onto a board which had Lucky Strike cigarette covers on it. If your dime ended up in the circle of the Lucky Strike logo, you won a prize. It was a game of skill.

Someone had filed a complaint saying they believed the operator of the concession had put wax on top of the board which would cause the dimes to slide. That was ridiculous because even if they slid, they could also end up in the circle and you could win.

The police went to the concession and asked the woman they found there if she was the owner of the concession.

She replied: "I'm not telling you anything."

"We're asking for the name of the owner of the concession."

"I'm not telling you."

They gave her a citation to appear in court the next day, but they couldn't put her name on it because they didn't know it. She still hadn't told tell them anything. She wouldn't tell them her name, where she lived or where she came from.

They set a trial for her in Municipal Court in San Diego County and my friend asked me to defend her.

I drove down to San Diego. The town where this happened was actually on the outskirts of San Diego; there was not even a motel in the town, so I had to go into a hotel in San Diego and stay there. The next morning I went to court and met my new client in front of the courtroom. I asked her what had happened. She explained that the policemena had asked her if she was owner of the concession and she had simply refused to answer.

The District Attorney assigned to the case was a young woman who I could see was quite competent because we had to wait until after she finished her closing argument in a drunk driving case. While the jury was out on the drunk driving case we had an opportunity to discuss my client's case.

I told the District Attorney she simply had no case against my client.

"Well, the lady wouldn't answer any questions."

"How are you going to prove that there was anything wrong?"

"Let me look at the police report."

She did, and when she came back she admitted, "You're right, there's not much of a case here. Why waste our time? I'm going to dismiss the case."

After the judge dismissed the case, I asked my client why she wouldn't answer the police:

"I watch television."

"Pardon?"

"I watch television."

"What has that got to do with it?"

"On television, the lawyers tell their clients don't answer any questions. So, I wasn't going to answer any questions."

"In the future, tell them your name anyway and what your address is."

"I'll do that, Mr. Cohn, but I'm just doing what they tell you to do on television."

Forty Minutes to Freedom

17

In one case I represented a man who admitted he had stabbed another man numerous times; and I obtained the fastest verdict of acquittal in a first-degree murder case in California history.

One day I picked up the paper and saw that a former client of mine, who I shall call Joseph Corleone, had been killed. The paper said he had been stabbed multiple times and that the person who had stabbed him had been arrested and charged with murder.

I was not the least surprised that something of that nature had brought an end to Mr. Corleone's life, given my experience with him.

I had represented Corleone in a prosecution for theft. His boss (another client of mine) had gone away on vacation and told Corleone to watch his property and to make sure no one stole anything. While his boss was away, Corleone hired a truck and cleaned out his boss' warehouse and home.

I obtained an acquittal, but when it became evident to me what sort of a man Corleone was, I advised him I would never represent him again. I thought to myself: "Someone who does that to his boss isn't going to last very long…"

Apparently, he hadn't. The news story also said Corleone had been awaiting sentencing on another charge at the time he was killed.

I turned the page, and thought that was the end of the matter.

Several days later, a couple I will call Mr. and Mrs. Sapiente, the parents of the man accused of killing Corleone, called me about representing their son, and I told them to come down to my office.

Their son, they said, had stabbed Corleone multiple times and killed him.

After the stabbing, their son had driven down the highway until he spied a highway patrol officer at a drive-in. The patrolman had just finished his hamburger and was working on his coke when their son parked his car next to the officer, walked up to him and placed a bloody knife on the patrolman's tray, announcing, "I just killed a man in San Francisco."

The officer wrapped the knife in a paper napkin, ordered the young man into the back seat and called the San Francisco Police Department.

The San Francisco police confirmed there had been a stabbing in the Outer Mission District, and that the alleged victim (Mr. Corleone, it proved later) was being treated at San Francisco General Hospital.

When Corleone died, their son was charged with first-degree murder.

Their son had already given the police a complete confession describing exactly how the stabbing had taken place.

On the face of it, there seemed little I could do.

However, the Sapientes continued to talk to me about their son and his relationship with Corleone, and the story was not so cut and dried.

The real story had begun in Los Angeles some years back when their son was working in a butcher shop as a meat cutter, married to a very young beautiful woman. The couple had three children: a girl, a boy and a baby boy. Mr. Sapiente worked and went home and took care of his children. He was a dutiful husband and bread-winner with a beautiful wife and three children he loved. So things remained, for a while.

That was before Mr. Corleone entered the picture. After their son's mother-in-law was involved in a shooting scrape, his wife came up to the Bay Area to be with her mother, and their son asked a distant cousin—Mr. Corleone, it turned out—to keep an eye on her while she was there. It was then that their son's young wife began an affair with Mr. Corleone.

When she returned to Los Angeles, the affair continued. Mr. Corleone relocated to Los Angeles and their son's wife continued seeing him, often staying away for days at a time.

One morning, their son was at home asleep when his wife awakened him and asked him to answer the door for her. When he opened the door, a process server handed him a complaint for divorce. Stunned, he demanded to know what it was about. His wife explained she had gotten mad at him and gone to see a lawyer, but had later thought better of it. She claimed she had told the lawyer to drop the divorce suit, but the lawyer had gone ahead with it. She assured her husband she would have it dismissed. Satisfied with the explanation, and still in love with his wife despite everything, he went back to bed.

She stayed with him for another six months. Then one day, when he came home she handed him the divorce decree and told him to get out of the house. She had had her lawyer take a default against him and she had been given custody of the children and all the community property, while he had to pay her support and support for the children. She had stayed with him just long enough to make the default impossible to open.

He sought a lawyer in Los Angeles. The lawyer told him there was nothing he could do.

When his now ex-wife moved up to San Francisco to set up house with his cousin, he followed her north and moved to San Jose, taking a job in a meat-cutting plant. He hired a lawyer to obtain visitation rights with his children and went to his ex-wife's new house in the Outer Mission to see his children. Like many houses in the Outer Mission, the house was built over the garage with stone steps leading up to the door.

He soon learned the disadvantage of this arrangement for unwanted visitors when his cousin threw him down the stairs, not once but twice. He returned several more times, and each time Mr. Corleone, who was twice his size, beat him.

Their son went to the District Attorney and to the police, but both refused to do anything. The police informed him that since the assault was a misdemeanor, he would need another witness before they could bring charges.

One night he went over to the house, and when his cousin threw him down the stairs, Mr. Sapiente grabbed a knife and punched holes in the tires of his cousin's Cadillac. When his cousin chased after him, he ran away.

Finally, their son found someone in the District Attorney's office willing to listen to him and the District Attorney worked out an agreement that their son could visit his children once every other week, and that his cousin would not be present.

So it went for several months. Their son would go over to his wife's house in the Outer Mission and pick up his children on his visiting days.

Then, the day of the killing, Mr. Corleone again came to the door and told their son he could only take his daughter and his older son, but the baby was too sick to go. While he was out with his two older children, his daughter told him that there was nothing wrong with the baby. It was just that his cousin didn't want him to see his own baby.

When their son drove his two older children home at approximately four o'clock in the afternoon, Corleone came to the door again. Their son insisted on seeing his baby but Corleone threatened to throw him down the stairs again.

Their son was not a fighter like Mr. Corleone, but this was too much for him to bear. He went to his car, opened the trunk where he had his meat-cutting knives in a box, took out a knife and rang the bell again.

This time when Corleone lunged for him, their son started stabbing Corleone, and Corleone fell. His daughter, who saw this, told her father to run away. He got back into his car and drove until he saw a highway patrolman, and handed the patrolman the bloody knife.

From what I knew, I thought there was no way I could win the case. The man had confessed, he'd done it deliberately, and he'd stabbed his victim more than once.

I don't like to take money from people if it looks as if I am not really going to be able to do anything for them. I tried to explain to the Sapientes that I saw no way of saving their son or even significantly reducing his sentence. I said I might be able to reduce his sentence some, and they could get the Public Defender to do that.

But they had read in the papers about a tough murder case where my client seemed a cinch to go away for quite a length of time, and I had gotten him off with manslaughter and probation and they didn't want to take no for an answer.

I told them it was just a waste of my time and their money.

They insisted they just wanted their son to know they were supporting him and for him to know they had obtained for him the best lawyer they could get. They insisted they would pay whatever it cost.

At that time I was charging twenty-five to fifty thousand for a murder case, but I thought there was nothing to this case. It was a short case, I thought, and I was not going to be able to do much good. I told them so and said I would charge them less than half my minimum.

I reiterated to them over and over again, to make sure they understood, that I guaranteed nothing, that from what I was told and what I had learned so far I did not think there was any way in the world that I could save their son, or even get him a lowered sentence. I told them it just wasn't in the cards.

They told me to just do the best I could.

They paid my fee and I went down to see my new client and hired an investigator to investigate Corleone's reputation. I found that my former client had even attempted to assault the Chief of Police of Belvedere. It seemed Mr. Corleone had not only been a hood, but a nut, as well.

The case came on for trial before Judge Harry Neubarth. While Judge Neubarth was not known for being easy on defense attorneys, defendants somehow got the feeling that they had obtained a fair trial from him and Judge Neubarth had shown me letters defendants had written him from prison thanking him for being such a compassionate judge.

The District Attorney was a man by the name of John Dean. Dean was a straight-ahead prosecutor. He saw what he was aiming at and he went straight for it. Nothing could make him swerve from his course.

He had a cinch of a case. He had a confession. The defendant had said he did it. He had a dead body. What else did he need?

John Dean was not worried about the jury. All he needed was twelve people who were alive and could listen to a confession and he had my client dead to rights—that's what he figured, at least.

I took a little time to pick a jury. There was one lady that I determined to have on the jury. She was middle-aged and well-dressed and gave the impression of being very intelligent and knowledgeable.

In the end, I had six good jurors and six I could live with.

Then Judge Neubarth informed us that the lady I had determined to have on the jury, Juror Number Seven, had told him that she wasn't sure she could serve on the jury. Her husband had served on the grand jury that had indicted my client.

I thought about it, and resolved to follow my instincts and keep her on the jury. I didn't know then how right my instincts would prove to be.

John Dean made his opening statement: he described how my client went to his car, armed himself with a knife, rang the door and, when Mr. Corleone answered the door, stabbed him multiple times; then how my client had confessed to the stabbing. That was the whole story.

Now, I made my opening statement.

"The District Attorney made certain statements as to what he promised you or told you that the evidence will show. Whether it shows that or not is up to you to decide.

"I am going to tell you what I think the evidence will show. As in most cases, a situation seen by two people is often different. In this case the evidence will show this very easily. Mr. Sapiente, my client, the young man sitting over there, was married to Mrs. Sapiente at the age of 19. She was 16.

"Mr. Sapiente was a hard-working young man taking good care of his family, taking good care of his wife. He loved his wife; he loved his children.

"Some time a couple of years ago, Mrs. Sapiente's mother got involved in a shooting scrape. Mrs. Sapiente went to Martinez to get her mother and then took her mother to Los Angeles.

"Mr. Sapiente had some distant relation in the area by the name of Vince Corleone who owned a car wash, a long distant relation, a distant cousin. Mr. Sapiente asked him to watch out for his wife. But Mr. Corleone was in Chicago at the time Mr. Sapiente's wife arrived and Mr. Vince Corleone asked his brother Joseph, a gentleman who was quite involved with the law, to stand in his stead.

"The evidence will show that Mr. Joseph Corleone, the gentleman who is deceased, had been convicted of several felonies. He was a vicious man, a big man — about 5 foot 10, about 180 pounds. My client was as tall as he is now, weighing 125, 126 pounds.

"After she was up here for a week, it seemed that Mrs. Sapiente started to stay out late nights—in some instances, all night. She took a new job, one involving Mr. Joseph Corleone. The evidence will show Mrs. Sapiente had been playing around all over town with Mr. Corleone. When Mr. Sapiente found out that Mr. Corleone was carrying on with his wife, he asked Mr. Corleone about this. Mr. Corleone beat him up—this was Mr. Corleone's attitude toward everything.

"We will bring witnesses here to tell you that he took someone out of a car and beat him up because he called Mr. Corleone a dirty name. Two days after the incident in this case, Mr. Corleone would have been in San Quentin—he was awaiting sentence for selling stolen cars and printing his own pink slips to do so.

"Mr. Corleone told everyone that he had a criminal background. He told my client he was going to have somebody kill him. The evidence will show that Mr. Corleone told Mr. Sapiente that he might not do it him- self, but he would hire some of his friends with whom he was associating.

"This becomes important because Mr. Sapiente knew all this. Mr. Sapiente knew that Mr. Corleone had burglarized his own boss' place, that he had fought with the Belvedere Chief of Police, that he had attacked the Marin County District Attorney's investigator. Mr. Sapiente knew all of this.

"Mr. Sapiente was crazy about his children—he wanted to come up and see them. Mr. Corleone called Mr. Sapiente's mother and father, who are sitting here, and told them that if their son kept coming up and trying to see his children, he would have their son killed. He threatened Mr. Sapiente's mother and father to keep the boy from coming up and visiting his children, and every time he went over to visit his children, Corleone threw him out.

"When Mr. Sapiente went to visit his wife, Mr. Corleone pulled a .22 rifle on him, and went after him with the rifle. Mr. Sapiente told the District Attorney, 'I'm scared. This man has threatened my life.'

"Nobody did anything about it. Not for this quiet little man who was absolutely nuts about his children—and who was still in love with his wife.

"The evidence will show that at all times Mr. Sapiente thought that Corleone was going to do him in. Mr. Corleone was a vicious ex-felon who had been found guilty of burglary, who had been found guilty of assault. We will show you he was a vicious man.

"The evidence will show you that it happened all on the spur of the moment. The man came at him and he thought he was in danger and he was protecting himself.

"He took the two children out for the day, and when he came back, he said to his wife, 'I want to see the little child, I just want to see the little child.'

"She slammed the door in his face. He rang the bell again. 'I want to see my little girl.' She opened the door, he put his foot in the door, he came in and he said, 'I want to see my little child,' he said, 'I want to see her, I haven't seen the child for several weeks,' and he is nuts about the child.

"Corleone, a big, husky, guy came out swearing at him in a rush. The kid didn't know what happened. The next thing he knew he had a knife in his pocket, he saw Corleone coming at him and stuck him with the knife. He went wild and stuck him. There is no argument there.

"He then sees what he has done, he has the knife in his hand, he takes the little girl, gets in the car and they drive away. He puts the knife down beside him. The little girl looks at him and says, 'Daddy, you better take that knife and throw it away in the bushes. Otherwise, people will know.'

"He says, 'What have I done in front of my child?'

"So he drove back and took the little girl up to the door. Then he drove down the street looking for a policeman..."

"We are going to ask you to acquit him of this."

But the key evidence was to come from an unexpected source.

About three or four years earlier, a friend of mine, whom I will call Dr. Anderson, a doctor in one of the big hospitals in San Francisco, had called me and asked me to do a favor. He explained another friend, also a doctor, was in need of legal help.

His friend had gone out to an Italian restaurant in North Beach and had dinner with his wife. He retrieved his car from the attendant and started driving away when a police car saw him and pulled him over.

The doctor pulled out his license and gave it to the officer. When the doctor refused to take a sobriety test the officer placed him under arrest for drunk driving.

I went down to the restaurant and brought a court reporter with me. I went to the manager, whom I knew, having been in the restaurant myself before. I told him about the doctor having being there.

"Yes, I know the doctor. He was in here."

"He signed his tab, do you have a copy of it?"

"I think I can get it."

The manager brought me a copy of the doctor's tab and there was no alcohol on it, except one glass of wine.

"Did you see him when he came in?"

"Yes."

"Was he sober?"

"Absolutely."

"Did you see him when he left?"

"Absolutely sober."

The court reporter was taking all this down.

I talked to the waiter. The waiter said, yes, the doctor had been there.

"What did he have to drink?"

"One small glass of wine. His wife had nothing, he had one small glass of wine, and that's all he had."

I took all that down.

I talked to the valet parking attendant.

"Do you remember the doctor?"

"Of course."

"When he came out and got his car, was he drunk?"

"Of course not, I wouldn't give a man a car if he had been drinking. He was cold sober."

The court reporter took all this down and transcribed it and I went down to the District Attorney's office and asked for the District Attorney handling the case.

I showed him the statements.

"Do you want to go to trial? I want to go to trial and I'll ask for a jury trial. Then, I'm going to sue for false arrest."

"You can't sue the District Attorney's Office, we're privileged."

"I can sue somebody…"

I knew the District Attorney very well. I was needling him.

"Are you sure this is right?"

"Check it out."

"I take your word for it, we'll dismiss it."

I called up the doctor who had referred me, and I told him it was all dismissed. He could tell his friend not to pay any attention to anything more about it.

"How much do I owe you?" he asked.

I told him he owed me nothing. It was fun to do and it was a nice thing to do for somebody. I didn't want any fee.

That had been four years earlier. Now the Sapiente case was in the papers every day. It had taken the prosecution two days to present their case. All they had to put on was that they had a dead body, and they had a man who said he had killed the victim and stabbed him eighteen times. They were just finishing their case when Dr. Anderson called me.

"Mr. Cohn, I'm going to tell you something. You did a favor for a good friend of mine a few years back, and I want to be of help to you if I can. I want to tell you something, but I don't want my name to get into this in any way. I don't want anybody to know I told you this."

"You have my word on it."

"I was at San Francisco General Hospital the night of the stabbing. I was there on another matter to see some patient of mine, and I walked by the emergency room and I happened to see the doctors running around in a panic. Something happened, I don't know what it was, but something happened. I know they were working on the victim there before he died. That's what I know. But don't tell anyone."

"Thank you very much."

The prosecution was about to finish their case by putting on the coroner. The coroner testified that the victim was dead when he saw him and that he died of multiple wounds.

"You did the autopsy, right?"

"Yes."

"You didn't have anything to do with the operations or anything they did for the person before he died?"

"No."

"So, you can't really testify as to what the cause of death was, what knife caused the wound that you say could have caused the victim's death?"

He testified he could not say which knife made the cut that he testified could have caused the death—and whether it was caused by my client, or in surgery.

I insisted the District Attorney bring in the doctor that had worked on the alleged victim in the emergency room in order to prove his case. I also subpoenaed the doctor's records. If I had called the doctor instead, I would have be unable to cross-examine him and impeach his credibility, but now he would be the prosecution's witness.

I made them bring in the records an hour before the doctor was set to testify. I went through the records, and I found that they had performed a tracheostomy on the Mr. Corleone, but they had put the tube in his stomach rather than his lungs, and that his brain was deprived of oxygen for a period long enough to kill him.

"Isn't it true, Doctor, that the man was intubated into the esophagus for six or seven minutes without oxygen to his brain?"

"Part of your statement is correct. He was intubated for about six minutes. The period without oxygen to his brain was approximately three minutes, as outlined earlier. This man had oxygen administered by a mask, which is quite a satisfactory way to administer oxygen."

"But he was intubated for six or seven minutes in the esophagus?"

"That's right, during the time in which we were doing a tracheostomy."

"And the tracheostomy didn't become effective or operative for the first six or seven minutes, is that correct?"

"No, approximately three minutes."

"If a person is without oxygen to the brain for six or seven minutes, it would be enough for a cause of death, wouldn't it be, Doctor?"

"Yes, it could. It is important to understand that at the time this man was without oxygen as far as his brain was concerned was three minutes, not six minutes."

"Did you time it, Doctor?

"Yes, we did."

"With a clock?"

"Yes, with a clock."

"You mean you knew you had the tube in his esophagus, you knew he wasn't getting enough oxygen, and you stopped there and started looking at your watch to see how long he was without oxygen to the brain, is that what you are telling us, Doctor?"

"That is not what I am telling you.

I introduced the death registry, which the doctor had signed.

"So you made this out, 'immediate cause of death, cardiac arrest?'"

"That is correct."

"'Due to blood loss and cerebral anoxia,' is that correct?"

"That's correct."

"And cerebral anoxia means that there was no oxygen to the brain?"

"That is correct."

"And at the time that the man didn't have any oxygen to the brain, that was caused by the fact that you had the tube in the wrong place, isn't that right, Doctor?"

"That is not correct. This man had died, had a cardiac arrest, before any tubes were placed in his throat, before any operation was done on him."

"Well, it says in your records that up until an hour before he died he was in good condition, Doctor."

"Well, you are talking about events removed in time by about 12 hours."

"You mean he died once and was brought back to life and he died again?"

"That is correct."

"Oh, I see. You are telling us that his first death was caused by the stab wound and the second death was caused by you, is that correct?"

"That is what you are telling me."

"I have no further questions."

When I had finished with the doctor, I had the jury angry at the victim, and protective of my client. They were feeling bad for my client, and now I had given them something to hang their hat on in order to bring in a verdict of 'not guilty.'

I was claiming self-defense … and that they had not proved that my client had actually caused Mr. Corleone's death.

The District Attorney wasn't prepared for that. He had expected it to be a cakewalk. All this was thrown in his face, and very quickly. We made our closing arguments, and the jury was sent out to deliberate.

After the jury was out for five minutes, the bailiff announced that Juror Number Seven had asked to see the judge.

"What is it you want to see me about?"

"I'm emotionally upset about this case. I don't think I want to be in the jury room while this is being discussed."

I told her, "You're a very bright lady, and you have civic duty to perform."

The judge told her to try it and if something really affected her or caused her any real problem, to let him know.

Thirty minutes later, the bell rang again. The bailiff entered and announced that the jury had a verdict. I told my client to brace himself. Usually when a jury comes to a verdict quickly, it's a prosecution verdict.

It had been about forty minutes since the start of deliberations when everyone was assembled and the verdict was read.

"We find the defendant not guilty."

After the judge had the clerk record the verdict and the bailiff release my client, one of the reporters came over to me:

"You've just set a record. The record for not guilty in a first-degree murder case had never been below an hour, and you got one in forty minutes. No one has ever been found not guilty in so short a time in the State of California."

After Judge Neubarth called me and Mr. Dean into his chambers to compliment us, I went out to find Juror Number Seven.

She explained why she had asked to speak to the judge.

"Mr. Cohn, when I heard the case I was upset because I was afraid somebody might vote to find the defendant guilty and I might have to hold out. I didn't know whether I had the strength to hold out. The moment I walked into the jury room, I wanted to find your client not guilty.

"After we selected a foreman, he gave everyone a folded piece of paper and told us each to simply write 'guilty,' 'not guilty' or 'unde-cided.' When he got them all back and opened them up we were twelve to nothing for 'not guilty.'

"Then we had to tell the bailiff we had the verdict, and to wait for everybody to show up, the lawyers and the court attachés. That's what took the forty minutes.

"I was relieved. I had been afraid someone was going to say 'guilty,' and I'd have to sit there and I'd have to fight them. I'm not the kind of a person to do that. And my husband, believe it or not, was on the grand jury that indicted your client!"

So, my instincts had been correct for reasons I could not have known; and a phone call from a friend who owed me a favor who had happened by the emergency room the night of my former client's death had brought in the fastest verdict of acquittal in California history. Who would have known?

Flower Drum Comic

18

Because I was an attorney for the American Guild of Variety Artists, the union representing the singers, dancers and other entertainers who appeared throughout the United States, I received quite a few cases from entertainers. Through one such case I came to know the comedian Jack Soo and gave him his big break in *Flower Drum Song*.

Jack was starring at a Chinese nightclub in San Francisco as a stand-up comic when he came to my office and told me that someone had rear-ended his car and given him a pretty severe neck sprain. The doctor told him it would last quite a while and wasn't too sure whether or not there would be some permanent damage.

Jack asked me if I would represent him in a lawsuit against the driver of the other car. He started telling me a little bit about his life and what he'd been doing and we became quite friendly. I took the case to make sure that if something serious evolved from that injury he'd be protected. I filed a lawsuit immediately because if you didn't do that in those days, you could sit around for years waiting for the case to go to court. The insurance companies would just stall, figuring they had use of that money for a few years. They also figured that people would be more anxious to settle if they had to wait for quite a while before they received any money.

I would see Jack at different times—he'd go to a doctor or we'd have a deposition.

One day Jack came to see me about another problem.

When he was working in New York, he had had a beef with a some-one who claimed he owed him money, and now someone from New York wanted him to call. Jack asked me to return the call.

The number turned out to be the office of a man who was producing a stage musical called *Flower Drum Song*. He told me he had gone through San Francisco a couple of weeks ago and seen Jack Soo's comic routine and loved it. He wanted to hire Jack to do the routine in this play.

I told him that I would contact Jack and go over this with him, and that I would appreciate it if he would send me a copy of the script so I could have an idea what this show was going to be about. That way, I could best advise whether or not Jack should change his career from being a stand-up comic in a nightclub to being an actor in a stage play.

When I told Jack, he wasn't interested.

"I've been a stand-up comic for many years. I'm not a young person anymore, and this is no time for me to go around changing careers."

I suggested he should wait to make up his mind until he saw the script. Then he could make a determination.

Within a couple of days I received a rough working script. I read it and I liked it. I thought it would be very good for Jack. Jack reluctantly agreed to read the script and it had a part he liked, Sammy Fong, the comic lead. However, the producers had already signed Larry Blyden for the part. I told him I'd see what I could do, but Jack was still hesitant to become involved in a stage play.

I told Jack if the play were successful, it could have a nice run, and there would be a road show which would travel all over the United States playing the big cities and he would probably be in that, too. There might even be a movie, and he would have additional income during that period. They wanted to pay Jack a fairly decent figure for doing his routine. Still, Jack was hesitant to give up his career as a stand-up comic for it.

I called the producer back and told him that Jack was not anxious to change careers, but I thought I could convince Jack to take the role if they would allow Jack to understudy Larry Blyden for the comic lead. If Blyden left the show, Jack would replace him.

A couple of days later the producers called me back and agreed, but they wanted Jack in New York in thirty days for rehearsals for the show. The financial arrangements were not earthshaking but they were very nice. They also told me that they didn't want Jack to use his real name, Suzuki, in the production, but to keep his stage name because they had hired Pat Suzuki, a top-notch singer, who was going to have a major role in the musical, and they didn't want two Suzukis in the production.

Jack had no problem with keeping his stage name, since he had been using it his whole entertainment career. However, he was still concerned that if the show didn't make it he would have wasted a lot of time and have been out of the nightclub business for quite a while.

He had another problem, too. His car had been wrecked in the accident and he'd hadn't been in a good enough financial position to buy a new car. He didn't have an automobile and his wife wouldn't fly. Plus, he didn't have enough money to live on while the show was in rehearsal.

I told him I could take care of it.

I called the insurance claims manager who was representing the other driver and I told him the truth: Jack had the chance to go back east and star in a Broadway production, but he needed money and I wasn't going to settle for less than what I thought the damages were. If the insurance company would not settle and Jack was unable to go into the Broadway production, I was going to add all Jack lost in that Broadway production to the damages.

The claims manager knew me well. I had settled many, many cases against his insurance company. He thought about it for a minute.

"How much could he lose?"

I said it could be a tremendous amount of money.

I told him what I was asking and he agreed to settle.

Next, I called a local politician, Roger Boas, who had a Pontiac dealership. I had supported him in his campaigns for Supervisor, and I told Roger the story.

"What I want is a brand new Pontiac Jack can drive to New York and get there safely without any problem. But he won't be able to pay you anything on the car until the show opens in New York, which could be two or three months."

"Tell him to come down and pick out any car he wants. I'll sell it to him and he can pay me when he starts collecting his salary from the show in New York."

I sent Jack down and he picked out the best Pontiac they had. He piled his family into the car and drove to New York. Somebody with Flower Drum Productions obtained an apartment for Jack and his wife and made arrangements for him to stay there until *Flower Drum Song* opened.

Jack had a ball. He had never been in a Broadway production before, but he loved it and all the people there liked him, because he was such an excellent comic. He had a marvelously droll style.

At the time I was representing some clients in New York, and Jack wanted me to come to the opening of the show. I couldn't make the opening night but I came two weeks later. When I got to New York, he had two tickets for me; fifth row on the aisle. Jack was doing his comic routine—the same one he did in San Francisco—and the audience loved it.

After the show he and I went out and had a drink and had something to eat. I told him I thought it was going to be a big hit and have a long run. He was the happiest guy in the world.

Even for the part he was playing, he was receiving almost double what he had been receiving from nightclubs for the same act, and he had studied and prepared in case anything happened to Larry Blyden.

A few months later Jack called me again. Someone had written a play for Broadway called *The Tenth Man*. It was written for Larry and he was leaving the show. Jack was now the comic lead. He wanted to know when I would be coming back to New York. He could hardly wait. The part was made to order for him, and his salary was now much larger than he had ever expected. "When are you coming out here?" Jack demanded to know.

A day or two days later, I start getting phone calls from friends of mine all over the United States:

"Nate, you know Jack Soo?"

"Yeah, he's my client."

"A story just came out that he's replacing the comedy star in *Flower Drum Song* and in the story he says he owes everything that's happened to him in *Flower Drum Song* to his attorney, Nathan Cohn. I'll send you a copy of the article."

Friends sent me articles from Chicago, Texas, South Carolina. Then, that Sunday there was a whole column about Jack Soo in the *San Francisco Chronicle*. There, too, it said he owed his whole career in show business to me, which I thought was very nice.

I went to New York a couple of weeks later and did see Jack in *Flower Drum Song*. He was better for the part than Larry had been. It was as if he was playing himself. He invited me to a cast party and I met the entire cast. He told everyone, "If it wasn't for Nate, I wouldn't be here. He's the one who made me do it."

The musical went on in New York for quite awhile. When it came to San Francisco, Jack got tickets for opening night and invited me to the opening night party. In fact, he invited me to every party.

The publicity people even promoted a softball game between the chorus girls in *Flower Drum Song* and the women at a radio station in San Francisco. The game was held at the baseball field in the Marina, and I was selected to be the umpire.

The Oriental girls from *Flower Drum Song* were small, and when they hit the ball they had to run twice as hard to get to first base as the other girls. I was the umpire, and when one of these young ladies from *Flower Drum Song* would hit the ball, the girls from the radio station would get the ball and throw it to first base. The runner would get there maybe four seconds later, but I'd still call "Safe." It was all a gag and I was having a ball. After I had done this four or five times, one of the young ladies from the radio station came over to me.

"Mr. Cohn, I understand you're a lawyer."

"Yes, I am."

"Well, all I can say is, if you make judgment calls like you do out here, I hope you never become a judge."

After the showing in San Francisco, *Flower Drum Song* moved to Harrah's at Lake Tahoe, and Jack invited me up for the opening there too.

I drove up one weekend and met Jack at Harrah's and he showed me his dressing room.

"Bill Harrah has given me a house with a cook, a maid and a butler."

"That's pretty good."

Then we got into his car, which was a big Cadillac.

"Wait a minute," I said. "From what I understand, Harrah's gives the star of the show a Rolls-Royce."

"Yeah, he wanted to give me a Rolls-Royce but I told him I'd rather have a Cadillac."

"Why did you do that?"

"If they see an Oriental driving a Rolls-Royce, they'll think I'm somebody's chauffeur."

His cook made a fantastic dinner and, after the show, we played blackjack in the casino and Jack had everybody laughing. Jack was a born comic.

Later on, when *Flower Drum Song* had run its course, one of the producers heard that the Palace Hotel was going to do theater-in-the-round, and asked me to see the manager to find out if he would be interested in having *Flower Drum Song* as theater-in-the-round there.

I knew the manager, had a talk with him and gave him the producer's name. Next thing, *Flower Drum Song* was in theater-in-the-round and I had to see it again. I saw *Flower Drum Song* so many times, I could probably have replaced some of the actors with their lines.

Then, Jack told me a Hollywood producer had decided to make a movie out of *Flower Drum Song*.

I told Jack that was great.

"Well, the people producing the stage play don't want to let me go from the tour. Can you call them and get me out of this? I want to be in that movie if I can."

I called the producers and explained Jack wanted to be released from the production to be in the movie. They said they still needed him for the production, so I made a suggestion. Jack's understudy was also an excellent comedian. Why didn't they contact the studio and tell the studio they would release Jack to them on condition that the studio paid the salary of Jack's understudy. That way they would have the understudy in the role and wouldn't have to pay either of the two salaries.

Two days later, the producer called back. "Your idea was good and Jack's going to be in the movie."

When the movie opened in San Francisco at the Golden Gate Theater, Jack called me: "Don't make any dates for that whole week because you're going to be with me and you're going to be busy." A couple of nights before the opening, the studio was throwing a party at Johnny Kan's restaurant on Grant Avenue for all the people connected with the movie alon with important people in San Francisco, because *Flower Drum Song* was supposedly located in the city of San Francisco. The author of the original play was also going to be there.

"If you want me, I'd be happy to attend, of course, but don't push it."

"I already did that."

"What do you mean?"

"They told me they didn't have any room for anybody other than the ones they invited. So I told them, 'Then you'll have one more seat. If Nate doesn't go, I don't go.'"

I sat next to the gentleman who wrote the original play. It was a hell of a party.

After *Flower Drum Song* had finally run its long course, Jack called me from Los Angeles and said that he had a new job in television. It was a detective series. Jack was going to be the sidekick. Jack was good, but it lasted only one season.

I got a phone call from Jack and he said he was going to be on *Barney Miller* for four episodes, and Jack told me to watch it—it was going to be on that night. I watched the four episodes and then the next week he was on again. He was so good in the first episodes that they made him a permanent member of the cast and he became one of the most popular actors in the series.

After he died of cancer a friend of mine sent me Jack's obituary that came out of his Los Angeles publicist's office, and in his obituary, Jack had them put that he owed his career in *Flower Drum Song* to his lawyer, Nathan Cohn.

The Orphan

19

In one case I was able to save not only my client, but also his co-defendant in what looked like a strong case for a death sentence or life in prison.

It began with a phone call from the head of a Jewish orphanage. The man told me he had heard about me and noticed that I had obtained good results in several murder cases.

There was a young man from the orphanage who was now facing a first-degree murder charge. He had met another young man and, from what this man told me, they had gone to rob a gentleman who was selling jewelry. When the two young men went to his apartment to commit the robbery, they found four people in the apartment with the victim. The second young man had a gun and put it on the guests and locked them in a closet. The young man from the orphanage watched and then the two of them robbed the man of his jewelry and his money. The other young man then tied up the victim. Unfortunately, he tied the man in such a way that if he tried to escape, he would choke himself. The man choked to death on his own vomit and died, and the two young men were apprehended and charged with first-degree murder in perpetration of a robbery.

I went over to see the young man in jail and he told me he didn't realize that the other young man would tie the victim up like that. He said he really didn't participate except in the robbery and in helping to tie the man up. He didn't realize that it was going to happen.

I told him I would see what I could do for him.

I met with him several times. On the Friday before the case was to be tried on a Monday, my client informed me he had talked to the other defendant, who was being defended by a Public Defender, and the other defendant had told him his lawyer had not come to see him up till that very day. I didn't think that was possible.

So, I called the Public Defender who said it was true. "I'm going to see him this weekend. That's all I need."

"Don't you think it's better to see him early and go over the case?"

"Oh, I'll find out. I'll take a day off and see him Sunday."

I wasn't going to tell another lawyer what to do, but I was still infuriated.

In the meantime, I had prepared my client for trial. I had a friend of my client's give him a pair of slacks and a shirt and sweater and I had him get a haircut from the jail barber. When he came into court on Monday, my client looked like a serious high school student. His co-defendant, however, came into court with his hair hanging on his shoulders and a zoot suit on—a black suit with wide shoulders and a long black coat and a chain hanging down with nothing on it.

I looked at the Public Defender: "What are you doing?

"What do you mean?"

"Your client looks terrible. If the prospective jurors are outside of the courtroom and saw your man come in dressed like that, they would convict him on the spot. I'm surprised that the jailers let him have that chain hanging down, because he could hurt himself or somebody with the chain."

"The chain is a very light chain, there's nothing to it."

"I know, but look at him. He needs a haircut. He needs everything!"

I asked the judge, Judge Orla St. Clair, to see him in chambers and I asked for a continuance to get a new jury panel that had not seen the defendant dressed in that manner, because that alone could prejudice them, and that prejudice would adversely affect my client.

Judge St. Clair knew what I was saying. He agreed to dismiss the jury and directed us to appear the following Monday for trial, but warned us that he would not grant any more continuances.

After the jury was excused, I went over to the Public Defender and his client, and advised his client to get a haircut and change his appearance.

"Well, that's the way he dresses."

"No, that's not the way he dresses. Get him a pair of slacks and a jacket or sweater of some kind."

"They charge for a haircut and I don't have any money."

I gave him ten bucks out of my pocket.

"Get yourself a haircut. Will that cover it?"

"Yeah, they don't charge that much."

"Just give him the ten bucks. Make it a very short haircut, and come in dressed like a reasonable person."

The next Monday we started the case, but the Public Defender was excusing jurors I liked.

I took him into another room.

"What are you doing? How many jury cases have you tried?

"Not too many, but I'm looking for people who don't like people who sell jewelry."

"How're you going to tell who likes people who sell jewelry?"

"What?"

"Look, let's do this. Who is the next person you're going to challenge?"

"I'm going to challenge Number Six."

"That's the best juror we've got!"

"Why?"

"He's my size and he's bald like I am and he seems to be a very intelligent man. I like to get jurors who can identify with me or my client. He's going to identify with me because he's my size and he's bald like I am and he seems like a reasonable man, so don't touch him. If you do, there'll be another murder case."

"What do you mean?"

"They'll have me before the court for murdering you!"

"Okay, I won't touch him."

"Just let me pick the jury."

He'd already challenged several people I liked, but I did keep this one man on the jury.

I defended my client on the theory that the death was an accident. However, after I cross-examined the prosecution witnesses to bring out the facts I needed for my defense, the Public Defender would give the witnesses another opportunity to tell their story against our clients.

I made a closing argument that this was an accident and not a deliberate murder. Then the Public Defender made his closing: "I don't understand Mr. Cohn's theory, but there were four witnesses who said they were locked in the closet. How do we know the witnesses weren't the ones that killed this man?"

I couldn't believe it.

The jury was out for a full day and at the end of the full day of discussion the jurors come back with a second-degree murder conviction.

The foreman of the jury was the heavyset man whom my associate wanted to remove from the jury. He came over to me after and said, "Mr. Cohn, I want you to know something. This was tough. Most of the jurors wanted to find your client guilty of first-degree murder. A couple of them wanted to give him gas. But I was able to get it cut down to second-degree murder, which was the best I could do. I couldn't get it down any more."

I thanked him very much.

I told the Public Defender to do me a favor and stay away from me because every time I looked at him I had murderous intent in my mind. He didn't know whether I was telling the truth or not, and he left.

Several years later, my client came into my office and brought me a couple of cigars, because he knew I liked cigars, and told me that he had been released from prison after serving a few years. He told me that the other defendant had taken up painting in prison. (The prison sold paintings which they put up in the reception area of the prison. The money would go into a fund so prisoners could buy cigarettes and other items.) He said that his friend was going to have to serve a little more time than he did, but his friend would be out in a month or two.

Several months later, the other defendant came into my office and he thanked me. He told me what had happened after his conviction. He said that after he started painting, a visitor came there to see someone else and saw the paintings and liked them. The visitor found out who the artist was and offered, upon his release, to sponsor him in a painting career.

The young man was very happy, and admitted, "If I hadn't gone to jail, I would not be in the position I am now, where I might make a career out of being an artist. I want to thank you for everything you did, because I realize that the lawyer I had really wasn't the best lawyer in the world."

And that was the last of that.

Cop-killer Harold Miller today
a strange bit of remorse over hi
of Police Inspector Denis Bradl
Miller says he's sorry it wasn't
Insp   May irad nstead.
The str y   red   convict s
Girard   at   up a   was alwa
me."
"P   hat   (Bradley) w
killed," he declared at City Prison.
"If it had to be anyone, I wish it v
have been Girard.

Crazy as a...

20

I had several notable experiences with the so-called insanity defense and several opportunities to utilize it. The first was early in my career. It concerned a disturbed cab driver.

One day the papers featured an article about a cab driver who took a shotgun and went up to the apartment belonging to the manager of his building. The cab driver rang the doorbell and when the manager came to the door, the cab driver shot him, killing him.

People came out when they heard the shot and they saw the cab driver standing there with the shotgun. He went back downstairs to his apartment where the police found him. When the police arrested him, the cab driver told the police that he had shot the victim because the Lord had sent him a message that the manager was evil.

My uncle, Newman Cohn, was the business agent for the cab driver's union. He knew the cab driver, and my uncle asked me if I would go down and see what I could do for him.

I went to the city prison to see the accused. Before I could tell him who I was, he said, "I know who you are."

I thought he realized that I was Newman's nephew.

"You're an angel. You've been sent down here to protect me."

We went into court and I pled the man not guilty by reason of insanity. I asked the Judge to appoint some psychiatrists to examine him because my talk with him had convinced me that he was mentally deranged.

"What caused you to believe that?"

"I went in there and he said I was an angel sent down to defend him. Any client that thinks I'm an angel has got to be mentally deranged."

The Judge duly appointed three psychiatrists who examined the cab driver, found that he was mentally deranged, and sent him to a mental institution.

I never heard from him again.

Some years later, a federal judge called me and asked me to come to his chambers and see him. When I walked in, he looked up and said, "Nate, I have a problem and I would like to know if you would help me."

"Of course, Judge, I would be happy to help you, if I can."

"We have a man who was arrested for robbing a bank and we're trying to get an attorney to represent him."

This was in the days before the Federal Defender system. The federal court would appoint lawyers to represent defendants without charge. I had performed this service many times before, and I was perfectly agreeable to performing the service in this case.

"This is the problem," he explained, "The appellate courts in the federal system have issued a decision which states that a defendant has a right to an attorney of his own choosing."

The judge told me that he had appointed some of the finest criminal lawyers in the city, but every time he appointed an attorney, the defendant refused to accept him as his counsel.

Finally, he had the bailiff give the defendant a yellow pages listing, and the judge told the defendant to pick one and that he would see if he could appoint that person to represent him.

The judge told me that the man had gone through the yellow pages and he had selected my name and wondered if I would represent him for the court without charge.

I told the judge I would be happy to do so.

I went over to the jail, where the defendant was being held, and visited him.

The defendant was agreeable to talk to, but he kept insisting if I got him out of jail, he was going to give me a million dollars that he had hidden away somewhere.

"Well, if you have the million dollars hidden away and you'll give it to me anyway, why not tell me where it is, and I can get it and bail you out?"

I talked to him for quite a while and I had made up my mind he was a sick man.

I appeared the next morning before the judge and the judge asked me if I had had time to talk to the defendant. I told him I had.

"Can we proceed to plead?"

I made a motion at that time that the defendant be examined for mental illness. I had gone through his records and I found that he had also spent some time in a mental institution in the East.

The judge granted my motion and had the defendant sent to a psychiatrist to be examined.

The psychiatrist made a report saying the defendant was suffering from mental illness and the judge sentenced him to a mental institution. When he was released, the case would be dismissed against him.

With that, the defendant smiled broadly, looked at the judge, and announced, "See, Judge? I might be crazy, but I sure know how to pick a good lawyer!"

Post-Partum Psychosis

21

Use of the "insanity defense" has received a great deal of attention in recent years. The newspapers and television have devoted quite a great deal of time to the case in Texas of a young woman who killed her children while suffering from post-partum psychosis. She received a life sentence. I handled one of the first post-partum psychosis cases many years ago. My client never spent a day in jail.

It began with a phone call from a man in the advertising business. He proceeded to tell me that what had happened. He was married, with a lovely wife and a four year-old child. His wife had become pregnant and they had had a second child, but the doctors had diagnosed her with post-partum psychosis, and she was unable to cope with the new baby's crying. He had left home early in the morning for work, and arrived at the office a short time later, where he received a hysterical phone call from his wife. She told him that she had taken one of his ties and put it around the baby's neck and strangled the baby because she couldn't stand the sound of the baby crying.

The man immediately called his doctor and the doctor had his wife taken to a hospital and placed in a psychiatric ward. He called the police to tell them what had happened; then he called Jack Rosenbaum, the columnist, to see if he could obtain a lawyer who could be helpful to his wife and himself.

Jack had suggested he call me.

I asked the man what hospital his wife was in. It was a hospital in San Mateo County. I told him I would drive out there immediately and meet him there in about forty minutes. I obtained my car from the garage and shot out to the hospital. He had described what he looked like and what he was wearing, and when I arrived at the hospital, I found him, very nervous, waiting for me outside.

I introduced myself and we proceeded to the psychiatric ward. His doctor was there with his wife. She was in very bad condition. I could see that. The doctor explained she had a post-partum psychosis, which women often have after the birth of a child. I told the doctor that I wanted the doctors and the nurses in the hospital to protect my new client. I did not want the police, the District Attorney's Office, investigators, or anyone else talking to her about what had happened without my being present. I then talked to the doctors and the nurses in that section, and told them what I wanted them to do. I suggested to them that if someone came to them, even if he looked like a doctor, even if he wore a white coat and carried a pad and a stethoscope; that unless they knew him to be a doctor or a nurse, not to allow him to talk to my client without my being present. They all assured me that they would be very careful, that they would not allow anyone to talk to her that they did not know for sure was a doctor on the staff of the hospital.

I then took the husband to lunch over in San Mateo and got all the information I could get from him, and told him what I thought should be done. He had never been involved with the law before, criminally. He was very bright and wanted to make sure he was doing everything he could do for his wife. There was nothing he could do for the infant.

After lunch, I went back to the office and called the office of the District Attorney of San Mateo County, and told them what had happened and told them if they had any questions, or anything that they wanted to talk about regarding my client or the incident, they should contact me and I would be available to discuss it with them.

The husband came down to my office the next day and signed an agreement with me to represent his wife. He told me that his neighbors in San Mateo County all seemed to be supportive of him. They brought him cakes and pies and offered to baby-sit for his other child.

Following an investigation by one of my investigators for background on what had happened, I went to a medical library to read up on newborn babies, post-partum psychosis, and psychiatric treatment of women with post-partum psychosis to make myself as familiar with the situation as I could.

I then contacted the D.A.'s office again, after talking to my client's husband about it. He told me that the doctor said his wife would not be able to appear anywhere for at least a week, and that I should put over any court action for at least another week to allow my client to appear in court.

I made arrangements for my client to appear for arraignment in court ten days later. It was arranged that she would appear in a South San Francisco courtroom before Judge Charles Becker. I told my client's husband and her doctor what I had done and they assured me that the husband would have her in court that morning, and would have her doctor with her, or, if he was unable to appear, a nurse.

Ten days later, I met my client, her husband and a nurse, dressed in regular clothes, and we appeared before Judge Becker. At arraignment, I suggested that we would waive a preliminary hearing and send the case directly to the Superior Court in Redwood City for arraignment.

At that time, I asked Judge Becker to set bail for my client. Judge Becker informed me that it was his understanding there was no bail in a first-degree murder case, and that the defendant had been charged with first-degree murder.

I had with me a brief that I had used in the L. case before Judge Carpeneti and explained to Judge Becker that bail could be set on a first-degree murder charge unless there was an actual evidentiary showing this was a first-degree murder case.

From the facts of the case, I argued, the main element of first-degree murder was missing: premeditation. Judge Becker asked the District Attorney for his opinion, but the District Attorney was not really prepared to argue the law I presented, and had no objection to bail being set. Judge Becker was about to remand my client to custody for transportation to Redwood City pending posting bail when I pointed out: "Your Honor, there are many photographers and cameramen present from the newspapers and TV. May I talk to the District Attorney for a moment?"

I explained to the District Attorney that if they began to fingerprint my client or take her picture or take her into custody, she might flip out, and if that happened in front of the cameras, they'd have to overcome the pictures that resulted, because I was going to plead her not guilty by reason of insanity, and those pictures would be the best evidence that she was not guilty by reason of insanity.

I suggested instead that he allow me to take her to Redwood City, put up the bail, and, later on, after everything calmed down, he could have her picture and her fingerprints taken.

Judge Becker agreed to make me a special deputy of the court, and placed my client in my hands to take her down to Redwood City and make arrangements for bail so she could be bailed out immediately and not have to be incarcerated.

The judge then arranged for us to go out the judges' entrance, to evade the crowd of reporters and cameraman in front.

My client and I and went out the back entrance, and the press didn't know we were gone until we got into my car. I called a bail bondsman who I knew to put up bail in San Mateo County, and he told me he would meet me in front of the County Clerk's desk where they accepted bail. He would have all the papers ready. All we had to do was sign the papers and my client and I could leave immediately.

It was close to lunch. I told the bail bondsman my client and I would have lunch and meet him in Redwood City in an hour and a half. He said he'd have everything arranged. I drove my client over to an excellent restaurant in San Mateo County. We had lunch, and then my client, her husband and I went down to the Redwood City Courthouse to the County Clerk's desk where they accepted bail. The bail bondsman was there with the bail all set. He posted a certificate of bail, and we all walked out.

The matter was set for us to appear a week later in Superior Court for arraignment. When we arrived, we found we had been assigned to one of the toughest judges in San Mateo County, Judge Edmund Scott. Although Judge Scott had a reputation for being very tough, I liked Judge Scott very much because I knew he was an excellent judge who knew the law thoroughly.

At arraignment, Judge Scott asked if I was ready to plead.

"Yes, Your Honor, I am."

Usually, lawyers will take more time to plead, especially when their client is out on bail.

"How do you plead?"

"Not guilty by reason of insanity. I assume your Honor will want to refer this to three psychiatrists.

"You assume correctly."

"What I'm going to do, so you will understand where we are, is that I'm going to waive a jury trial and present it before the Court alone, without a jury."

Everyone in the courtroom seemed to gasp at what I did.

"Mr. Cohn, do you really want to do this?"

"Yes."

"Do you want time to talk to your client or to think about it?"

"No, Your Honor, that's what I want to do, and I'll do it right now."

"Okay, do you have any psychiatrists you want to recommend?"

"No, but there is one psychiatrist who is the leading psychiatrist of the California psychiatric hospitals here in San Mateo County, and there are several others I'm sure Your Honor is familiar with. I won't even suggest them, but whoever Your Honor suggests would be agreeable."

The judge asked the prosecutor. "I'll go along with Mr. Cohn. I'm leaving it to the Court."

The Court assigned the case for investigation to three psychiatrists. One was the doctor who was in charge of the psychiatric hospital in San Mateo County. I had used him before as a psychiatrist and I had great confidence in him.

The Court continued the case for five weeks to get the reports.

The doctors called me and asked me to make arrangements for my client to visit them to be interviewed. All of them asked if there was anything I wanted brought to mind.

"Yes, one thing I'd like you to keep in mind is this. A mother is very protective of her infant child. Even the wildest animals will fight to the death to protect their children, and any woman who kills her child in this fashion has to be out of her mind, because a mother's instinct is to protect her children, and not to allow anyone to hurt them."

"Do you have anything else?"

"No, you know more about this than I do. You go ahead."

They all agreed, and five weeks later the doctors had written their reports. I received a copy of the reports, and every doctor who had examined the patient and given an opinion mentioned that what I had said was correct, and that the defendant had been legally insane at the time she had killed her baby.

We discussed the matter before Judge Scott.

"From the bench, I'm going to find the defendant not guilty by reason of insanity. What we do on these cases is we then place them in a hospital, and they stay in the hospital until they are capable of returning to the general public."

I made another suggestion to the judge: "In this case, we have an odd situation. This lady has now, from what I gather from the reports, gotten over this mental problem and she is basically normal right now. She does need psychiatric help. Why can't she get it outside the institution? Let her go home and once she is cured it will be dismissed, rather than put her in a mental institution to remain there and come back to court at that time."

Judge Scott looked over at the psychiatrist, who was there at my request.

"What do you think?"

"I think Mr. Cohn has an excellent idea. I think this lady could be treated outpatient as well as in the hospital. It might be to her advantage and her husband's advantage and her other child's advantage, because, from what I can see now she is no danger to the other child."

"I will not place her in a hospital, but I will let her be an outpatient. When the doctor determines that she is no longer a danger, you will advise Mr. Cohn, and I will dismiss the case."

Thus the case was eventually dismissed and my client never spent an hour in prison. However, not everyone was pleased with the result. My client's husband had told me at the beginning of the case how supportive his neighbors had been. But when it came out in the papers that his wife had been found not guilty by reason of insanity and had spent not one minute in prison, the neighbors changed their attitude and they became upset. It got so bad the couple had to sell their house and move to another county.

The Birdman of Alcatraz

22

nother highly unusual case I handled was when I represented a
man who was the subject of the Hollywood film, *The Birdman of
Alcatraz*, Robert Stroud.

I became involved with Mr. Stroud when the Presiding Judge of the
federal Circuit Court called me and asked me to see him in his chambers.
He asked me if I would be willing to handle a very interesting matter
without a fee.

He told me that there was a man at Alcatraz called Stroud who had
filed a petition in the Circuit Court, and the Judge wanted to know
whether I would represent him in court on his petition.

He told me that during his incarceration Stroud had become one of
the foremost authorities on the care, feeding and treatment of canaries,
and had written a book on the subject.

The Judge showed me the petition Stroud had written. The English
was excellent, and the petition was amazing in that, although it was all
hand-printed, the printing was so precise and neat it looked as though
an artist had executed it.

Stroud's petition sought the right to correspond with his brother and
to have a typewriter in his cell so that he could type the manuscript of a
book he was writing.

I told the Judge I would be happy to accept the assignment.

Several days later, I went to the pier and took the boat to Alcatraz.
When I arrived on the island, I was met at by a car, which took me up
to the prison. It was so quiet there that I was startled by the silence.
There didn't seem to be a sound anywhere after the boat docked as I
was driven up to the prison.

Stroud himself was a tall, thin man who appeared to be in his sixties.
His every motion was slow and precise. He sat down in the chair opposite me and shook my hand.

I introduced myself and explained I had been asked by the court to represent him. Stroud opened a box he carried with him, which had contained wooden kitchen matches and now contained kitchen matches and some hand-rolled cigarettes. He lit a cigarette and told me about himself.

He had been arrested for murder as a young man and had gone to jail. It was in prison that he had first started reading books to improve himself.

Because he had been on good behavior, he acquired a canary and he proceeded to read all the books he could on the care and treatment of canaries. Through observing the canary, and through studying, he became an expert on canaries. Eventually, he wrote a book which became a success with people who have canaries and even with veterinarians who treat canaries and he began to receive letters from all over the world asking for advice on the care and treatment of canaries.

The inflow of letters became a mammoth undertaking for the prison and the warden became upset. According to Stroud when the letters started coming in droves, the warden stopped them. He told Stroud this was not a business venture, he was in to serve time. The Warden also removed his canaries from his cell.

Stroud became enraged, sullen and despondent, and, after a meal, he somehow managed to take a spoon to his cell with him. He worked on the spoon for quite some time and turned the spoon into a weapon. One day, when leaving the mess hall, he put it to use, stabbing a guard he hated, killing him.

Stroud received another murder conviction and life sentence. Luckily for Stroud, because of the publicity he had received on account of his book, he had funds and was able to appeal the decision of the trial court, and obtained a new trial. Stroud was tried again and again found guilty, but this time received a death sentence.

Stroud was able to avoid the death sentence because of the publicity his book had achieved, and his sentence was commuted to life imprisonment. As he saw no possibility of parole and did not wish to waste his time, he was now working on a trilogy about prison life. It would tell of his life in prison, the way prisons are run and the way they should be run, and of the evils of the present prison system, including the sexual activities of the inmates.

Stroud said the authorities did not want him to write this book, and that they knew if he did not have a typewriter and had to write it by hand he would probably never be able to finish it.

His brother on the outside had acquired a publisher and was ready, willing and able to assist him in publishing the book.

He assured me I would be paid handsomely from the proceeds of the book, and that I would be doing a service to humanity and to the prison system if I were to assist him in writing the book because the book would be the cause of necessary improvements in the system.

Stroud was an incredibly self-educated person. He had even learned to play the violin without a teacher in the times he had recreation.

My impression of Stroud was that he had been in prison a long time. He was undoubtedly very intelligent, but he had one or two ingredients missing—as became evident.

I prepared a petition which was no better than the one he had already prepared—the one he had prepared had obviously taken much research and much time to print and prepare—and filed it with the Circuit Court of Appeals and they granted me a hearing.

During my talks with Mr. Stroud, he was adamant he wanted to go to San Francisco and argue the case himself. I told him I would see what I could do, but the court saw no reason to bring Stroud to the hearing.

The hearing was held at the old Post Office building in San Francisco and three justices of the Court of Appeals heard his petition. The U.S. Attorney arguing for the prison system against Mr. Stroud was Joseph Karesh, who was chief deputy in the criminal division of the U.S. Attorney's Office.

I thought I had made an excellent presentation to the Court, until Joe got up to speak. "Your Honor, Mr. Cohn is probably correct in his law and he presents his case well, but Mr. Cohn doesn't realize some physical facts. If you allow Mr. Stroud to have a typewriter in his prison cell, it would be the same as giving a prisoner a gun and ammunition. Each one of the typewriter keys can be removed, and those keys, when removed, can be filed down to a sharp edge and then you would have a tremendous number of stilettos. Even if he only removed one or two, which might not be noticeable, you would still have a dangerous weapon in the hands of a dangerous person, as far as the typewriter goes.

"As for the letters, the reason Mr. Stroud's letters to his brother were stopped was because of the content of the letters, not any antagonism for Mr. Stroud and not because he was going to write a book.

"I would like Your Honors to see the letters that he was writing to his brother, and I would like you to read them. I have prepared copies for Mr. Cohn, and after Mr. Cohn reads these letters, I would like him to tell me if he still thinks that Mr. Stroud should be able to send these letters out of the prison to anyone, including his brother.

"The government is perfectly willing to allow Mr. Stroud to write to anybody he wants as long as he does it in a moderate manner."

With that, Joe handed me a series of letters, which I could see at first glance had been written by my client. The printing was as meticulous as on his petition.

I read the letters and I was amazed. Mr. Stroud, who had appeared to be such a quiet, retiring person, had written the most explosive letters to his brother one could ever imagine. He had called him names using the foulest language one could imagine. Every possible swear word was contained in those letters.

"Well, Your Honor, would it be possible to give permission to Mr. Stroud to write to his brother and correspond in a more pleasant manner?" I asked.

"I don't think we'll be able to give him a typewriter," the Court responded, "but we will make an order that he be allowed to write to any person he wishes and correspond with anyone he wishes, so long as he does not use foul language or threats."

I thanked the Court and went to bring the news to Mr. Stroud.

When we sat down in the attorney's visiting room, Stroud looked at me intently and asked what had happened.

I told him that the Court had refused his request for a typewriter and that the reason for it was that each key could become a dangerous weapon in the prison. He grinned from ear to ear: "That's true."

I told him that the Court had made an order that he be allowed to write any letters as long as he wanted, to correspond with his brother or anyone else he wanted, so long as he didn't do it using foul language, abusive language or threats.

He smiled again. "That's fine. Mr. Cohn," he added, "I'm going to remember you. When I write my book, I'm going to make you famous."

Two years later, a book was written on the life of Mr. Stroud called *The Birdman of Alcatraz*. A motion picture was made from that book, also called *The Birdman of Alcatraz*, but at no time in either the book or the motion picture was my name ever mentioned.

The Tale of the Golden Dragon

In one of the most difficult cases I ever tried, my client was identified as the shooter in a murder by no less than seven eye witnesses. Yet, I was able to obtain an acquittal.

A young Chinese woman had come into my office and announced that her father wished to hire me to represent her brother, Kenneth Yue, who had been charged with murdering Vincent Chu. The woman had been referred to me by another Chinese client who had referred quite a few Chinatown criminal cases to me. Fortunately, I had been successful in all of them.

She told me a little bit about the charges and I advised her that if I took the case I would have to charge a fairly decent fee and as I would just be taking their money if there were no chance at all of doing any good, I would have to talk to her brother first to see if there were any possible defenses.

The young woman told me her brother would be coming into town in a couple of days.

"Coming in from where?"

"New York."

Her brother had been arrested in connection with another shooting in New York's Chinatown and charged with possessing an unlicensed handgun under New York's Sullivan Law. Kenneth had been found guilty after trial and was serving a five-year prison sentence in New York. Now they were bringing him out to San Francisco from a New York State prison to stand trial for murder.

"When are they coming out?"

"They should be out any day now."

I told her to let me know when her brother was in the San Francisco County Jail and I would go see him.

This was what Kenneth told me when I visited him: Yue and seven of his friends had eaten dinner at one of the restaurants in San Francisco's

Chinatown, then decided to walk down to Washington Square where there was a festival. On their way, they walked by St. Louis Alley. When they looked down the alley they saw three boys, approximately 18-20 years old. Kenneth and his friends recognized them as Joe Fongs, or "Joe Boys." The Joe Boys were "ABC's," American-born Chinese. The boys with Kenneth Yue were "Wah Chings." Wah Ching means "young Chinese." The Wah Chings were "FOB's"—fresh off the boat.

Kenneth and his fellow Wah Chings walked down the alley to confront the Joe Boys. Somehow, the boys with Kenneth had three guns. Somehow, the guns were drawn. They were talking to the Joe Boys when all of a sudden the place exploded. One of the Wah Ching boys had apparently shot and killed Vincent Chu. The other two Joe Boys ran out of the alley down the street, wounded. Someone called the police.

Kenneth and his friends went back to their cars and drove down to a bowling alley in Millbrae where they went bowling. On the way to Millbrae, they heard about the shooting on the radio.

Kenneth and his friends bowled for a while, then went over to Lyon's Restaurant in San Bruno, where they discussed their situation.

One of the boys thought someone might have recognized him back at the alley and Kenneth and his friends decided they would all spread out. A few remained in San Francisco. Kenneth went to Chinatown in Los Angeles.

According to the police, Kenneth was in Los Angeles for awhile. Then the Wah Chings decided he should ship out for New York's Chinatown where he became involved in another episode involving some other kids and a gun, and was arrested and sent to prison.

The Wah Ching boy who thought he might have been recognized hired a criminal defense lawyer in San Francisco named George Walker. George is one of the top criminal defense lawyers in San Francisco and had won quite a lot of cases. He was one of the first members of the American Board of Criminal Lawyers and one of its first presidents.

George knew what to do for his client, and promptly negotiated a deal with the District Attorney that his client would turn state's evidence if granted immunity and testify as to the identity of the shooter. Soon, four of the other Wah Ching boys who had been with Kenneth that night also agreed to testify. They all named Kenneth Yue. And they all received immunity.

There had been three guns that night in St. Louis Alley. The other two boys who were shooting and had wounded the two surviving Joe Boys were identified by the Joe Boys and arrested. George Walker represented one of these two boys and Harriet Ross the other. Harriet was a Public Defender and is now in private practice. She is also one of the best criminal defense attorneys in San Francisco. A client represented by Harriet can be assured of having the equal of any attorney around. Harriet was also one of the first members of the American Board of Criminal Lawyers and became its president.

I explained to Kenneth's sister that I didn't think there was a snowball's chance in hell of Kenneth being acquitted.

That did not satisfy her. She insisted her father's friend had said I could win the case.

I explained I had been lucky with some of the cases the gentleman had sent me but in this case we had seven people saying Kenneth did it.

In the end, I agreed to represent her brother for a moderate fee, although I didn't feel that I was going to be able to do much for Kenneth.

When I went over to the county jail I also found Kenneth had no clothes of his own, so I had his sister buy him a blue suit and several shirts and several pairs of socks and several ties and a new pair of shoes. I wanted to make sure that he had a clean shirt and a new tie and clean socks every day of the trial and was wearing a brand-new pair of shoes. Kenneth's sister brought in a light blue suit without cuffs, and I took it over to the county jail and made Kenneth stand on a chair while I pinned the cuffs—to the amusement of the deputy sheriffs—and Kenneth was able to wear the suit in court when the trial began.

When I went down to court to get the discovery in the case, I ran into Harriet Ross in the Hall of Justice. She told me the prosecutor had offered her a good deal if her client would testify. She asked what I thought she should do. I told her to go ahead and take the best deal she could get and let her client testify. I ran into George Walker, too, who was representing the other boy charged with shooting. I told George to take the best deal he could get.

That made two who were given deals in exchange for testimony in addition to the other five that had already been granted immunity. All seven would testify that Kenneth Yue shot the deceased.

The district attorney, James Lassart, was one of the best attorneys in the office. He was like a fullback going through the line and came straight at you.

Predictably, he started the trial by calling these boys who had been granted immunity.

On cross-examination, I asked the same question of each: "Who is your attorney?"

"George Walker."

"Oh, George is one of the finest defense lawyers in California. He must have worked an excellent deal for you..."

They admitted that they had agreed to testify my client shot Vincent Chu in return for the District Attorney agreeing not to charge them.

That was the first thing I had to do: let the jury know what a great lawyer George was for running down to the District Attorney and negotiating immunity for his clients.

There was something else about these witnesses. They were inveterate liars. They just had to lie. But I had pored through everything I could find about them, and I knew more about them than they could imagine, and every one of them had to lie about something—every one of them. One didn't do something he had done. Another wasn't someone I proved he was. They lied and said they drove the car or lied and said they didn't drive the car, or they lied and said they didn't go bowling, or they lied about whether they had gone to the restaurant or what they had ordered in the restaurant. They lied and I kept showing up their lies.

On one side of the courtroom were Wah Chings. On the other side were Joe Boys. Someone asked me if I was worried about it, but I knew they weren't going to bother me. "I'm a lawyer. They are all liable to need me sometime themselves."

None of them threatened me or even said anything when I made them look bad on the stand. None of them seemed to get upset.

But after Lassart had called three of the Wah Ching boys who had been granted immunity and realized I was killing them, he brought on the two shooters. I continued in the same fashion, and brought out the special deals they had obtained through their great lawyers, George Walker and Harriet Ross. I made it look as if they were testifying because of the deals they had been offered. The two remaining immunized Wah Ching boys never made it to the stand.

After several days of testimony from these boys, if any of them had testified they were now in San Francisco, the jurors would have gone outside to look at a sign just to check.

I put my client on the stand, who testified that the gun which did the killing was indeed registered to his father, but that he had loaned the gun to one of the boys who had been given immunity.

During a recess in the trial I went out into the hallway across from the courtroom where we were trying the case. There I ran into a very good friend of mine, Deputy District Attorney Tom Norman, and we chatted. Just as Tom left, I heard two Chinese kids about two or three feet away, around the corner:

"What do you think of that Coh-hon?"

"Yeah, he's something."

"You know who he reminds me of?"

"No."

"He reminds me of Perry Mason."

"No, Perry Mason is much fatter..."

I broke up.

I argued to the court that my client said he didn't do the shooting and I pointed out that although the other witnesses said he had done the shooting, each had received something for saying so.

I made a motion *in limine* before the court to exclude anything regarding my client's New York conviction because the New York incident took place after the events in this case and was not relevant to this shooting.

In my closing argument, I pointed out all the different things that the other boys had lied about and asked the jury directly whom were they going to believe.

The jury was out several days. Finally, at 11 o'clock at night, the judge called them in to ask if they could come to a decision. He gave the *Anderson* instruction, which, in essence, tells the jury there is no assurance that another jury will be better, and that those in the minority should listen to those in the majority and see if they can come to a decision.

The *Anderson* instruction has been struck down since then, but it was common at that time. As I got up to make my motion for mistrial on the grounds of the impropriety of the *Anderson* instruction, the bell rang and Judge Mullins halted my motion. "We will continue this after the jury comes in..."

The jury acquitted my client.

I felt wonderful, but his family couldn't take Kenneth home. He was still in custody for New York, so I told his sister to get the suit and clothing she had bought and to hold them for when he came back.

As I left the Hall of Justice, it was very late and Halls of Justice are not in the safest locations. Downstairs I met one of the jurors, a woman who was waiting for a cab. I asked her where she was going. She told me if I could drive her to Market Street she could catch a streetcar which would take her right to her front door. I agreed to drive her to Market Street and we made conversation.

"I guess your client's family is very happy."

"Yes they are."

"I guess he will be back with his family tomorrow."

"Well, he really won't."

"Why not?"

"He's really in prison in New York."

"Why didn't we know that?"

"Because it has no relevance to the case."

She became upset: "I wish we would have known that he was in prison for a shooting in New York … I wish we would have known that!"

"Well, it has no relevance. You see that happened after this incident, so it has nothing to do with this shooting and is nothing that can be used to prove my client's guilt in this case."

"Well, that's a fine way to try to run the justice system!" she shouted, and slammed the door as she stormed out of the car.

Not long after Kenneth Yue's trial, a group of Joe Boys entered one of the big restaurants in Chinatown called the Golden Dragon. The owner of the Golden Dragon was known as a big supporter of the Wah Chings. When the Chinese kids came in from Hong Kong, they would hang out in the Golden Dragon and he would help them get jobs.

The Joe Boys shot almost everyone in the Golden Dragon that night because, it was said, I had won an acquittal for a Wah Ching. That shooting became known as the "Golden Dragon Massacre."

Some of the Joe Boys involved in the shooting were arrested, charged and convicted for the Golden Dragon Massacre shootings.

A few weeks after the "Golden Dragon Massacre" trial was over, I received a telephone call from a very close friend of mine, an immigration attorney in Chinatown named Jack Chow. Jack also had offices in Hong Kong and he had helped bring many Chinese to the United States. When Jack was in Hong Kong and word was out he was in town, people would line up from his office all the way down the street and for another block waiting to see him about emigrating to the United States.

Jack was a good friend of mine and sent me quite a bit of criminal work from Chinatown because he didn't handle criminal cases.

Jack asked, "Nate, are you going to be busy tomorrow?" I told him I had nothing in the afternoon.

"I want to come over and pick you up tomorrow. Will you be ready? I want to take you somewhere."

"What's it all about?"

"I can't tell you." I asked him again to tell me what it was about, and Jack insisted he couldn't tell me. But Jack was a good friend, so I agreed to meet him.

When I went down to meet Jack the next afternoon, he was seated in the back seat of a limousine. Next to the driver in the front seat was a Chinese man. I got into the back seat next to Jack and asked him again what this was all about.

"Just do me a favor. I need you for a while."

We drove into the hills north of San Francisco, in Marin County or perhaps Sonoma County. Finally, we arrived at a big house surrounded by oak trees. There was no one about except some Catholic priests.

Jack explained, "I want you to do me a favor. This is a retreat. There is a young man here who is the witness who identified the shooters in the Golden Dragon Massacre and I want you to talk to him."

"What about?"

"The City of San Francisco put up a reward of $100,000 to anyone responsible for the capture and the conviction of the Golden Dragon shooters and this is the young man who told them who it was."

Inside the house I found a Chinese youth. The other man who had driven with us in the front seat was an interpreter.

Jack talked to the interpreter, then I talked to the interpreter, and then I talked to the youth. The youth could understand quite a bit of English, but Jack had the interpreter available to make sure he knew precisely what was going on.

The youth wanted to hire me to get him the $100,000 reward from the City of San Francisco for identifying the shooters at the Golden Dragon.

"I'll take it on one condition," I told him. "If I get you the money, I will charge you 10% of what I get for you. If I don't get you anything, it is free." Both he and Jack thought my terms were very reasonable.

There was one hitch: the boy had not filed a claim with the City for the money. The time had already elapsed to file a claim, and you can only sue after a timely claim has been turned down. But Jack told me he was sure I could handle it.

I knew the City Attorney very well. We had tried many cases against one another when he was Deputy City Attorney. I also knew the police detective who was in charge of the Golden Dragon Massacre investigation. It turned out that the police hadn't wanted the boy to file a claim because, on cross-examination, the defense attorney could have brought out the fact that he had something to gain for his testimony.

I explained all this to the City Attorney and the City Attorney agreed my client could file a claim if the Police Department also agreed; I filed a late claim and my client received his $100,000.

The check was made out to the boy and to me.

I told Jack to bring the boy to my office to get the check, but to also bring someone who spoke both English and Chinese so I could talk to him.

At that time I had a young lawyer in my office named Jay Rogers. Jay had been a finance officer for the United States government. They would send him in when there was a catastrophe, a hurricane or an earthquake, and it was his job to give out money.

But Jay was a funny guy. He didn't like to give out government money, and he got upset with the job and quit. Jay then went into the Air Force and became an Air Force finance officer in Alaska. After he had served four years, he went to law school, and because of his background, he became an attorney for the Federal Home Loan Bank. After a few more years he decided he wanted to become a trial lawyer. When Jay asked me for a job, I had an opening and I hired him. Jay was a genius.

I told Jay I wanted him to sit down with this boy and that the boy was going to receive $90,000. I wanted Jay to explain to him that if he put his $90,000 in CDs he would make about $5,000 a year, and that $5,000 a year would provide him at least $400 a month, and that way, he would never be broke for the rest of his life.

Jay explained all this through the interpreter. I could see the youth nodding up and down and smiling. Finally, I gave the him his check.

"Do you understand what he told you?" I asked the youth.

"Oh yes," the interpreter said, "he told me you have $10,000 coming."

"Fine. Here's your $90,000. Now, do what Mr. Rogers told you."

The youth left the office and I repeated he should be sure to go to the bank and take care of getting the CDs.

A few years later, Jay came in to see me. He said he had read in the paper that the young man had been killed in Los Angeles holding up a grocery store.

I was involved in one other case which involved a shooting of a young man by another in a gang setting: I represented a boy who had been charged with first-degree murder for shooting a young Latino boy in San Francisco's Mission District.

My client's parents retained me. They were very fine religious people and had never been in any trouble. I had represented them many, many years before in an accident case, and obtained an excellent jury result for them. After the accident case, they had come to me when their son was charged with stealing a bicycle and I was able to obtain an acquittal on that charge.

Their son had convinced them that he was not in the vicinity at the time of the shooting. He also assured me that he had not been in the vicinity and thought it might have been his brother who had done the shooting, as his brother was in the vicinity of the shooting and owned the gun which police had found in a drawer in the bedroom shared by the two brothers.

Based on what my client told me, I was going to base my defense on the fact that the witnesses had misidentified the shooter, and I selected a jury of people who were sophisticated and who could understand a misidentification defense. I had a good feeling about the jurors I had selected.

I reserved my opening statement until the end of the District Attorney's case—which turned out to be very fortunate as the case transpired.

The District Attorney called several Latino boys to the stand who testified they saw my client standing on the curb that evening watching lowriders driving up and down the street. The boys recognized him, they thought, as a boy who had hurt one of their friends in a fight a few nights earlier. They testified they went around the corner, parked their car, and four of them went over to where he was standing in order to accost him. But, as they approached him, he pulled out a gun and shot the leader of the group in the chest. The wounded boy ran into the street and the other three boys ran in different directions. They testified the shooter deliberately stepped up on the curb and shot the wounded boy again, this time killing him, then went around the corner and got into a car.

Another witness who had seen the shooting testified he wrote down the license number of the car and gave it to the police. The police obtained a search warrant, went to my client's house, and found the gun that had fired the shots in a drawer in my client's room.

At that point I was still confident I could show that the shooter was not my client.

Then the District Attorney put a witness on the stand that had not been on the witness list. My client had assured me he didn't know the witness and that the witness could not testify to anything harmful to the defense.

But when this witness took the stand he testified that he was my client's closest friend; that they had gone to school together and been close friends for over six years. And he testified he was with my client on Mission Street at the time of the shooting, standing next to my client the entire time. He testified unequivocally that my client pulled out the gun and shot and killed the victim.

After we finished the examination of this witness, I took my client into a room where I could talk to him confidentially and I asked him what in the world he thought he was doing, and why hadn't he told me that this boy was a friend of his and that he was there at the time of the shooting.

"Well, I didn't think he would say anything that would cause me any trouble because he's a good friend of mine."

"Your good friend, and your reluctance to tell me the truth, may have put you in jail for a long time. Now I have to switch my whole defense. The only option we have now is self-defense. I would have selected a different jury for self-defense: rugged men and women who would recognize the necessity for a person to defend himself against someone who was threatening them."

Fortunately, I had not made an opening statement, but I still had the wrong jury for this case.

Then I proceeded to make the case for self-defense. I established that the witnesses had seen my client standing on the street and that the four Latino boys had walked over to him—four against one. One of the witnesses testified that the leader of the boys had gone into the trunk of the car and pulled out a shiny metal aerial.

After my client realized that his lying to me about this witness had put him in deep trouble he finally told me what had really happened. He was standing on Mission Street when these four boys had come up to him. One of the boys had a shiny metal thing in his hand, which my client thought was a knife. They were coming toward him and he pulled out his gun. They kept coming, so he pulled the trigger because he was afraid that they were going to kill him.

Fortunately, my client hadn't taken the stand. Fortunately I hadn't made an opening statement setting forth the ridiculous story that my client had first told me.

I cross-examined the three Latino boys and I showed the jury that they had gone over to my client with the intention of causing him harm, and the leader of the four had a shiny, long object in his hand which could have been interpreted to be a long sword or stiletto.

Of course, the fact that after the boys started running across the street my client shot at them again negated the self-defense argument unless the jury believed that the original shot was the one that killed the victim and that the other shots missed him.

The jury went out and, as I was afraid, the jurors did not believe the self-defense argument. They were out for almost a day before coming back with a manslaughter conviction.

As neither the judge nor the jury had any notion that my client had been less than honest with me, I made a motion before Judge Vavouris for probation, and Judge Vavouris granted my client probation on condition that he serve a year in the county jail.

The verdict came back in the early part of November and my client was sent to the county jail the second week in November. Several weeks later, my client's parents came to me and asked if I would do whatever I could to get their son out of the county jail so he could come visit them during the Christmas season. They were very religious people and said they would appreciate my just trying. So, I told them I would see what I could do.

I went over to the Hall of Justice intending to file a petition at the County Clerk's office asking the Court to release my client for two or three weeks during the Christmas season so he could spend time with his parents. But, as I was walking toward the County Clerk's office, I saw my client at the Hall of Justice walking around at liberty.

"What did you do?" I called out.

"What do you mean?"

"You're supposed to be in custody. Did you escape or something? If you did, you have to go right back."

"No, no, no. The county jail was packed with prisoners and they wanted to get rid of some of them. They have a sheriff's committee for parole and due to the fact that I had been found guilty of manslaughter and had gotten probation on condition that I would serve a year in a county jail, they felt that this was not the usual manslaughter case and they gave me parole and released me."

"Do you have to go back?"

"No, I've been paroled and I'm loose. I'm through."

"You only served about a month."

"That's true—not even a month."

Unfortunately, several months later his parents called me about him and wanted to come down and see me.

Their son had moved to the Central Valley because he wanted to get out of San Francisco. They told me he was afraid that some of the Latino boys would find out where he was and come after him. He started using drugs. There was a hold-up at a drive-in and one of the customers at the drive-in was killed and their son was charged with the shooting. Their son didn't want to call them about it because he had already cost them money they couldn't afford, and he thought that the Public Defender would be able get him out of it and he could call them after it was all over. But the jury found him guilty of murder in the first degree and he was given the death sentence.

The boy's father told their son they would get him a lawyer to appeal it, but the boy didn't want the father to spend any more money and he didn't want the mother and father to visit him in prison because, he said, he had gotten himself into this situation.

"Do you want me to go over and talk to him in prison?"

"I asked him, but he said no, he didn't want to face you."

"He's not responsible to me. However since I'm not an appellate lawyer, I would not handle the appeal. But if I can be of any assistance to him…"

"No, we're going to try to see him. Even though he doesn't want to see us, we're going to try to see him anyway next week and we'll talk to him. And if he feels he would like to talk to you for any reason, we'll pay you to go over and see him."

"You don't have to pay me. If he wants to talk to me or if I can be of any help in any way, call me and I'll do it without fee. But I'm not going to handle the appeal because I'm not an appellate lawyer."

Two weeks later the father called me. "He does not want to see you under any circumstances and he will not put your name down on the visitor's list."

"If you hear anything or I can do anything, let me know."

As of this writing, I haven't heard from them.

I often think that if I had not successfully defended him on the first charge that he would have been found guilty of second-degree murder or manslaughter without probation; and that he might never have gone down to the Valley, and he might never have participated in this robbery and not be looking at the death penalty.

He
Stole the Show
(Literally)

24

When I started to represent him, Steve Cochran had starred in several movies which were doing well at the box office, and an Italian film director wanted him to star in a movie made in Italy. Steve would receive his expenses and, in lieu of salary, the rights to distribute the movie in the United States.

They made the movie, *Il Grido (The Cry)*, but after the movie was completed, the director started a feud with Steve and wanted to the keep the U.S. distribution rights for himself. He thought it would be a big success, and he set up a showing in San Francisco at the San Francisco Film Festival, but he wouldn't give Steve a copy of the film so he could see the picture as it had been completed.

Steve wanted me to stop the movie from being shown at the film festival, which was being held at a theater in the Marina District. A friend of mine who was in the theater business was director of the festival and I called him and said unless Steve had an opportunity to see the film before it was shown, he would bring an action to enjoin the festival from showing it.

The festival director knew that what I said, I would do, and made arrangements for Steve to see the movie the morning before it was to be shown. Steve invited me to go to the movie with him. It was an excellent movie, and Steve, who could speak Italian very well, interpreted for me, and we became quite friendly. Steve was pleased with the picture and said it could be shown.

However, the movie was not delivered to Steve to distribute in the United States as had been agreed. It was kept in the Consul General's office in Los Angeles.

A short time thereafter, I received a phone call from Steve telling me that some friends in the movie industry had made arrangements to view the picture with the idea that they would distribute it. Some of Steve's friends were actors who played gangster parts in the movies and they attended the preview dressed up in gangster attire, managing to convince the people at the Consulate they were hoods, and Steve and his friends physically seized the film.

When Steve called me for advice on what to do, I told him to stop play-acting and take the film back to the Italian Consulate, and I straightened the situation out.

After that, Steve had me check all his film contracts. He lived in Beverly Hills, and when I would go to Los Angeles I would visit Steve and go over his legal problems.

One evening when I was at his house Steve had two young Mexican girls with white servant outfits waiting on us.

I asked Steve, "Where did you get these … girls?"

"My wife and I went down to Ensenada in my yacht, and a radio host there interviewed me and I mentioned to him that I would like to get some kids to come down to my boat and clean it before I came back to the United States. The next morning I had all these young kids down at my boat ready to work for me.

"I hired some of them to clean the boat and I paid them off, and my wife and I came back to Los Angeles. When we got into the harbor in Los Angeles, I realized that these two young girls had stowed away on my boat. They were afraid that they would be arrested for coming into the country illegally so I brought them home. They wanted to stay here for a few days in Los Angeles, so I allowed them to stay in my house and I would pay them as servants, and they could see L.A."

I stopped in my tracks.

"Tomorrow morning, as early as you can get up, get those girls out of your house. Take them down to the train or a bus for Mexico and put them on there. They go to Ensenada, that's not that far from San Diego.

"Don't have anything to do with them staying here, and let them go back to Mexico. If you run into any authorities, explain to them what happened, and that's it."

"Okay."

A couple of days later, my associate, Ed Bardin, who ran my office in Beverly Hills, called and said that the Immigration had stopped the girls and the U.S. Attorney's Office was commencing an investigation of Steve for bringing the girls into the country illegally. I told Ed to contact Steve and to tell him to advise the U.S. Attorney that he would cooperate completely, except that he would not say anything until I was present.

I called Steve and told him that the U.S. government was investigating his actions and that I wanted him to go with me and Ed Bardin to Ensenada to investigate what happened, for the benefit of his defense.

I flew down to L.A. and I rented a car, and all three of us went to San Diego where I hired a shorthand reporter who worked for the federal government, and an interpreter who interpreted for the federal government, and took them with us down to Ensenada. We took statements under penalty of perjury from the radio announcer and from the two girls who were involved and the interpreter and the shorthand reporter went back to San Diego. We had dinner in Ensenada, stayed overnight, then went back to L.A., and I returned to San Francisco.

A day or two later, I received a phone call from Ed, who said the U.S. Attorney was all upset and was threatening the two of us with prosecution.

"Relax." I called up the prosecutor.

"You went down and started talking to my witnesses! You had no right to do all that."

"They're not anybody's witnesses. I have a right to talk to anybody that I want to in investigating my case. You don't own the witnesses." I also explained that I had an interpreter that worked for the federal government and a shorthand reporter that worked for the federal government.

"You don't think I'm stupid enough to try to get those people to say anything not true. Those are two people who work for the federal government."

"I didn't know that."

"You have no right to witnesses. I have as much right to witnesses as you do."

He calmed down and had to agree that I was correct.

A few days later, he called me to tell he was calling Steve to testify before the federal grand jury.

"You have a right to do that," I told him. "Tell me when, and I'll bring him."

He set a date for the next week and I brought Steve down to the federal courthouse where the grand jury was.

When we arrived, I gave Steve a piece of paper. On the piece of paper, it said: "On advice of my counsel, Nathan Cohn, I refuse to answer the question on the grounds it might tend to incriminate or degrade me."

I asked Steve, "Can you read that?"

"Of course."

"Now, you're an actor, and I want you to do a little acting.

"What's that?"

"They're going to ask you some questions. Now, you can answer a question like your name, your address and your business, but any other question I want you to read this paper back to them.

"The first time you read it, I want you to accentuate the first word. The second time you read it, I want you to accentuate the second word, and every time you read it, accentuate the next word: 'ON advice of my counsel…,' 'On ADVICE of my counsel…,' 'On advice OF my counsel…'

"You want me to do that?"

"That's what I want."

Ed and I sat outside of the grand jury room, waiting. We were not permitted inside the grand jury room, but, after a while, we could hear the grand jurors inside laughing.

Finally, it was over. Steve had been told that if he wanted to ask me any questions of me, I was outside, and he could come and talk to me, but he never did. He just read from the paper.

The grand jury did not indict him. In fact, they were quite amused by his performance.

And I told Steve that in the future I didn't want to hear about any other girls on his boat under any circumstances.

⊢——·——⊣

At one time, he was going with a young lady who was a movie actress and who played the secretary of a private detective on television. She was co-chair with Debbie Reynolds of a yearly dinner to raise money for the Thalians, a theatrical group who raised money for blind children. The dinner was to be held at the Beverly Hilton Hotel. I was in L.A. on another matter, and Steve wanted to take me to this dinner. He told me that his girlfriend was co-chair and he had made arrangements for us to have an excellent table.

I said I didn't have a tux, so Steve sent me to the tailor in L.A. that he got tuxes from. After I finished in court, I went back to Beverly Hills, put on the tux and went to the Beverly Hilton.

At the hotel, as you went into the main dining room, there was an anteroom. There, they had built a bridge, and the floor beneath the bridge was filled with photographers, and as the celebrities went over the bridge, they stopped at the top of the bridge and posed for pictures.

Steve and I went over the bridge, and the photographers took our picture. Afterwards I went down on the floor where the photographers were while Steve excused himself to go to the bathroom.

I watched as all the movie stars went over the bridge and had their picture taken.

A little later, a cameraman came over to me.

"Can I take your picture?"

"Wait a minute, you don't want my picture."

"What do you mean?"

"I'm not involved in a movie studio. I'm not an actor. I'm not involved in movies at all. I'm just here as a guest."

"Can I take your picture?"

"Look, I'm nobody. I'm a lawyer from San Francisco. Nobody's interested in my picture.

"Can I take your picture?"

After three or four attempts to explain it to him, I was getting nowhere.

"Go ahead." He took my picture.

"Why in the world would you want my picture?"

"You must be important. Anybody as bald as you who would come to this place without a toupee has got to be an important person."

We sat down, and at the next table was Hugh O'Brien, who was starring on a television series as Wyatt Earp. He was with a very attractive lady who was the ex-wife of a big-name movie actor, and he had had a few drinks. He was giving her a bad time, and she was just trying to be nice. It just ticked me off.

O'Brien came over to give his regards to Steve.

"Steve, how are you?"

"I want to introduce you to my close friend and lawyer, Nathan Cohn."

I looked at O'Brien and he looked as though he thought he was the greatest thing that had ever happened.

"You're that actor in that television series, Wyatt Earp."

"Yes, I am."

"You just ruined the series for me."

"What?"

"In the series, you look like a tall, good-looking guy. Now, I see you're a little shrimp."

Nate and actor Steve Cochrane plan to take the world.

Steve had to look away to keep from laughing. O'Brien couldn't believe it. He looked at me as if to say: "Who is this guy insulting me, a big movie star?" If looks could kill, they'd have buried me in the next ten minutes.

Steve also had a good sense of humor.

One time I went down to San Pedro on a matter for Steve and I took along a young lawyer from my office by the name of John Gardenal. John was Yugoslavian and there were a lot of Yugoslavian immigrants in San Pedro, and I thought we might run into someone John could help with the language. Steve had a little problem which I went down there to solve, and we spent a couple of hours and got everything straightened out.

Afterwards, Steve suggested we go to have dinner in San Pedro. I took John and my associate Ed Bardin and we went to one of the restaurants there. When the bill came, Steve had the waiter give me the bill.

"You don't want me to pay this bill."

John couldn't believe it. He knew I never had clients pick up the bill, and John was shocked at hearing me tell Steve it would be better for him to pick up the bill.

"Why would it be better?" Steve asked.

"Because if I pay the bill, I triple the amount and put it on your bill. Now you're saving two-thirds the amount of the dinner by paying it."

One time, he called me at my hotel and left a message he wanted to talk to me. I called him back. He had an office and a secretary, because he was producing some of his own movies. A secretary with a haughty voice answered: "I'm sorry Mr. Cohn, he isn't here now, he's on his yacht."

"Is that so?"

"You can tell Mr. Cochran I have two yachts."

"You have??"

"Yeah, a front yacht and a back yacht."

She didn't know what to say, but when she told Steve he broke up.

Steve married a beautiful Swedish girl and wanted me to meet her.

I called up Ed and said, "Come along with me. I'm going to introduce you to Steve's wife."

"Really?"

"Yeah."

When we arrived, I introduced Ed to Steve's wife. "This is my associate in Beverly Hills."

I told Ed to give Steve and his wife his card and explained to her that if I was not available I wanted to make sure she had both my card and Ed's card.

Ed asked me afterwards what that was all about.

I reminded Ed he knew Steve, and if some night she got mad and shot him in the head, I wanted her to have his card so he could defend her.

Steve would sit upstairs, and he would have this beautiful woman—she looked like Debbie Reynolds—run down and get us drinks, do this, do that.

"What are you doing?" I asked Steve. "If you want somebody to run for you, hire somebody to do it."

"That's why I got married! She loves to wait on me."

"Yeah, that'll go for about a month, and then she won't be so happy about it."

But women flocked to him.

Steve had great parties at his house, and sometimes I liked to bring some down-to-earth atmosphere to them. On this occasion, I brought a friend of mine, Al Mundt, with me. Al was a husky seaman and looked tough. We were sitting, having a drink and watching the action, and a pretty girl was sitting next to Al.

"Have you met Mr. Mundt?" I asked.

"No, I haven't."

"He's one of the head men in the Mafia…"

He looked liked he might be, and he was playing along.

She grabbed her purse, put it on her lap and ran out.

Steve saw what had happened.

"What did you do to her?

"I just told her that Al was one of the head men in the Mafia…"

Steve had a good laugh.

I had told Steve never to be on a boat with a young girl, but he didn't listen to me. He went sailing down to the lower part of South America, and he had three girls in the boat with him. From what I heard, he became ill on the boat and he was afraid to call for medical help. He went to his cabin and went to bed and died in his cabin. The boat was floating around off Chile with no one running it because the girls did not know how to run the boat. Fortunately, another boat saw the girls waving, and they took the boat into Chile, but Steve had passed away.

That, sadly, was Steve Cochran.

A Man
Called Lucky

25

I guess one could say that my luckiest client was a man eponymously named "Lucky," although it looked like his luck had positively run out when I took the case.

Lucky Jang owned a bar in Chinatown, which, naturally, was named "Lucky's," and Lucky was very likeable. He was so likeable, in fact, that he had been married five times. Lucky also had a daughter by a previous wife, a most beautiful young girl.

Then, it looked like Lucky's luck was at an end. Lucky's fifth wife was shot in the back five times and Lucky was facing a murder charge.

The next day, my secretary told me a young woman had come to see me. The young woman had been referred by my wife—she was her hairdresser.

Accompanying her were two other very attractive young ladies and a movie-star gorgeous girl of sixteen or seventeen. They turned out to be Lucky's wives two, three and four, and Lucky's daughter.

They wanted to hire me to defend Lucky. They were also all in agreement that Lucky's last wife was to blame. All the divorces had been amicable they agreed, but Lucky's last marriage was a mistake.

It seemed Lucky and his last wife had gone to Chinatown for dinner. There, his wife berated him while Lucky drank.

Afterwards, Lucky and his wife went home to the Richmond district, both loaded. But she didn't stop putting him down. She announced she was going to go bowling and started ironing her bowling shirt.

Somehow, one of them got a gun, brought it into the room and put it down. She kept antagonizing Lucky, and finally he grabbed the gun, and shot her in the back five times. When Lucky realized what he had done, he called the police and told them.

Lucky was now facing the gas chamber.

I didn't think there was a chance of winning the case and I told them so; but the hairdresser had heard from my wife about the difficult cases

I had won, and they wanted me to represent their ex-husband.

Never a one to resist flattery by four beautiful women, nor ready to face my wife's disappointment at letting her hairdresser down, I went to see Lucky at the county jail.

Lucky swore he had been drunk. He also said he had been out of his mind: his wife had been driving him crazy. She had said he wasn't a man anymore and that he couldn't allure her; and, loaded with alcohol and driven to the breaking point, he had reacted and shot her. That was the long and the short of Lucky's tale.

Lucky had been charged with first-degree murder, and the case was assigned to Judge Joseph Karesh in Superior Court. A bright, honest, intelligent District Attorney was assigned to the case, Owen Woodruff, who later became a Federal Magistrate Judge. His word was as good as gold, and he was an excellent cross-examiner and trial lawyer.

I selected the best jury I thought I could get, and I tried the case on the theory that my client was simply too intoxicated to form the intent to commit first-degree murder.

I put his ex-wives on the stand, who testified what a wonderful man my client was, and I put his daughter on the stand to let the jury see how beautiful and sweet she was.

I also established that the deceased was a decidedly nasty person, which of course doesn't have too much to do with whether you shoot them or not; but it helped the jury to understand how it happened. The jury came back with a manslaughter verdict.

At that time, if a gun was used in the commission of a crime, the defendant could not get probation unless the judge found special circumstances, but I petitioned the court to find special circumstances in Lucky's case. The judge, after having heard the witnesses, agreed that special circumstances existed, and Lucky was granted probation by the court.

At that time, the law also stated that in order for a defendant to receive probation in a shooting, the district attorney had to agree. I argued to the court that sentencing was a judicial function, and the court should not have to have the approval of the district attorney to do a judicial act.

"Well, if I find in your favor," Judge Karesh inquired, "and don't uphold the law, they'll probably appeal it. Could you handle an appeal to the court?"

I said, "Of course."

Judge Karesh granted my motion. "We might as well get this settled right now. I am going to grant him probation on the condition that he serves four months in the county jail."

To the District Attorney he said, "You can appeal it. Do whatever you want."

And they did appeal it. The appellate court held that sentencing was a judicial function and that the legislature could not take that away from the judge and give it to the District Attorney.

And Lucky Jang, true to his moniker, had gone from the possibility of the gas chamber to a short jail sentence and probation. His luck hadn't run out after all.

Cop-killer Harold Miller today
a strange bit of remorse over hi
of Police Inspector Denis Bradl
Miller says he's sorry it wasn't
Insp   Max G ard, instead.
The st   y-   ed ex-convict s.
Girard   at   p   was alwa
me."
"I   hat   p (Bradley) w
killed," he declared at City Prison.
"If it had to be anyone, I wish it
have been Girard.

The Gayola Case

26

In the days before San Francisco became a mecca for gays and long before anyone thought of marrying them at City Hall, San Francisco had a substantial gay population. They frequented San Francisco's gay bars, and the owners of these bars, or some of them, believed that they were being harassed by the San Francisco Police. The owners of one of these bars charged two police sergeants and two patrolmen with shaking them down to leave their bar alone and the case hit the newspapers as the "Gayola" case.

One of the police sergeants came to me to represent him and the other went to my close friend James Martin MacInnis. The two patrolmen hired an attorney named Harry.

When I tried cases with Jim, he would let me direct the case, and I had the order of the defense pretty well figured out.

MacInnis was tall, handsome, athletic and possessed of a golden tongue. Jim went first because he made such a beautiful impression. Women loved him.

Harry would be next. I would come last in order to close all the doors and make sure that everything was in perspective when we finished the defense.

I suggested that we not do anything fancy in this case. I knew that Harry ran two or three different directions at the same time in some cases. Jim agreed with me.

The District Attorney's star witness was the bartender who claimed the officers had demanded a bribe from him. I cross-examined him. Jim cross-examined him. Harry cross-examined him pretty thoroughly, and we finished with the bartender's testimony on a Friday.

On the following Monday, Harry fairly burst into the courtroom: "Boys, I won this case."

"How did you win the case?"

"Well, I've got this friend of mine who's an investigator. He's gay and he went into the bar with a recording device and started talking to the bartender." He related some inconsistencies with the bartender's testimony.

"Okay. What about the rest of his testimony?"

"Well, that was all the same."

I decided to make things clear to Harry. "Harry I'm going to explain it to you one time. I don't want to have to do it again. I don't want that recording around. I don't want that wire around. Just throw it in the Bay. I don't want it to be introduced in court. Those were two small items. You're putting him back on the stand and the jury will hear the same story all over again on everything else!"

The next morning, Harry came over and said, "Nate, I've gone over it again. I've given it a lot of thought."

"Harry, I don't want to even talk about the wire. I don't want to even hear about the wire anymore. I want you to take that wire and put it in your office and just leave me alone."

The next day MacInnis came up to me. "Harry wanted me to talk to you about getting the wire in."

"Jim, will you do me a favor?"

"Sure."

"Tell Harry, if he mentions that wire once more, I'm going to wrap it around his neck and throw him over the railing at the Hall of Justice!"

Jim explained it to Harry and advised him not antagonize me, because I might very well do precisely what I said.

I heard no more about the tape.

After we finished with a witness, the judge asked, "Mr. MacInnis, do you have any other questions?"

Jim stood up. "No, Your Honor. We have no further questions at this time."

I wanted to give Harry the message, so I stood up. "No, Your Honor. We have no more questions at this time."

Harry jumped up. "I've got a question or two."

Harry started opening up doors for the D.A. After the third time Harry had done this this, making it harder for me to close them each time, I leaned over to Jim and I said, "Jim, our co-counsel is an idiot."

"Yes, Nathan, but he's our idiot."

In the end, it was the testimony of the owner of the bar that won the case for us. He testified that he wrote down in his ledger the money he had given the police. He had the book and it showed that money had been paid to the defendants. I looked at the book. The writing was in pencil.

"Did you write this in the book yourself?"

"Yes I did."

"Did you do it at one time or did you do it over a series of times?"

"No, all at one time."

"On the same day?"

"Yes."

"Within the same ten or fifteen minutes?"

"Yes, right away."

"Did you use the same pencil to write this in the book that you used for the rest of the book that you wrote above that?"

"Yes, I did."

You could see that the entries were written with different pencils. One was broader and one was thinner. I had cut him off every way.

I called Dr. Kirk to come over. The jury could see with their eyes that these were different pencils. One was thin, one was flat and wide, and he had claimed that he had written both entries at the same time with the same pencil. But Dr. Kirk would carry it over the top.

Dr. Kirk testified for the defense as a forensic expert, and he examined the writing on the stand. First, he put a magnifying instrument on his head with lenses that he flipped down. I asked him to compare the two entries. One had been written with a number one pencil and one with a number three pencil.

Dr. Kirk established completely that this was the owner's testimony was not true. The pencil that had been used to write down the money that had been allegedly paid to the officers was with a different pencil than the other one and he claimed that they had both been written at the same time. Kirk destroyed the man's testimony.

On a lighter note, I also brought in Joe Vanessi, who owned Vanessi's restaurant on Broadway, which was in the same vicinity as the gay bars. Both sergeants had eaten there quite a bit. I brought him in to establish that even although they ate there, they paid for their food, and they didn't ask for anything or take anything. Joe was also a client of mine at times.

"Oh, no. These gentlemen are very honest," he testified. "They wouldn't take anything. I couldn't give them a Christmas present. I couldn't give them a cup of coffee. No, they're very honest."

Finally, when I finished with him on direct examination, Harry and James MacInnis left him alone. When the D.A. got up to cross-examine him, Joe looked at the judge and asked, "Who'sa thisa guy?"

The judge informed him, "This is the District Attorney. He is going to ask you some questions."

"Aaahh. Thatsa nice."

He was a great witness, and the jury got a kick out of him.

There were other humorous moments. In one instance, the two patrolmen testified that they went into the bar and there was a gay man sitting at the bar with two little poodles. There were also several other people at the bar.

"Are you saying that everybody in the bar was gay?" The D.A. inquired. "What?"

"Are you testifying that everyone in the bar was gay?"

"Well, the men were. I'm not too sure about the two dogs."

Everyone broke up.

The jury acquitted all the defendants. After the acquittals, my sergeant and his fiancée and I went to a bar with Jim MacInnis and his sergeant and his sergeant's wife. We were sitting at the bar, having a drink and celebrating.

"You know Jim," I said, "let me tell you something. I can read you like a book. In your mind you're sure that your brilliance, your wit, your oratory, your intelligence, your personality, you won this case.

"In my mind, I believe that my intelligence and my strategy, my cross-examination and bringing in Dr. Kirk, won the case.

"We both believe that Harry was probably the dumbest one, the most inexperienced and the worst lawyer of the three, and that we're so much brighter than he is. But, did you notice one thing?"

"What was that, Nathan?"

"When the case was over you met your client and his wife and came down to this bar with me and my client and his fiancée. Harry had one of the most beautiful young ladies I've ever seen in my life waiting to spend the weekend with him up in Lake Tahoe. I've come to the conclusion that maybe Harry was the smartest one in this whole case!"

My client had a pair of cufflinks made for me, a replica of his sergeant's badge. He said I had saved his badge so I should have these cufflinks with his badge number on them. It was a trial I thoroughly enjoyed.

Which reminds me of another policeman I represented after he got in a jam. He got into a fight with another policeman and beat him up and was charged with assault and battery.

He told me the reason for the fight was that the officers in his station made fun of him and were anti-Semitic. He said that one of them had made some anti-Semitic remarks on the date in question, and had invited my client out to the alley. That didn't set too well with me because I was Jewish and I don't like anybody picking on anybody for any reason.

Afterwards, another friend of mine who was at the same station told me that my client's story was ridiculous. He said they didn't pick on him because he was Jewish; they picked on him because he was off his rocker. My friend told me what had happened on this day was that somebody was making fun of my client and another policeman said, "There's something I want to talk to you about. Can I meet you in the alley later outside the station?" Before he knew it, my client hit him with a punch to the face that knocked him down and kept beating on him. The funny part, my friend told me, was that in all the fights my client had ever had with the other cops, this was the first one he had won, and he got arrested for it!

When we went to court I realized my client was not hitting on all eight cylinders. The first day I objected several times and each time I objected, the judge sustained the objection. At the end of the day, I objected and the judge overruled my objection. My client nudged me and said, "See, Nate, I told you they'd get to the judge."

I pretended I hadn't heard him.

In the middle of the trial, an advance sheet came out containing a decision by an appellate court that the defendant in a criminal case is entitled to discovery from the prosecution. I took this advance sheet in to the judge and demanded to see the District Attorney's file. He gave me the file and I was able to glean enough information to win the case.

My client had also been taken before the Police Commission and the Police Commission had taken him off duty and stopped his salary. I went to the Police Commission and they told me the man had a problem: he thought everyone was against him. Some of his fellow officers made fun of him, and he thought they were against him. I suggested to the commissioners that what they do is remove him from the Police Department and drop the charges, and it would be all over, but they felt they had to proceed.

The jury found him not guilty.

Two months later I was walking on Third and Market—and who was directing traffic but my client! I walked up behind him and said, "What the hell are you doing out in the middle of the street? Why aren't you on the sidewalk where it's safe!" He turned around, mad as hell. Then he saw me.

"Oh, hello, Mr. Cohn, how are you?"

An Exposé Exposed

27

One Sunday I was watching *60 Minutes*. The first story was an exposé of a carnival. That caught my interest, as I had represented many carnivals.

The show began with an interview with a gentleman who *60 Minutes* claimed was a Deputy Attorney General of the State of California charged with investigating carnivals. The piece alleged that all the concessions at a carnival owned by Lloyd Hillegoss were crooked. They had a picture of the alleged Deputy Attorney General going into the Attorney General's office in San Francisco and they tried to identify him as an employee in the Attorney General's office, but I realized who he was. He was a man who worked in the DA's office in Sacramento investigating whether or not people were entitled to welfare. Apparently, he had gone to a carnival and for some reason grew angry with the concessions and had convinced someone in Sacramento to pass a law that said that if a carnival concession was controlled by a mechanical device it was illegal.

I also knew Hillegoss, and none of his concessions were illegal. I was amazed that *60 Minutes* would put such a story on. After the show was over, Lloyd Hillegoss called me and asked me if I had seen the story. He said he had made a copy on his recording machine and I asked him to come to my office the next day with another copy of the program with him.

He came into my office with several copies of the show.

I called up a friend of mine in the California Attorney General's Office who had been there many, many years and I gave him the name of the person who allegedly was in the Attorney General's Office and asked him if he would check to see whether this man was in the office now or had ever been in the office. He said he would call me back. He called me back thirty minutes later to say that the man was never in the office and no one there had ever heard of him.

I wrote a letter to *60 Minutes* informing them that under the laws of

California they had defamed my client and that I demanded a retraction within ten days and the same amount of time that it took to broadcast this *60 Minutes* segment. I wanted them to make clear that the allegations were completely untrue. I told them that my client did not have illegal concessions and that they had misrepresented this person who they had claimed was a California Deputy Attorney General.

A day or so later a lawyer representing *60 Minutes* called me back and told me he wanted more time to investigate my complaint. I informed him that under the law of California he had only ten days to retract, and if he did not retract the allegations, I would file a lawsuit against *60 Minutes*.

"I understand that *Sixty Minutes* is seen by at least eight million people in the United States," I continued, "and I'm going to file a lawsuit, and when I get to the point of damages, I'm going to ask for one dollar damages for each of those eight million people, so you could be hit pretty heavily."

I reiterated I wanted the retraction the next week and I wanted the same amount of time they gave for the original broadcast.

The next Friday, he called back to tell me to watch *60 Minutes* on Sunday and I would see a retraction.

"I hope it's the same amount of time that the story took," was all I could say.

"Yes, I made it clear that it has to be."

They retracted the whole thing.

That took care of that for the moment.

But that was not the end. Shortly thereafter, my client, who had a carnival that traveled up and down the West Coast, was investigated by the federal government who claimed he had not paid taxes on his trucks, which ran on the highways of the United States. My client told them that he didn't think he had to pay because his trucks were not trucks that transported merchandise but trucks that transported the outdoor rides for this carnival from one place to another and when the government came to him, he opened all his books to them and let the agents inspect them.

The I.R.S. claimed he owed $40,000, and the next thing I knew he was indicted. It was in all the headlines in all the San Francisco newspapers. Lloyd asked me to defend him, and I said I would.

The lawyer who had arranged for the retraction from *60 Minutes* now called me and said if he had known my client was going to be indicted for tax fraud, he never would have allowed his client to retract the story.

I reminded him that an indictment is not a conviction and that my client was entitled to the presumption of innocence.

"Besides," I added, "I have heard he has an excellent lawyer representing him and he might not be convicted."

"Who's that?"

"Me."

The Assistant United States Attorney on the case was a very capable young lady who had won, I believe, all her cases. I suggested that my client pay the $40,000 and the government drop the case, but she refused the offer, and we went to trial in federal court before a jury.

My defense was that in order to defraud the government one must have an intent to defraud, and since my client believed that his trucks were not in the taxable category, there was no intent to defraud.

I used the chief investigator for the Internal Revenue Service to help my case. I asked him whether it was true he had investigated all the people who knew my client and talked to them about my client.

"Yes."

"Didn't every one of them tell you that he was an honest person?"

"Yes."

"Didn't you find out that right now he had a doctor who was worried about his heart condition?"

"Yes."

"Look at his face now, it's all red. Do you know anything about heart conditions?"

"Not really, but I can understand what you're saying."

I brought out the fact that California law differentiated trucks that used the highway to transport merchandise from trucks that were built to carry specific things, such as my client's rides.

I didn't put my client on the stand, but I explained to the jury that he had a bad heart and that I didn't want to put him the stand and have the stress cause him a heart attack, winning the case but losing my client.

The jury went out and found him not guilty.

After the verdict, I immediately took my client up to 20th floor of the federal building where the press room was and I took him into the press room. I knew the newspaper people there.

"When my client was charged with a crime," I reminded them, "there were headlines which went out all over the United States saying he was charged with tax fraud. I think it's only fair that the same amount of publicity be given to the fact that he was found not guilty."

A couple of the fellows said, "We'll see what we can do," but nothing appeared in the papers.

After a week and a half my client called me. "When are they going to print it?"

"Why don't you call the newspaper and tell them that when you were indicted they wrote big articles. Now you've been acquitted there's not a word." He called me back an hour later and said he had talked to some of the editors of several of the newspapers and they said they would take care of it.

About two weeks after that, on the obituary page of the *Chronicle*, there was a two-inch story about his acquittal.

I also called the attorney for *60 Minutes* and informed him that my prediction about the prosecution had proved correct, after all.

When I was preparing my defense in the Hillegoss case, I did a lot of research. In checking out the cases to see if I could find a case that met my requirements, I ran across a case from a Southern state that was surprising.

A Congressman from the state had introduced a bill into the legislature that if a person was charged with a tax fraud case they had a right to have that case heard in their home federal district, but they had to give notice within 15 days that they wanted to select the place of the trial. It kind of surprised me because in most of the cases I had read, the venue of trial was determined by rules rather than by Congressional legislation. I kept it in mind for an opportunity to use this law.

Some time later, another tax fraud case came along where I could work this law in.

An investment adviser had found a tax shelter that few people had noticed. If you invested in an invention, the investor could write off an enormous amount of taxes as a shelter. The government finally grew aware of this and changed the law, but some investors were still using the now-closed loophole to set up tax shelters. The government indicted the two heads of the operation and their secretary, along with two salesmen who sold the tax shelters. One of the salesmen was referred to me, as he had been indicted in San Diego for conspiracy for selling the tax shelter and for tax fraud for using the tax shelters in his own income tax reports. There were many, many counts. When he gave me the indictment, I remembered the case from the South that I had read in the Hillegoss matter.

I called a friend of mine who was a top federal criminal trial lawyer in that state and asked him what the law was about. He informed me what had happened was that in his state the Internal Revenue Service had set up a collection office in a small, redneck town where jurors hated the people from the adjoining large city. They also hated anyone charged with a crime and anyone charged with tax evasion. The U.S. Attorney would try all the tax fraud cases in this little town and the juries would convict the defendants no matter what, and some of the people in the larger cities nearby prevailed on their Congressman to pass the law.

I immediately prepared a petition requesting that the tax fraud case against my client be transferred to San Francisco because he was a resident of the San Francisco federal district. I showed my co-counsel in San Diego the law and three of them also filed petitions for their clients who lived in San Francisco. The others lived in San Diego. When I filed my petition, the U.S. Attorney had never heard of this law, but the judge gave the U.S. Attorney time to investigate and the judge came to the conclusion that I was right. The U.S. Attorney told the judge he was going to make a motion to appeal the decision to transfer the tax fraud cases to San Francisco.

I handled the appeal, but I didn't say anything about the conspiracy counts. The appellate court held that I was right, and returned the case to the district court to transfer the tax fraud cases to San Francisco. At the hearing in the district court, I sat in the background and listened. I knew exactly what was going to happen. The U.S. Attorney informed the court that three of the defendants had stipulated to transfer the conspiracy cases to San Francisco where the conspiracy cases could be tried with the fraud case. The judge went through the first three defendants and asked them if they so stipulated. Then he asked me.

"No, I don't. My client's tax fraud case is being transferred to San Francisco, but I won't stipulate to the conspiracy case being transferred. I'm ready to try the conspiracy case right now."

Finally, the judge called the attorneys into chambers.

"We have a little problem here. Mr. Cohn had the tax fraud against his client switched to San Francisco, but he wants to go ahead with the conspiracy case here in San Diego. Is that true?"

"Yes, your honor. "

"Are you ready, Mr. Cohn?"

"I'm ready next week, or this week, if you like."

The Judge turned to the U.S. Attorney. "I suggest you call Washington and see what you're going to do about this."

The U.S. Attorney called Washington and they decided to dismiss the conspiracy charges against my client. The only charges against him were the fraud charges and tax charges.

In the meantime, we had taken a deposition of the chief witness for the prosecution. He testified he had not come into contact with my client in any way.

We had traveled to Santa Ana to take his deposition, because he was very ill and the prosecutor did not know if his witness could make it for the trial. When we took his deposition, I saw what condition the man was in, and I felt very badly for him. So, I told him that I wasn't too much involved in the deposition because I understood he had never met my client, and if he wanted to stop the deposition at any point to let me know and I would protect him in the deposition. He appreciated my offer.

When I walked into the courtroom in San Francisco where the case was going to be tried, the other three defendants and their lawyers were all sitting at the defense table. The prosecution lawyers were sitting at the table to the left of the defense table. There was also an empty table to the right of the defense table. I had my client and his wife with me and told them not to go near the other defendants, but to stick with me; and when everyone was seated, I addressed the court and asked the judge if it would be possible for my clients and me to sit at the table to the right of the defense table. I told the judge that I was kind of messy and I didn't want to get my papers mixed up with other papers.

"That's fine. Sit there."

I told my client to sit with me at the table by ourselves and his wife was to sit in the audience right in back of our table and that at no time should he or his wife go over to the other defendants and talk to them or go out to lunch with them, but to stay away from the other defendants.

First, I asked the judge to instruct the jury that my client was not part of the conspiracy case, only the tax fraud, and that we would be tried at the same time, but still there was no conspiracy charge against my client.

At different times when I thought it might be important I would ask the judge to tell the jury that we were not part of the conspiracy. The judge would remind me that he'd already told that to the jury, and they would be reminded.

When the main witness for the prosecution took the stand, he remembered me and acted as if I were his closest friend, and he testified he had never seen anything nor could he testify to anything involving my client.

He testified the other defendants had had various meetings at different times, but I was able to bring out the fact that my client was not at those meetings.

The jury found the three defendants over at the defense table guilty on all counts, but they found my client not guilty on all the counts against him.

My shortest tax fraud case involved a star in many Las Vegas shows and never made it to court.

I received a phone call from a client of mine in Las Vegas. When she called, she was really upset.

"What's the problem?"

"I think I'm in trouble."

"What kind of trouble could you be in?"

"The Internal Revenue."

"Well, don't you file your tax returns?"

"No, what happened was, I get these slips from the places I play and they deduct from my salary monies which I thought took care of the income tax, so I didn't think I had to file any forms because they took all the money out." She said somebody had asked her about having filed tax returns and she became nervous.

I told her I would be in Las Vegas the next day.

"Don't talk to anybody. Don't say anything to anybody about it. I'll come there tomorrow and see if I can straighten it out."

"Please do. I'm scared to death."

The next morning I got up early, flew into Las Vegas and took a cab to the hotel where she was starring and she explained the situation to me.

I had been told by an Internal Revenue person that if you go to the Internal Revenue Service before they start investigating you for any criminal activity and you file whatever forms should have been filed, they will charge you for taxes owed, but they will not bring a criminal proceeding, so I asked her to give me all her papers.

She gave them to me and we took a cab down to the Internal Revenue office. I told the receptionist that I wanted to see someone in charge who would be able to advise us.

She was very nice and sent us in the office of an Internal Revenue agent, and I told him the truth.

"The young lady called me yesterday. I'm not a tax man. I've tried a lot of criminal cases, but I'm not an accountant. I thought that the best thing to do was to come right over here and let her explain the situation so we could find out what she has to do."

"You're right. As long as you came in here voluntarily before we file any charges against her, we will not go after her criminally."

"She thought that by getting these slips showing deductions were taken out that she was paying her income taxes."

He looked at the slips: "What you do is get a tax accountant and let him make out the income tax forms and have these slips showing what was paid. If there's anything due, she pays. If there isn't anything due, she might actually get a refund.

"No charges? Nothing?"

"No, nothing is going to happen."

"Which is the best tax accountant around here?"

"I can't recommend a tax office to you, but I'm sure that other people in the vicinity could recommend who's a good accountant to do this type of work."

I went out and looked through the yellow pages and found that there were several accountants who advertised that they were expert in income taxes. One of them was nearby, so we walked over there and I told him the story and gave him the information.

I told her I would bill her the next day or so, and she thanked me profusely. Then I took a cab back to the hotel.

The next day I went back and charged her for my services and my expenses.

A couple of weeks later she called me. She said I'd never believe what happened.

"What?"

"The accountant found out I had paid too much money, and I received a very substantial refund from the government!"

If only all my tax cases had ended that way!

10-A Court

28

For many years, prostitution cases were heard, not in the Hall of Justice, but in what was called "10-A Court," a holding facility for prostitutes at the Health Building across from City Hall.

At that time, if the police arrested a woman for prostitution they would take her to this holding facility, give her a blood test and hold her for 48 hours until the results of the blood test came back to see if she had any venereal disease. She would not be eligible for bail until that time elapsed. After that time, she could be bailed out and she would be brought to a Municipal Court in the same building across from City Hall on Polk Street, and into a small courtroom called "the 10-A Courtroom" where she would be charged, arraigned and tried.

Several cases I handled in "10-A Court" were highly unusual.

One began with a telephone call from a very prominent San Francisco public official. He said he was sending me a couple of clients and asked me to see what I could do about helping them.

I was a little startled, because I had never represented a public official in any legal capacity, and we weren't that close, but I thanked him and asked him to have the prospective clients come see me.

Later that afternoon, two very beautiful young ladies walked into my office: gorgeous, but very flashy. They introduced themselves as having been sent over by the public official.

I let that rest, but I listened to their story.

They told me that they were two young ladies of pleasure who were dating several of the more important people in San Francisco. These important men were older and not that good looking, but it was a business arrangement. They did not tell me the names of the people they were dating and I didn't ask, and, frankly, I didn't want to know.

The two ladies told me that one evening they decided to take the evening off to go to a musical which was showing on Geary Street at the Curran Theater.

They had dinner at the Clift Hotel, and while there they noticed two very good-looking men at the bar. After the musical, they returned to the Clift for a drink and again they noticed the same two young men come into the bar after they did.

They started to chat with these two young men. The men advised them that they were from out of town and that they were there on business in San Francisco, attending a company executive meeting. They explained they were both single and held top executive positions.

The four talked and had a few drinks, and the young men offered to drive the ladies home. The women informed the gentlemen they were models, and said that they had modeled for some of the larger department stores and for several of the better-known photographers and invited the two men up to their apartment and offered drinks.

One of the ladies went into the bar area to prepare the drinks, while the other went to the refrigerator for ice. When they returned, their two guests had taken off their coats and were sitting on the sofa. The two men appeared to them to be well-dressed, clean-cut, and exactly what they had represented themselves to be—young executives.

When my clients brought the two men their drinks one of the young men stood up, reached into his back pocket, pulled out a badge and told the ladies they were under arrest for solicitation of prostitution.

The women were absolutely stunned. They told me they had not even suggested anything like that to the two men, but were, in their words, "having fun on a day off."

The two police officers arrested them, handcuffed them, called for a police car and took them down to the police station at the Hall of Justice at around 2 a.m.

The ladies called a bail bondsman, but he couldn't do anything for them until the 48 hours had elapsed. After the 48 hours had elapsed and they were bailed out, they went home, soaked in a tub, cleaned themselves up, and called their friend, who sent them to me.

They swore they had not suggested anything to the officers or had any kind of conversation with the officers regarding prostitution, but the officers admitted to them they they had been tipped off that these young ladies were committing acts of prostitution and had been sent out to arrest them.

They were angry at the phony charge, more so than if they had been virgins.

I listened to their story and I explained the legal process, as neither of them had been arrested before. I then informed them what my fee arrangements would be, and I advised them that my fee would have to be paid in advance, that I ran the show and they would have to listen to me and to follow my instructions if I was to be their attorney.

The first thing I did was to call one of my secretaries into my office and introduce my new clients to her. The secretary had come from a very wealthy family and was extremely well-dressed at all times, in good taste, and she was quite an attractive lady herself.

I told her to take the two ladies down to Joseph Magnin's and to obtain for them two-piece suits in solid colors—different colors for each of them—with white blouses. I wanted them to come back looking like young business executives or college students from wealthy families.

I also instructed my secretary to take them to her hair dresser and cosmetologist and have their hair dyed dark brown or black and to remove most of their make-up and to make arrangements to instruct the young ladies on how to fix their faces with very little make-up, to produce a clean-scrubbed look.

My secretary did not say a word other than "Okay, Mr. Cohn."

I instructed the two ladies to come back the next morning so that I could see how they looked.

The next morning when my secretary came in, I asked her how it had gone.

My clients had followed every instruction she had given them without saying a word.

When they came back, they looked like two young business executives or college upper classmen dressed for an important appointment. Everything from their shoes to the top of their hair conveyed class and culture.

I told them I was very pleased with their appearance and I told them that from now on, every time we went to court, I wanted them dressed in that manner. They didn't say a word other than "Yes."

After the arraignment, pleas, motions and discovery, the case was set down for trial at the Municipal Court at City Hall before Judge Carl Allen. Judge Allen was stern and wanted trials to be held in his court without commotion or theatrics.

The selection of the jury was a more touchy matter. San Francisco, at that time, was not a liberal city as far as prostitution was concerned. The average woman on a jury was very antagonistic towards prostitutes, and the men on the juries did not want the women on the juries to see that they were complacent when it came to prostitution, so they would be very harsh in cases involving charges of solicitation of prostitution.

I selected what I believed would be an excellent jury. One of the jurors had been an admiral and had just retired from the Navy. I had given a lot of thought to whether to keep him on the jury and I concluded that it would be good to have him on the jury. I reasoned that admirals had servicemen under them and knew that prostitution was, world-wide, the oldest profession, and that they might be more liberal and might view the young ladies' story with more acceptance.

Usually, I don't like retired officers. They are often very prosecution-minded and inclined to vote for conviction rather than acquittal, but I liked his looks and I thought I would leave him on the jury.

The young ladies told the jury the same story they had told me, and the two officers testified they had been picked up in the bar at the Clift Hotel; that the ladies had taken them to their apartment where the ladies had offered to commit prostitution on the payment of $100 each.

I asked the officers if they had paid my clients the money.
"No."
I asked them if they had any marked money ready for payment. They hadn't.

On cross-examination, I was able to show that these two officers were overzealous young police officers eager for an arrest.

The jury was out several hours. The admiral, who had been selected as foreman of the jury, came back with the verdict: not guilty on all charges.

After the verdict, I went across the street to a bar with my clients and they bought me a drink. I was very pleased with the results and I was sure my clients were very pleased with the results. Throughout the trial they had been very demure and and well-mannered and they did look like two beautiful young executives.

Three days later, my secretary buzzed me and told me that my two clients were back in my office and wanted to see me. I told her to have them come in.

They looked exactly as they did when I first saw them. They did not look like college girls or business executives, but I decided not to mention it.

"What can I do for you?"

"We both felt that you represented us so ably we wanted to bring you a present. In fact, we have two presents for you."

"I don't want a present. I charged you a fee. You don't owe me anything."

"No, no, we want to do this."

They gave me a box of cigars and a second package. theytold me not to open the second package until they had left.

As the ladies left my office, one of them turned to me. "You know, Mr. Cohn, we really appreciated what you did and everything that you did was obviously for a good cause, but I just wanted you to know one thing. The one thing we resented was when you had your secretary select our clothes for us and tell the hair dresser how to fix our hair and tell us how to apply makeup. That we really didn't like. And I want you to know, Mr. Cohn, that each of us makes more in one night than your secretary makes in a month!"

With that, they smiled and left.

I opened the package. Inside the box were twenty photographs of what would be best described as suggestive photographs of men and women in a variety of sexual poses (but not photographs of my clients.) I looked at the photographs and put them back in the package, thinking I would have some fun by giving them to a close friend of mine who was a square. He would probably have a heart attack when he took a look at the pictures.

But I enjoyed the cigars.

⊟——·——⊟

Following that case, which received a little publicity, I started to receive phone calls from other young ladies who had been arrested for prostitution. I received one call two days later from a young lady who asked me if I would come over and visit her at 10-A. She was there in quarantine, and wanted to retain me.

I told her I was going to be at City Hall that afternoon and would come by.

I met her in the 10-A holding area. There was an attorneys' room there to meet with clients, and the guards brought her in. She was a very beautiful young lady, a blonde.

I told her, "Before we do anything, I hope you realize that you will have to pay a retainer in advance." I quoted her my usual retainer in this type of case.

"Oh, your fee is fine, but I never pay these fees in cash."

"Pardon me, but what do you mean you never pay them in cash?"

"I make arrangements with the attorney to supply services either to him or his friends."

"You are a very beautiful young lady and no doubt your favors would be very impressive, but I don't operate that way. If you want my services, I expect you to pay me in cash. Then, if I want your services, I'll pay you in cash, but I'm not really interested in bartering attorney's fees. I don't believe in that."

"That is what I have always done," she responded, surprised. "I've been arrested several times, and I've always done that."

"Well, I'm sorry. I don't do it."

She thanked me and wished me good luck.

A few days later, I had to appear in 10-A Court on another matter. While I was sitting there, I heard the court clerk call up the young lady that I had visited in the lock-up.

She looked very pretty. Then, a young lawyer came bouncing over. "Your Honor, I represent this young lady."

I broke up. When everybody started looking at me I realized that I was one of only three people in the room who realized how this gentleman was going to get his fee.

———·———

One day I was just about to leave the office when I received a telephone call from a very important businessman in San Francisco. He said that he was referring me a client and that he would appreciate anything that I could do to help this young lady.

By this time, I had become used to having ladies of pleasure, as one might call them, referred to me by important people.

I thanked him for the referral, and the next morning a very attractive, well-dressed young lady came into my office. I would never have imagined that she was a practitioner of her profession.

She introduced herself to me and told me she had been raided in her home in one of the most respected and exclusive districts of San Francisco.

She had a beautiful home in St. Francis Wood, nestled among the wealthy and important in San Francisco. Her clientele, from what I gathered, were the top executives in San Francisco, whom she knew well.

It seems a man had come to her door and showed her what purported to be a search warrant and forced his way in with several other men. They went through the house, taking everything out of every drawer and throwing it on the floor.

She became worried, she said, because they looked like hoods, and she called the police. Fifteen minutes later, a squad car arrived and two uniformed policemen came in. She informed the officers what was going on. The other men identified themselves as undercover detectives and showed badges. They told the uniformed officers they did not have a search warrant, but that she had invited them in and told them to go ahead and look around.

The house was a mess. They had thrown practically everything she had on the floor. Obviously, no one was going to invite them to do that.

They arrested her for prostitution. It seems they had found some photographs of men and women in compromising positions. They had also found some condoms in one of her closets.

In addition, they found an address book with the names and addresses of some of the more prominent people in San Francisco, including several city officials.

The officers called it a "trick book." They knew women who practiced prostitution keep an address book of their clients and their phone numbers.

However, my client had been very clever. She put the names and addresses of several top city officials in San Francisco in her book, including the Chief of Police, the District Attorney and the Mayor. She figured that if a policeman picked up this address book and saw those names, he would be reluctant to make it available to the press.

When the police called some of the important names in the book and mentioned the lady, they, not surprisingly, claimed they had no knowledge of her.

When the case came on for hearing, the District Attorney and I went into the judge's chambers, where I explained that the police officers had taken a piece of paper which was useless, and had used it to search the lady's house, and then, later on, claimed she had invited them in; and I pointed out that they had practically destroyed her house. I explained that they had arrested her because they had found some condoms in her dresser drawer and some pictures of her while she was in the nude, and an address book of the names, addresses and phone numbers of very important people in San Francisco.

The police couldn't designate it a trick book, because if they did, they would embarrass a lot of important people.

I told the judge that I felt the matter should be dismissed because the search was conducted illegally—thus, what they obtained in the search was obtained illegally—and there was no real evidence that any solicitation of prostitution had, in fact, occurred.

The officers had arrested her for keeping a house of prostitution, I pointed out, but she was the only woman in the house, and it was a little difficult to show she was keeping anything.

The judge agreed to dismiss the case, but before we left chambers, the judge asked me to stay behind. She said she wanted to talk to me about something else.

"Let me ask you," she said. "I looked at that book, and I saw all those names. Are those fake?"

"Yes."

"You mean she put those in there to kill the idea of anyone claiming it was a trick book?"

"Yes."

The judge broke up. She thought it was the funniest thing.

One day, I received a phone call from Jake Ehrlich.

"I'd like to see if you can do me a favor. There's a big corporate law firm downtown that sends me criminal cases, and the head of the firm got himself in some real trouble. I'd like to see what you can do."

"Anything I can do, I'll do."

"Here's the situation. The man got in trouble and he gave a wrong name to the police. If I show up in court with him the press will figure it out and this man could be destroyed."

"What happened?"

The lawyer had been at a motel in the Marina district with three girls, and the police had broken in and arrested the three girls, and had given the lawyer a citation to appear.

It seemed the police had found the lawyer in the bathroom trying to wipe lipstick off his body when they broke in. He had gone to this motel with these three girls and had hired them by the hour at $100 an hour each. There, they stripped him and lay him on the bed, then they stripped down to the buff and rubbed lipstick all over his body from their lips. After thirty or forty minutes of this activity, he would become aroused, and one of the girls would have sex with him.

He apparently did this every so often, and he hired the same three girls each time, who were familiar with his peculiar desires.

On this night, several police officers followed the girls and saw them take him into the motel room. The officers waited approximately thirty minutes, listened to the action, then broke through the door and arrested the girls and found the lawyer in the bathroom furiously rubbing himself with towels, trying to remove the lipstick from his body. The lawyer broke down when the police questioned him and admitted that he had paid the girls $300—a $100 an hour each—to come with him and perform this act.

The man was shocked and worried. He had a family and children, was the number one man in this large law office with a top reputation, so he gave the police a false name.

"If I go into court with him, that will draw attention to it and the press might think there's a story," Jake implored. "If the press looks into it, that will destroy the man. You know Judge Underwood very well. Would you take the case and handle it for me?"

"Sure. I'd be happy to."

On the day of the appearance, I asked Judge Underwood if I could see her in chambers with the D.A. present. She agreed, and in chambers I explained the situation: the three girls had been arrested for solicitation of prostitution and the man involved had given a false name. I explained he was a married man with a high position, and he was afraid if it came out, he would be destroyed.

"This is all I'm asking. We try the case and if there is no case against him, then we dismiss it. If there is a case against him, I'll bring him and he'll have to be sentenced. Is that fair?"

Judge Underwood agreed.

When the case came up, the District Attorney made his opening statement, explaining to the court that the two officers would testify that they saw the three girls enter a motel room with a man, and the girls looked to them to be prostitutes. The officers knocked on the door and there was no answer. The officers knocked on the door a second time and announced, "We know you're in there. Police, open the door." With that, the District Attorney said, one of the women opened the door and the officers told the girls they were under arrest for prostitution.

I recognized one of the officers. I had helped him out a jam one time. When he took the stand, the District Attorney asked him what had happened. He testified they saw the three girls with a man. He and his partner did not know who they were, but they saw them enter a motel room. Then, they broke in the door and there they were.

"You broke in the door?" The D.A.'s case was disappearing.

"Yeah."

"I thought you knocked."

"We didn't knock, we just broke it in."

"Did you have a search warrant?"

"No."

"Did you have any kind of warrant?"

"No."

"Did you ever see the defendants before?"

"No."

"Did you ever see the man before?"

"No."

"Did you have anything to base your breaking into the motel room on?"

"No."

The judge invited us into chambers.

"You've got no probable cause," Judge Underwood told the District Attorney.

"When I talked to them, they told me they knocked on the door. I didn't know that."

"What do you want to do?"

"Judge, you have to dismiss the case," I insisted.

Judge Underwood suggested that if I could convince any of the three girls to plead guilty to some misdemeanor that involved sex, she would accept it and ask for a fifty dollar fine and dismiss the rest.

I talked to my three clients and explained it to them, and they were very happy.

"One of you is going to have to plead to something. Which one of you has the worst record?"

One of the girls spoke up: "I already have a long record for solicitation and prostitution. One more charge on my record won't hurt me. The other two of us don't have any record, so they don't have to plead. What can I plead to?"

I laughed. "I have a suggestion. Why don't you plead to a misdemeanor of visiting a house of ill repute?"

"You want me to plead to being a visitor? I love that! Just imagine these people looking at my record. They will see me being arrested several times for solicitation and acts of prostitution. Then, I plead guilty to visiting a house of prostitution. I love it. In fact, I would love to have it on my record!"

I laughed and we all went back into the courtroom and I informed the judge and the District Attorney that we were ready to plead and that I was pleading my client guilty to the penal code section we had agreed to.

The District Attorney objected. "You can't plead to that. That's for visitors!"

"That is what we're pleading to!" He got the humor of the situation and laughed. Even the judge thought it was funny.

She pleaded guilty to being a visitor to a house of ill repute and she was fined fifty dollars, which she paid, and the case was over.

Afterwards, Judge Underwood asked to see me in chambers. The judge assured the District Attorney it had nothing to do with anything on his calendar, that it was something personal.

In chambers she asked if I could tell her the name of the lawyer that I had refused to reveal.

I told her that I could not do that. If I happened to say something to her and it got out, it would ruin his reputation.

"I won't do it because I don't want to be responsible for ruining a man's life who has a family and who hasn't committed any real crime."

"Okay. Can I ask you one more question?"

"What is it?"

"Just answer me yes or no. Was it Joe Karesh?"

"No, Judge, it wasn't."

"That is all I wanted to know."

She had run for a Superior Court judgeship and Joe Karesh had decided he would run for the same vacancy on the Superior Court, and he had defeated Judge Underwood. During the campaign he had mentioned that Judge Underwood was in her seventies and that he was only in his fifties, and he could serve longer. She did not mind anything else in the campaign, except that Joe Karesh had mentioned her age, and it made her very angry with Joe.

When she heard it was not Joe Karesh, she was satisfied.

As for the man whose career I saved, he never even called me to thank me.

—·—

Then there was the case of one lady who told me she had been arrested for prostitution for an unusual price.

She told me that she was not guilty, but that she did not want to discuss the matter. When I obtained discovery in court, I found that the complainant claimed that she had performed an act of prostitution with him and that he had paid her $9.27 for the act.

When the gentleman took the stand, he testified that he had had an act of intercourse with my client. He said he had met her, that they had gone to her room and that she had charged him $9.27. He said he wasn't displeased with the services and he wasn't against prostitution. He just wanted his money back. He had figured that if he had her arrested, she would have given him his money back and he would have gotten sex for free.

With that testimony it wasn't even necessary to present a defense case. We rested at the end of the prosecution's case and the jury went out.

A short time later, the jury came back with a not guilty verdict.

After my client paid my fee and thanked me, I took the opportunity to ask her about case. "That was an odd situation…"

"Why?"

"Well, a man going into court and claiming that he paid you $9.27. You told me you were not guilty, so that obviously was not true."

"No, no, you didn't understand what I meant. I meant I was not guilty because he asked me."

"It doesn't make any difference who asks who. It would still be solicitation if he asked you and you agreed to do it."

"I didn't know that."

"Did you actually perform an act with the man?"

"Oh, yes."

"But, why in the world did you charge him $9.27?"

"That's very simple."

"What's simple about it?"

"That's all he had."

Hypnotism on Trial

29

Cop-killer Harold Miller today
a strange bit of remorse over hi
of Police Inspector Denis Bradl
Miller says he's sorry it wasn't
Insp___ Ma___ ira___ instead.
The st___ y___ red___
Girard ___ at me up ___ onvict si
me." ___ was alwa
"___ hat ___ op (Bradley) wa
killed," he declared at City Prison.
"If it had to be anyone, I wish it v
have been Girard.

One of the most historically significant trials I was involved in was not a murder trial, but the defense of Arthur Ellen, the top hypnotist entertainer in the United States, on charges of practicing medicine without a license.

I first heard of Arthur Ellen when I was in Los Angeles to visit my son who was attending USC. I went down to Los Angeles with Hank James, and we went to the Stanford-USC game on Saturday and went to the Rams-Forty Niners game on Sunday.

As attorney for the American Guild of Variety Artists (AGVA), I also dropped by their L.A. office one day to let them know I was in town and to see if there was anything I could do. Irving Mazzei told me there was a show in Los Angeles which included a hypnotist who simply had to be seen, and he made arrangements for tickets for Hank and me to attend this show.

AGVA had arranged a table up front. Arthur Ellen was the star act.

Arthur had arranged eight chairs on the stage about four feet apart, then he asked for eight volunteers from the audience to come up on the stage. One of the volunteers caught my attention. It was Bimbo Guintoli, who owned Bimbo's 365 Club in San Francisco. I nudged Hank.

Bimbo walked up to the stage, and as he was walking up, he removed something from his left lapel and put it in his pocket. It was a platinum-and-gold pin which said "365." Arthur told the volunteers to sit in an empty chair, then to put their feet down flat on the floor and their hands in their lap, and to relax.

After that, he told them, "You are going into a deep sleep, a deep sleep. You are now in a deep sleep." Seven of the people on the platform went into a sleep. Their heads were hanging down. But not Bimbo. Bimbo sat there looking at all of them. Finally, Arthur asked Bimbo, "Sir, obviously you're not cooperating. Would you please leave the stage?"

Bimbo didn't leave the stage but continued staring. Arthur asked him again, and again Bimbo stayed put. "Please, sir, would you leave the stage?"

Finally, Bimbo left the stage.

Arthur went through his routine and had his subjects doing amazing things. I hardly believed what I saw. He was one of the greatest hypnotists I had ever seen.

Afterwards, I suggested to Hank that we go over to the Beverly Hilton and have a drink. There was a pianist playing at the top of the Beverly Hilton Hotel.

When we entered the elevator at the Beverly Hilton to go to the top, who was in the elevator but Bimbo, his wife, his daughter and his son-in-law!

I started chiding Bimbo about his actions during the show and Bimbo tried to explain himself: "I booked that man into my club. I wanted to see if he was a fake. It looked to me like he was legitimate."

"It was legitimate. I could see that from where we stood."

"Well, I don't see how he could do it. It was just talk. All he said was a few words and these people were out."

"He's a stage hypnotist. He knows what he's doing. He was very good. He will do well in your club."

Bimbo had the prettiest nightclub west of Chicago. They had great food and great shows.

I kept kidding Bimbo about what happened, and Bimbo laughed so hard he didn't know what to do.

A few weeks later, Bimbo called me and said that Arthur Ellen was opening at his club, and he wanted me to come as his guest, along with Hank.

Bimbo set aside a beautiful table for us for Arthur's opening show.

There were people we knew at many of the tables. At the table nearest us was a restauranteur and his wife, a very attractive young lady.

Arthur told the audience: "Put your feet flat on the floor. Put your hands in your lap. Completely relax. You're going into a sleep. You're going into a sleep. Your going into a deep sleep. A deep, deep sleep," and half of the audience had their heads forward, asleep. Arthur Ellen saw the beautiful restauranteur's wife at the table next to us and went up to her and put his finger on her forehead. "You, whose forehead I'm touching, on the count of three, you will wake, go up on the stage, sit in one of those chairs, and then go back to sleep."

He touched her forehead, counted, "One, two, three," and as he walked away she stood up and walked and went to one of the chairs and was back asleep with her head down. Arthur did the same to several other people and brought them all up on the stage.

At the climax of his act, he took two chairs and put them about three or four feet apart. He took this beautiful young restauranteur's wife, touched her on the forehead and said, "You, whose forehead I'm touching, on the count of three, you will stand up and do what I say."

He took her over to these two chairs. He told her: "You will be stiff as a board. Nothing will bend in your body. You will be strong as iron." Two of his assistants took the bottom of her legs and two others took her shoulders. They put her across these two chairs with nothing underneath the middle of her body.

He told one of his assistants to put their feet on the woman's stomach and stand on her. He helped his assistant up and now there was this heavy person standing on this slim beautiful young lady's body, her feet on one chair, her head and shoulders on the other chair and somebody standing on her stomach who had to weigh over 150 pounds. I could hardly believe it because the lady herself was very slim.

When everyone saw that, they knew that Arthur's hypnotism was a legitimate thing—it really worked. When he brought her out of the trance, she had no idea what had happened, and when she went back to her seat everyone applauded enthusiastically.

A couple of days later, Arthur came to my office. He told me that he had talked to Bimbo and he had a little legal matter that he needed someone to advise him on, and Bimbo told him that I was very competent and that he should come and see me.

He said he had called up American Guild of Variety Artists, and they told him the same thing. I was able to solve his problem quickly, and we became friendly.

After he played Bimbo's, Dick Swig, who was the General Manager at the Fairmont Hotel, booked Arthur into the Venetian Room. The Venetian Room was the most elaborate, prestigious venue for entertainment in Northern California.

About three months after he played the Venetian Room, Arthur called me a said he was going to open again at the Venetian Room. I had never heard of the Venetian Room having the same act twice in the same year, regardless of how great the act was. When Nat King Cole played the Fairmont, he might come back the next year, but never three months later.

I invited Arthur to speak at one of my annual criminal law seminars I organized in San Francisco. Every year I would have four or five hundred lawyers, judges, law students, and other people attending my seminars, which were the first of their kind. The lawyers were let in for $10 a person at that time. The judges were let in free. Any law student, or other person who wanted to attend to see what was going on could get in for a dollar. We even had court reporters who would come in and practice their reporting while the seminar was going on.

I invited Arthur to speak on how the trial lawyer could use a hypnotist to his advantage in trying a criminal case. Arthur demonstrated a great oratorical ability and he told the audience just what they could do and how they could do it.

When Arthur finished speaking, I told him I wanted to ask him one question.

"When you played the Fairmont in the Venetian Room did you ever hypnotize Dick Swig?"

Arthur got a big smile on his face and said, "Yes, I did."

"Well, that answers why you were re-engaged three months later!"

Arthur returned to speak for many years at my seminars. Then I told Arthur instead of simply giving a talk on hypnotism, I wanted to him to demonstrate to the audience how hypnotism actually works, and, instead of lecturing, he went out on the platform and arranged six chairs while I went to the microphone and announced he would perform a demonstration of hypnotism.

Soon he had half the audience asleep. He chose six members from the audience who were asleep and had them come up on the stage. Four of the six were either attorneys or judges well-known to the audience, so everyone knew this was not a set-up.

He had one well-respected attorney stand up and commanded him: "Now, put your hands together. Put your hands one opposite the other. Start turning them around. The left hand goes around the right hand and the right hand goes around the left hand. The harder you try to stop, the faster your hands go."

After a while, Arthur asked him, "Can you stop?"

"I'm trying to stop!" He couldn't.

"Do you believe in hypnotism?" Arthur asked.

"No."

The audience roared.

When he was finished, he had them return to their chairs and told them that when they woke up they would not remember what they had done and it would all be erased from their memories. Afterwards most of them said they still didn't believe in hypnotism.

The next year, Arthur's performance was even more impressive. He told the six people on stage in a trance that they were at a horse race and each had a horse in the race. If their horse won, they would win a good deal of money, and he wanted each of them to cheer on their horse.

He took the microphone as if he were a track announcer. When he announced, "Number one is in the lead," the man with that horse stood up and shouted, "Come on! Come on!" When their horse was ahead, they cheered, when their horse was behind, they pleaded. It was the funniest routine I'd ever seen on a stage.

At the end of the race Arthur disqualified the horse that won. The dignified lawyer looked like he'd lost his last friend.

When he was back east appearing in a nightclub, however, Arthur's life changed. A gentleman came up to him and said he was a doctor. The doctor had a patient, a very pretty young girl, who for no reason that the doctor could discern, could not walk. The girl had had a minor operation on her leg, and after the operation she could not walk, but he could find no physical reason why she could not.

The doctor had seen Arthur Ellen's show and wondered if Arthur could hypnotize his patient and find out what the problem was. Arthur said he had never done anything like that before but would be happy to try it if it could help.

Under hypnosis the girl told them that she recalled two nurses wheeling her to the operating room; then she recalled one nurse saying to the other, "What beautiful legs this young lady has. When she becomes an adult, she'll have the most beautiful legs you've ever seen."

The other nurse had replied, "Yes, but wouldn't it be terrible if this operation caused her not to be able to walk again."

Arthur told the girl to erase from her mind what had been said by the nurses. Arthur told her that there was no reason why she couldn't use her legs, and when she awoke from her hypnotic state, she would not remember any of this, but would be able to walk very well.

When she awoke, she got out of the bed and walked beautifully.

Arthur then realized that he could help people who had certain mental problems, and decided that he would, in addition to performing, help doctors.

Arthur continued to perform around the United States; then he would go home to Los Angeles where he had several doctors who used him with patients who could be aided by his talents.

Arthur was the first to call for the acceptance by the medical profession of hypnosis as an aid to medical treatment. However, once it was accepted, psychiatrists began to realize that in some cases a hypnotist could hypnotize a patient and in five minutes find out what was causing a problem; under hypnosis, the patient would tell him what his problems were and a doctor could advise him on treatment.

These same patients could go to psychiatrists and have many, many sessions, paying inordinate sums per hour to learn what a hypnotist could learn in one session. The psychiatrists went to the legislature to pass a law providing that only a doctor could use hypnotism to treat a patient.

By this time, Arthur was concentrating on his work with many Los Angeles doctors helping their patients.

The only time he would go on the road to perform was to go to Harrah's Club in Stateline, Nevada where he would be the guest of Bill Harrah for three or four weeks on Harrah's ranch.

Arthur could hypnotize smokers and tell them that they didn't like the taste of cigarettes and stop them from smoking and he could find out what caused patients to overeat and give intructions under hypnosis to help them lose weight. A psychiatrist would require several fifty-minute sessions to find out what caused you to eat so much, but Arthur could find out in one session and tell you what to do.

A group of psychiatrists became upset with Arthur because they were losing money, and they convinced the Department of Consumer Affairs of the State of California to hire investigators to see Arthur as patients, carrying tape recorders.

Arthur was arrested in January of 1967 and charged with practicing medicine without a license. When Arthur asked me to represent him I grabbed a plane to Los Angeles to meet Arthur and went to court with him. I had bail set by a judge in Los Angeles and Arthur was out on bail by late evening.

The case went to trial before Judge James Harvey Brown in July of 1967.

When I entered the courtroom, I was surprised. Practically every seat in the audience was taken by young, well-dressed people. I knew that Arthur was a public figure, but there had not been that much publicity about the trial and the charge was a misdemeanor. Even though it was extremely important to Arthur, it was not that serious a case.

The bailiff said that most of these people in the courtroom were assistant city attorneys or assistant district attorneys. When I asked one of them why so many district attorneys were there, he laughed said they heard that I was trying the case and they wanted to come over and see what I looked like.

I had a pretty good idea in my mind what type of jury I wanted, and I did fairly well: there were six men and six women. Of the six women, four of them would be described as heavyset or even fat.

Arthur was very nervous, but I told him I didn't know whether we would win the case, but I had a good feeling that we wouldn't lose the case.

The first witness was an investigator who had gone to see Arthur claiming she wanted to lose weight. I had investigated the case very well and on cross-examination I was able bring out that she was not a professional investigator. She only worked for the agency on assignment and was paid by the assignment.

I also brought out the fact that she *had* changed her diet since she had visited Arthur, although she still claimed that she hadn't been hypnotized and that her change in diet had nothing to do with Arthur's hypnotism.

Another investigator testified that she had been hypnotized but that she did not think it had done anything for her.

In both cases I had the District Attorney play the tapes of their conversations with Arthur. On the tapes, Arthur stated clearly that he was not a doctor and was not giving them medical treatment. He informed them he would hypnotize them to put something in their mind that would stop them from eating so much, but he made it very clear he was not a doctor.

The next witness was psychiatrist. He testified that Arthur Ellen was treating patients and practicing medicine without a license.

I thought I recognized the psychiatrist. I put two and two together and in my mind I got twenty-two, so I took a shot and I asked him if it was true that he was the President of the psychiatrists' association.

"Yes."

Then I asked him if he had been trying to pass legislation that only doctors could hypnotize people. He had. Then I brought up the fact that Arthur had been working for years, since 1958, to convince the medical profession to accept hypnotism as a tool to assist patients.

He said he didn't know about that.

I asked him whether or not Arthur had opposed him in the Assembly hearings on his bill, and he had to admit Arthur had.

"You and Arthur Ellen were on opposite sides at those hearings?"

"Well, yes."

"Now doctor, you understand that my client is being charged with practicing medicine without a license?"

"Yes."

"And on direct examination you suggested that what he did in these sessions with these two ladies who were investigators was practicing medicine without a license."

"Yes, I did."

"Is it true that practicing medicine means treating sickness and disease?"

"Yes."

"These ladies saw him because they wanted to lose weight. Is being overweight a sickness or a disease?"

"A disease."

I didn't need to ask him any more questions. I had achieved my purpose. The four female jurors who were all quite a bit overweight just glared at this doctor.

During the recess which followed I explained to Arthur my comment at the beginning of the trial: "Arthur, that's what I meant about not losing the case. I thought he would say what he did and if he did say that the overweight people are sick, the ladies on the jury who are a overweight are not going to be happy with that."

I also decided to call several of Arthur's patients to demonstrate what Arthur's hypnotism could accomplish. The first witness was a lady who had suffered a heart attack and had become addicted to sleeping pills. Arthur had hypnotized her and helped her break the habit.

The next witness was a businessman who testified Arthur had helped him clear up an aggravated case of tension, and taught him to give up sleeping pills and cigarettes. He had already undergone heart surgery once, and looking at him and listening to him you could easily understand that if Arthur hadn't hypnotized him and stopped his smoking, he wouldn't have been there in the witness chair that day.

The next witness was a lady who had brought her grandson to Arthur when the boy was sixteen years old. She testified that the boy was a high school dropout, could not communicate with his parents, refused to do any work, and was considered a delinquent in his neighborhood.

I had a trick up my sleeve for the District Attorney with this witness.

The night before, my friend Ivor Morris and I had gone to a restaurant for dinner. When we were walking back to the Biltmore Hotel downtown, we saw on the street a young man of eighteen with a goatee and rings in his ears and nose. His hair was green.

I said to him, "What are you doing tomorrow?"

"What do you mean?"

"How would you like to make $50?"

"Who would I have to kill?"

"You don't have to kill anybody. I'll tell you what to do and you make $50."

"How do I know I'll get the fifty?"

"I give you my word that you will."

"Tomorrow morning, I want you to go to the courthouse, to Judge Brown's courtroom and I want you to sit in the back of the courtroom dressed as you are now. Don't change anything. Keep the rings in your ears."

His head kept jerking as he stood there.

"You come there, sit there as long as I tell you, maybe just a couple of hours, and you'll make fifty bucks."

"How do I know?"

"Here's $10 now. You come tomorrow, you get another fifty."

"You got it."

The grandmother was on the stand testifying to all the terrible things her grandson had done to the family and to himself before she took him to Arthur. With her present at each of several sessions, Arthur was able to help him soften his attitude towards his parents and school. He graduated from high school and was now attending college and had learned to play the guitar with such skill that he was currently making records.

Judge Brown inquired, "Would you say that Mr. Ellen helped this young man?"

"He only saved his life," she responded.

When I finished with the witness, the prosecuting attorney looked in the audience and saw the boy who I had hired to be there.

The prosecuting attorney then did something that a top trial lawyer would never do: he asked a question to which he did not know the answer.

"Is your grandson in the audience?"

"Yes, he is."

"Would you point your grandson out to me?"

She stood up and she pointed not to the young man I had sitting in the room, but to a well-dressed young man with a suit on whose hair was short and nicely combed. He looked like a Phi Beta Kappa college boy.

The District Attorney was so confused he stumbled through the rest of his cross-examination and excused the witness.

Next, I called Pamela Mason, the former wife of the famed actor James Mason. Mrs. Mason's television and radio shows had an enormous following in Los Angeles. On the stand she testified that her life had been one long, punishing diet after another because of a compulsion to overeat. She said that hypnosis had helped her to break this destructive habit and added, "Now, I can leave the leftovers I was once compelled to eat, and I don't have to clean up my son's plate too."

Judge Brown asked Ms. Mason about Arthur's methods.

"All he does is get you into a frame of mind where you become will-ing to look into yourself. You then realize you have the strength to disci-pline yourself. If there was anything he said that I thought wasn't of value to me, I wouldn't have done it."

The District Attorney knew better than to attempt to cross-examine Mrs. Mason, who was quite a star in Los Angeles.

The next witness was Jack Wells, a television and radio personality with a vast following in the Southern California area. I knew that Arthur had told me that Mr. Wells was very easy to hypnotize. In fact, when Mr. Wells saw his dentist, he would call Arthur up and Arthur would hypnotize him over the phone, so the dentist wouldn't have to use novocaine.

I thought it would be good to have Arthur hypnotize him in the courtroom so the jury could see it. But before trying something like that in the courtroom, I had to test it out. Mr. Wells came to the courtroom a little early and Arthur, Jack and I went into the stairwell of the building and I asked Arthur to hypnotize Jack.

Arthur said, "One, two, three. You're in a deep sleep"—and Jack was out.

"Wait a minute. We can't do that."

What do you mean?"

"It doesn't look possible that you can say: 'One, two, three. You're asleep.'"

"I've been hypnotizing him so much that he's easy. That's how we do it."

"No, no. You're going to have to do something more than that. You have to carry on for a little bit or the jury won't believe it."

"If you want me to do it, I'll do it. But, we don't have to."

I was a little uncertain now how the demonstration would come across.

We went back into court and I called Mr. Wells, I told Judge Brown I wanted to demonstrate hypnotism.

"Not in my courtroom."

"We want to show the jury how hypnotism works so they can see it."

"Not in my courtroom."

I wasn't angry, I was relieved. If Arthur got up and did what he had done in the stairwell the jury would think it was phony.

I did bring out through Mr. Wells that he was a chain-smoker and had been markedly underweight for a man his size, which was six foot two, when he went to see Arthur. "Hypnoconfidence," he said, not only stopped the smoking habit, but gave him a new perspective on his food consumption. It raised his weight from 150 to 193, the ideal level for him, and it had remained constant for a two-year period.

Jack testified that all Arthur did was put it in his mind that he could do these things and he did them. He said that he thought Arthur was one of the finest men he'd ever met.

I also put Eddie Albert, the TV star, on the stand. He testified he had booked into a Broadway show, but he was extremely nervous and apprehensive. All his experience had been in movies and television. He was so prone to stage fright about this new venture that he expected the act to flop. Now here he was, raising his right hand in the courtroom and gazing calmly at the courtroom. He looked at all the jurors and told them in detail what hypnosis had helped him achieve. He had mastered his fears. He had gone into his new stage medium with complete confidence and was no longer chained to sleeping pills and tranquilizers. Hypnosis had opened a whole new horizon for him. The jury was charmed with Mr. Albert.

The prosecution made no effort to contradict his testimony.

My final witness was Dr. David B. Cheek from San Francisco, an obstetrician-gynecologist, and a fellow of the American College of Surgeons. Dr. Cheek was an author of twenty-six professional papers on the uses of hypnosis in medicine. He flew to Los Angeles for the final stages of the trial to testify that he was not only familiar with Arthur Ellen's long career, but had referred patients to Arthur. He told the court that he had listened to the tape recordings made by the state agents and heard nothing that would constitute the practice of medicine. He concluded, "Mr. Ellen is a fine gentleman. He knows his work and I wish there were more like him."

The jury was out for four hours. When they came back they told Judge Brown that the members of the jury were hopelessly deadlocked and that there was no chance of coming to a verdict. Judge Brown dismissed the jury and declared a mistrial.

I talked to the foreman of the jury afterwards and he told me the jury had been ten to two for acquittal. One of the holdouts had a young daughter who had been treated by a psychiatrist for two years without any appreciable improvement. Somehow, reflecting the prevailing ignorance of hypnosis, the man associated Arthur with the practice of psychiatry. He said he wouldn't vote acquittal for a person who was involved in psychiatry because of what had happened to his daughter. The other holdout was was a friend of this man's who said he went along with his friend.

When Judge Brown dismissed the jury, as Arthur and I were starting to leave the courtroom, the bailiff nudged me and said, "Mr.

Cohn, would you please ask Mr. Ellen if I could have one of his cards."

Arthur found a card in his wallet and I gave it to the bailiff. The judge saw the bailiff put the card in his pocket and smiled at us. Arthur smiled too, probably for the first time since the long episode had begun.

On August 24th, 1967, I appeared with my client before Judge Harold J. Ackerman, and the Deputy District Attorney admitted there was not enough evidence to make a second trial worthwhile and dismissed the charges.

Arthur returned to his practice in Los Angeles.

Cop-killer Harold Miller today
a strange bit of remorse over hi
of Police Inspector Denis Bradl
Miller says he's sorry it wasn',
Ins...   Max...   ra... instead.
The s... gy...   red   onvict s.
Gir...   at...   up a   was alwa
me."
"I'm s... y that cop (Bradley) wa
killed," he declared at City Prison.
"If it had to be anyone. I wish it v
have been Girard.

Divorce Court

30

T he law of divorce has changed a great deal from the days when I began practicing law. At that time, in order to obtain a divorce, it was necessary to prove the spouse's cruelty. That led to some very tortured claims.

One client, for example, claimed that her husband drank tea with his little finger sticking out and that caused her to be upset.

Even after a divorce was granted, it was only an interlocutory decree. That meant you could not get married for a year, when the final decree would issue.

Thus, I would receive phone calls at three a.m. as follows:

"Mr. Cohn, what do I do? We came to Reno to get married. I didn't realize it, but the final decree isn't up for two more days."

"Do whatever you want to do."

"You mean I can do anything I want?"

"Do anything you want, just don't get married. If you get married then you're in trouble."

"Anything?"

"Anything you want to do, just don't get married."

I had people call me up in the middle of the night saying they had received their interlocutory decree three or four months before, and they wanted to know if they could take their wedding ring off.

There were several divorce cases that stand out as unusual.

One concerned a close friend of mine, whom I shall simply call Rick. Rick was a colonel in the Air Force. He was stationed at the Adjutant General's Station in San Bernardino. As part of his assignment, they would give him a plane and he would travel three hundred miles from San Bernardino before he could open his orders which no one else knew; that he would travel to another base to check for leaks in intelligence at the base. He would report to the Chief of Staff or the President of the United States.

However, he had a wife who was a manic-depressive, and was abusing their children. He wanted a divorce. He went to his commanding officer and told him he wanted a divorce. The General said they couldn't take a chance on that. If he had to go to court and they asked him questions under oath, he would have to answer them and he might give away government secrets.

Finally, Rick told his commanding officer he had to get a divorce or he would resign in order to do it and his commanding officer said they would see what could be done. Rick said he had a friend who was a lawyer in San Francisco who had been in the Air Force Judge Advocate General's Department and perhaps he could get him to take care of it.

The next thing I knew, I was receiving calls from people asking if I was in some trouble or if I was being considered for a big job with the government. They said there were a lot of people investigating me.

Rick explained to me what had been happening and I flew to Los Angeles. Rick sent an Air Force car and driver to pick me up and take me to San Bernardino where we drove to the courthouse.

Rick's wife had a lawyer who had been a Navy flier, so he wasn't going to do anything to cause any problems for the government, and the Air Force had given Rick permission to move forward with the divorce.

Finally, the case went to trial. I was attempting to prove that Rick's wife was a manic-depressive. After several days of trial, the judge announced he would appoint an independent psychiatrist to evaluate Rick's wife and her treatment of the children. I told the judge that was fine.

When I received the report, it was not from a psychiatrist, it was from a psychologist. Nor did the psychologist did know much about psychiatry. In fact, he knew nothing: he was using words with the wrong connotations.

I wrote a letter to the judge: "I'm not a psychiatrist or a psychologist but what he says has nothing to do with either psychiatry or psychology." The judge agreed to release the psychologist and appoint a psychiatrist.

He appointed a local psychiatrist, and I had the opportunity to cross-examine him. The psychiatrist testified that he thought it was perfectly all right for Rick's wife to have the children, and that he didn't think it was in the best interest of the children for the father to get them.

I asked him if he understood that she had been diagnosed by psychiatrists, psychologists, hospitals, the Air Force hospital, and Army hospitals as a manic-depressive.

"Yes, I understand that."

"A manic-depressive is a psychotic. Is that true?"

"Yes, that's true."

"A psychotic does not become cured. They stay that way the rest of their life. Isn't that true?"

"Well, yes, but everybody's a little psychotic."

"Pardon me?"

"Everybody is a little psychotic."

"What you mean is everybody is a little neurotic, not psychotic."

"No," he said, "a little bit psychotic."

"So what you're saying is the lawyer over there and me, we're a little bit psychotic?"

"Yeah."

"How about the clerk, the bailiff, and the court recorder?"

"Yes."

"How about the judge?"

The judge interrupted. "Don't answer the question. You're excused."

Rick won his divorce and custody of his children.

⊢——·—⊣

I had a similar experience in a case before Judge Foley in San Francisco.

My client had a wife who was manic-depressive, and she was mistreating their child. The child, a thirteen-year-old girl, kept running away from home. So, my client sued for divorce and custody of his daughter.

The wife's lawyer brought in a psychiatrist who had examined her. He testified there was nothing wrong with the man's wife. He said she should have custody of the child.

I asked the psychiatrist: "This lady is a manic-depressive. Is that correct?"

"Yes."

"As a manic-depressive she can't be cured. She's psychotic."

"That's true."

"Well, isn't it dangerous for a woman who's a manic-depressive to have a little girl who just ran away from home? They just found her sleeping in the Golden Gate Park."

"No, not really. Your client is a manic-depressive too."

"Pardon?"

"Your client is a manic-depressive too."

"Did you ever examine my client?"

"No."

"Did you ever give my client any kind of written examinations or written tests?"

"No."

"Did you ever give my client any psychological tests?"

"No."

"Any psychiatric tests?"

"No."

"Did you ever meet my client in person?"

"No."

"If you didn't do any of those things, how can you diagnose that the man is a manic-depressive?"

"I talked to him on the phone."

"You did?"

"Yes."

"How long did you talk to him?"

"About five minutes."

"In that five minutes, you made up your mind that my client is a manic-depressive—without seeing him, without giving him any psychological or psychiatric tests, without looking up his background, without knowing anything about his medical history?"

"Yes."

"What did you talk to him about?"

"About his wife's condition."

"Still, you came to the conclusion he was psychotic from a five-minute conversation with my client about his wife?"

"Yes, I did."

"Let me ask you a question: I've been talking to you for more than five minutes…"

Judge Foley interrupted. "Nate, I don't think you had better ask him the next question."

I didn't ask him the obvious question. I asked: "If you only talked to my client for five minutes over the telephone, and you only talked to him about his wife, and not about himself, and if you never gave him a physical examination and a psychiatric examination, upon what did you base your opinion that he was psychotic?"

"It's simple. Any man who would have all the complaints he had about his wife and wouldn't sue for divorce is psychotic."

"Doctor, do you know what kind of case this is? Don't you realize this is a divorce case?"

His eyes grew wide.

Judge Foley excused the doctor and granted custody to my client.

A Good Turn Deserves a Good Judgment

31

Leonard was in the lingerie business and sold lingerie to many of the larger stores in California. During World War II when the Japanese were interned, Leonard took over two stores of his Japanese customers and ran them all during the war. When the customers were released from the internment camp, he returned the stores with all the profits made during those years to his customers. He was always doing somebody a lot of good, and when a young man started a department store Leonard put his own money at risk to provide the young man with lingerie. When the young man's stores became a large chain, the young man insisted all the lingerie be purchased from Leonard and, as a result, Leonard did very well in business.

One day, Leonard asked me for a favor. He had an employee named Joe working for him and Joe's son had been killed in an automobile accident in Stockton on Halloween night. Leonard said that he had checked with his friends in the Highway Patrol, and everybody had told him that it was Joe's son who had been at fault and not the truck driver who had run into him. But Joe together with his wife, Marjorie, had spent $10,000 for the boy's funeral; he knew that I had been successful in some personal injury cases and asked me if I could at least recover their funeral expenses.

I contacted the insurance company. They told me they would pay nothing on the accident and their experts and the Highway Patrol all said it was the boy's fault.

A day later, Leonard called me and said a friend of Joe's told Joe that he had been riding east on the cross-street when the accident happened and he had seen the accident. The man said Joe's son had come to the intersection at which he turned to go to his parents' home, and had signaled that he was going to make a left turn. As he made the left turn, a truck loaded with tires came at too fast a pace and smashed into the boy's car, killing him.

"Have him go directly to the Highway Patrol office and report it to the sergeant there and let me know what happens," I advised.

Joe's friend, an elderly man, went to the Highway Patrol office and talked to the sergeant, but the sergeant was upset, saying they already had a report on the accident and were done with their investigation.

I had an investigator take a statement from Joe's friend under penalty of perjury and I filed a lawsuit against the trucking company and served the trucking company with the lawsuit.

At that time I also filed what was known as a 998 motion, a motion with an offer of settlement. Death cases in Stockton at that time did not bring in large verdicts, so I served them with an offer to settle for $50,000.

The lawyer for the defense, a very capable lawyer out of a big office in Stockton, told me that the insurance company was not going to pay five cents. Neither the insurance company nor the company the driver worked for would pay any money.

I suggested that they pay $15,000 which would cover the funeral expenses and I would waive any fee, so that the parents could receive funeral expenses. He contacted the company and the company refused again.

My witness was elderly, and since it would take a couple of years to get a trial in Stockton, I set depositions for the defendant and the witness in Stockton, so if he did not last long enough to testify in court, at least we would have his deposition.

My witness testified that he had seen the truck and the truck was going at a high rate of speed. The truck driver slammed on his brake when he realized the car in front of him was making a left turn, but he was going too fast to stop from hitting the car and he smashed into it. My witness testified he had not reported it immediately because he had had an appointment and was late, and he figured that there would be other witnesses as well.

He remained firm in his testimony through cross-examination. At the end of his testimony, the defense lawyer asked him: "How old are you?"

"I'm 74 years old."

I was 72...

"Do you wear glasses?"

"Yes, I do."

"Did you have glasses on that night?"

"Yes, I did."

"What kind of glasses do you have?"

"I have trifocals."

The defendant testified that he was driving down this country road and he was going at a moderate rate of speed and that he saw the car in front of him make a signal for a right turn and he thought the car was going off to the right, and it did; but when it got to curb line, it abruptly turned around and went the opposite direction, to the left, and he was unable to stop his car before he smashed into the boy's car and killed him.

After the depositions, I tried to settle the case again. The defense reiterated the company would not pay one dollar.

The court sent us a notice that we were assigned to non-binding arbitration. At the arbitration, an excellent lawyer came out with a decision for the defense. But, since it was non-binding, I immediately filed a petition to set aside the arbitration and go to trial.

Next, I had to appear before a Superior Court judge in Stockton for a settlement conference. After some back and forth, the judge asked what was the lowest figure I would accept.

I told him the truth: I was trying to get funeral expenses for the mother and father of the boy who was killed and I would pay costs. Whatever was left should be at least $10,000, and I would give it to the father and mother.

After talking with defense counsel for half an hour, the judge confessed, "Nate, there is no way you're going to be able to settle this case. The defense figures that if you go to a trial with a jury, you'll get nothing up here. Nate, I'm afraid they're right. I don't think you can come up here and try this case with a jury and collect anything with a jury trial. I don't know what to tell you to do. I just don't see you getting any kind of a verdict in Stockton in this case."

I waited until almost the time of trial to see if I could settle the case again and prepared for trial.

I hired a college professor who was an expert on automobile reconstruction cases. I had just one question I wanted him to answer, and that was: could the accident have happened as my witness said it had? He said it could have.

The morning before we started the trial, I asked the defense lawyer again if they would settle the case for $15,000.

"This is your last chance," I warned him. "Once I start, I don't care what happens, I won't settle with you for anything: we're going to have to go to a jury verdict."

"There's nothing I can do," he repeated. "The companies won't pay anything."

I thanked him and we proceeded to select a jury.

There was one juror I was a little worried about. He was a truck driver and I was worried that he might sympathize with the defendant, but he seemed so honest that I left him on the jury.

I called the Highway Patrol officers who had investigated the accident. They had drawn diagrams and and brought them along with them. I also introduced the diagrams and pictures that I had, and had the officers go over the entire accident. They were both extremely honest men. They didn't hedge one way or the other, but told it exactly as they saw it and I put their drawings into evidence.

Since the defense was going to make my witness' age an issue, I decided what I was going to do was to try the case with no papers on the table in front of me. I'd do it entirely by memory, with only a yellow pad to make notes. I wanted the jury to get the impression that my witness could remember things very well also, even though he was 74 years old, only two years older than I.

When I put my witness on the stand, he testified exactly as he had before. He said he saw the truck going down the road heading in a northerly direction at an extreme speed, and that the car with Joe's son in it slowed down and came to a stop at the intersection with the left signal light on to make a left turn and made a left turn. By this time, the driver of the truck was going so fast that he couldn't control it, slammed on his brakes and skidded into the boy and killed him.

When the defense finished its cross-examination, I asked my witness on redirect: "By the way, how old are you?"

"I'm 74 years old."

"What do you do for a living?"

"I dig wells."

The heat at that time in Stockton was in the high 90's and even 100 on a couple of days.

"You dig wells in this heat?"

"That's when people need wells."

"By the way, do you wear glasses?"

"Yes, I do."

"What kind do you wear?"

"Trifocals."

"I'm 72 years old, and I wear bifocals. Is there much difference?"

"No, not a lot of difference."

The jury had big smiles on their faces. They knew what I was trying to do.

Joe and Marjorie testified that they lived west of the intersection and that their son lived quite a ways south, but in the same part of Stockton. He would come over to have dinner with them at least every month and sometimes more often. He'd been to their home many, many times and he'd driven the same route to get to their home each time and he knew that their home was to the west and not to the east and that he would have had no reason to turn to the east. The evidence showed that Joe's son had no alcohol in his system and that he was completely familiar with the road.

After that, I brought in my expert and my expert stated unequivocally that, from his investigation of the accident, the accident could have happened exactly as my witness said it had. With that, I rested.

The defense attorney put the defendant on the stand I knew the defendant had been issued a ticket two years earlier for drunk driving, but the defense had made a motion *in limine* to prevent me from introducing this evidence which the judge had granted, so I could not mention the citation.

When he took the stand, the defendant testified that he was driving home and he was going to have to go out again that night, which was Halloween night, to deliver a tire to a big rig. He lived quite a ways north of where he worked and from where he worked there was a freeway right in front of the office. Across the street was the highway patrol and right there was a restaurant that he ate in very often. He knew all the highway patrolmen, who also ate there.

On this day he'd gone to work late because he was going to have to deliver this tire at night. He had eaten breakfast around one o'clock in the afternoon, so when he got to work he didn't eat lunch, but had only had one beer, across the street in the restaurant the highway patrol officers frequented. But, instead of taking the freeway from in front of his business office north directly to his home, which was just a half a block from the freeway, he decided to go south half a mile and then west over to an old two-lane highway and then north on the two-lane highway, where the accident happened.

I drove that route and I couldn't understand why anyone would go that circuitous route—south, then west, then coming back north.

An idea came to me which I made use of in my closing argument. As the plaintiff you have the obligation of the burden of proof, and, due to that fact, you get to present your closing argument first.

When I made my closing argument, I went through the evidence and described what I thought had actually happened. I went over all of the damages and told the jury what I thought should be returned as damages. I came up with the figure of $370,000.

Then I told the jury: "Let me tell you one more thing and that is this—I could have waited for my rebuttal, but I didn't think it was fair to the other lawyer to not do it at this time—I'm going to call to your attention the route the defendant took, and call to your attention that this was Halloween night. I will also call to your attention that he was friendly with the Highway Patrol and knew that on Halloween night the freeways are loaded with highway patrolmen making sure that people use the freeways safely. I want him to explain to you the reason his client went south for almost a mile, then west for a few blocks to this old country road to go down to his home when he could have done what he did every night, which was: get on the freeway and go directly to his home a half block off the freeway. Let him explain why he did that and then you can come to your own conclusion. I'm not going to tell you what conclusion I came to. I'm going to let you come to your own conclusion."

When the defense attorney got up to make his closing argument, he did not know really how he was going to answer my challenge, so he ignored it, and in his argument he tried to get the jury to think about my witness and to take him apart every way he could. Then, at the end of his argument, he told the jury: "Mr. Cohn asked the witness how old he was. He was 74. And Mr. Cohn said he is 72 and wears bifocals. Well, this witness and Mr. Cohn are two different people. You've seen Mr. Cohn here in court, you've seen how he moves around and what he does. You can realize that Mr. Cohn and the witness are not equal."

But he had played into my hands: "I told you that I'm 72. And it's true the witness is not equal to me. You've seen me in court. You can also see quite easily that the witness was out digging wells in 100 degree heat at 74, and you know darn well I couldn't dig any wells in that heat! I can hardly walk in the heat." They broke up.

After the jury was sent out, I took my clients to a little coffee shop in the courthouse and we had coffee there. A couple of hours later, the bailiff came for us. "Mr. Cohn, the jury has a question for the judge and the judge would like you to come back."

By the time counsel, parties and the jurors were assembled, the foreman advised the judge they no longer had a question—they had resolved it—and now had a verdict.

"Give the verdict to the bailiff and the bailiff will give the verdict to me."

The judge read the verdict but didn't move a muscle. Then the judge gave the verdict to the clerk and asked him to record the verdict.

"The verdict is for the plaintiff. And the verdict is the sum of $425,000."

I couldn't believe it. The judge asked the defense if they would liked the jury polled.

The clerk then asked the jury one by one if this was their verdict and all twelve of them said it was their verdict.

After the judge excused the jury, the jurors came out of the jury box and came to where I was standing with my clients at the plaintiffs' table and they congratulated my clients.

I asked the foreman, "What was the question you wanted to ask?"

"Well, what I wanted to ask was if we could give more money than you asked. You asked for $375,000 and we decided to give $425,000. However, we found an instruction that said we were not bound by the amounts that either lawyer mentioned in their arguments."

The defense made a motion for a new trial and a motion to reduce the verdict, but the judge denied both motions, and I made a motion for interest and costs. Under the law in California, you are entitled to interest at 10% from the time you made your 998 request. I had made a 998 request for $50,000 two years earlier and I was entitled to 10% of

$425,000 for two years, which was $85,000; and I was also entitled to all my costs and expert fees.

The defense appealed the decision and I contacted Judge Boone, a former judge in Santa Rosa. He had sat *pro tem* as an appellate judge when he was a Superior Court judge in Santa Rosa, but he loved appellate work and he resigned from the bench right after his term was over so he could go back to appellate work. He had handled some appeals for me where I'd won and the other side appealed, and he had done very well and I won all the appeals.

The judgment was affirmed, and I received a check from the defendants, including interest, costs and fees for $600,000 on a case that could easily have been settled for $15,000.

I was trying to do a good turn for Lenny and for Joe and his wife Marjorie and instead I made myself one of my better fees.

Perhaps the most unusual fee I received was in a case in which I represented a Baptist minister.

The minister of a Baptist congregation had decided to build a new church. When the minister announced his intention to the congregation, an engineer who was a member of the congregation offered his services. The engineer said he would like to show the plans to an architect and he would be happy to do anything he could for the church.

However, when the minister told the Baptist leaders about his plans they advised him that the church had its own organization that designs and builds churches, and they would design and build the church for him. When the minister informed them about the engineer's offer, they said they had their own engineers who work from their own designs and they could not use an outsider, even if he were a member of the church.

The engineer, it turned out had done work on his own, sued the minister for his services and the minister came to me for representation.

I was puzzled as to why he had chosen me, and being a forward person, I asked him directly.

"I'm sure there are some lawyers in your congregation."

"Yes."

"I'm Jewish. I'm not a member of your congregation. I'm not even Baptist. Why did you come here? Why not hire one of your church members?"

"I did that the last time. That's how I got into this trouble! I've heard you are a very good lawyer, that you are a gentleman and that you are honest. That's what I wanted."

I guessed I had my answer. I called in my number one secretary, Flora Piatro, a Catholic girl.

"The Reverend is a Baptist, I'm Jewish and you're Catholic. Do you have any objections to my handling a case for his church?"

Of course she didn't, and we all had a laugh.

There was one final formality. I asked the reverend for a dollar bill.

"Now, you've got a lawyer. Give me whatever papers he served on you."

I filed an answer, took the plaintiff's deposition and set the case for trial.

I knew a judge who was Baptist and was also an excellent judge. I wondered if I would be lucky enough to have the case assigned to him. To improve my odds, I asked my client for a favor.

"There is one judge I would like to have. I won't tell you who it is, but you just might have a closer connection than I have, so I would like you to pray over the weekend to see we get that judge."

His connection worked and the case was assigned to the judge I was hoping for. I told my client, "You seem to have someone up there helping you!"

"Perhaps you had something to do with it," he countered.

"You fellows have to pray. I've got a direct line."

When we selected the jury, it included four Jews, and I told my client that we had the case in hand because the plaintiff could never get nine jurors to vote for him now. I knew that at least the four Jews would be unhappy with someone suing a church, even if it wasn't their church.

My prediction proved correct. When the jury went out, they returned twenty minutes later with a verdict for the defense, including costs.

When I sent my bill of costs to the attorney for the plaintifff, I advised him that I intended to collect everything we were entitled to— every dime, including interest— because it was terrible to sue a church of any denomination.

With the case against him sucessfully concluded, my client asked how much he owed me.

"Nothing."

"Don't I owe you something?"

"Nope."

"Well," he shrugged, "I brought you a little something, anyway.'

It was a Bible, beautifully inscribed—the most precious fee I had ever received—and one which I keep in my desk to this day.

The $400,000 Slap

32

Not all my notable trials were criminal and not all were gut-wrenching. Sometimes my civil trial trials proved as dramatic in a different way—for example, the case of the $400,000 slap.

I was sitting in my office one day and in came an extraordinarily beautiful young lady. She was probably better looking than 99% percent of movie stars.

"Mr. Cohn, do you remember me?" she asked.

I looked at her and thought: "No, I don't. If I had known her, I surely would have remembered her."

She gave me her name and said, "I was a reporter for a judge in Contra Costa County where you tried a case. I had been working for him for quite a while and I had seen most of the lawyers, and I made up my mind if I ever had an important case, I would come to you."

Here I had a beautiful girl saying I was the best lawyer she had ever seen—my ego bristled.

"What can I do for you? I'd be glad to help you."

She said that she had been driving over in Contra Costa County and she had violated some law. She had gone to court and the court had advised her she could pay the fine or go to traffic school and they would dismiss the ticket. She decided to go to traffic school.

While at traffic school, she met a good looking and well-to-do young man. They sat next to each other, and after classes they had a couple of dates.

They fell in love and he invited her to move in with him, an offer she accepted. He was a successful businessman and had a beautiful apartment. They lived there with her two children, and every day they would drive the children to school and she would go to work.

One night, after working hard all day, she had to get a transcript out. She had to dictate the transcript into a recording machine so that the typist who would type the transcript would be able to read it. It had been a long day and she had to do it correctly and slowly. Her boyfriend wanted to go out to dinner and then go dancing.

She told him she couldn't go—she had to finish the transcript. He kept bothering her. She told him to leave her alone so she could do her work: she had to get it done. Finally she grew exasperated and said, "I'm going to get a cab and spend the night somewhere else because I've got to get this done."

She went to pick up the phone to call a cab, but he came across the room and grabbed the phone out of her hand. In doing so, the phone clipped the side of her face and he slammed the phone down on the receiver.

She went into the bedroom and got a .22 he had purchased so he could teach her how to shoot a gun on a rifle range. She put the .22 on him and told him to stay put while she called the police.

The police came over and she told them that he had hit her with the phone.

Her boyfriend told the police that she had a gun and had pointed it at him.

She replied she was only pointing the gun at him to protect herself, and the police arrested her boyfriend.

In the end, he apologized and the Court slapped his wrist, while she took her children and left his apartment to get her own place.

The man, on the rebound, met someone else and married her within a very short time.

My client felt very bad. She had been having psychological problems since the incident, so she went to Kaiser Hospital. The psychiatrist at Kaiser told her she had a traumatic neurosis caused by the blow to her face. They treated her, but they could only do so much for her, so they sent her to a psychiatrist in Walnut Creek.

The psychiatrist also told her that she had a traumatic neurosis and she had to overcome it.

She met a young fellow in the new place where she was living; they dated, and she married him.

She had some investments with the ex-boyfriend that she split up with him. They had bought an airplane together and they had bought a piece of property up in Oregon, so she had money coming from both of those investments and she wanted her money.

Her husband told her that he would take her to the lawyer who he had used to get his divorce. In the meantime, the young lady had gone with her husband somewhere and passed out. The doctor told her it was caused by the traumatic neurosis said she should take things easy and keep going to the psychiatrist.

When she saw her husband's lawyer, he informed her she had a possible lawsuit against her ex-boyfriend. The lawyer asked her when the incident had occurred. She replied it happened the previous June or July. This conversation took place in November.

The lawyer asked her if she wanted to sue her ex-boyfriend, and she told him she did.

The lawyer filled out a contract for her to hire him on a contingency fee basis to sue the former boyfriend for her injuries. When he filled it out, he put down that the incident happened June or July of that year. In the meantime, the ex-boyfriend, who had no desire to cheat her out of anything, made arrangements to give her back any monies she had invested.

She saw her lawyer several times and kept asking about the case, because her condition was growing worse. She kept seeing the psychiatrist for the traumatic neurosis, and she had reached to the point where she couldn't work as a court reporter anymore because she was too nervous and upset.

Her husband's lawyer kept telling her the lawsuit was "being prepared."

Finally, her lawyer filed the lawsuit in July. Her ex-boyfriend's lawyer made a motion to dismiss it because the incident had happened in June, which was more than one year before the lawsuit was filed, and the case was dismissed as outside the statute of limitations.

Her lawyer told her he was very sorry that he had screwed up, and now she was coming to me to represent her in a malpractice suit against the lawyer.

I had told her I wanted to help her, but I wanted this case like I wanted to be hit in the head with a sledgehammer.

I told her, "Let me see what I can do."

I called her lawyer. He told me that he had reported it to the insurance company, but that he had screwed up. I tried to help him by giving him some suggestions. I said he might go to court and have a judge extend the statute of limitations, and I found several cases that I thought might be helpful, but the cases didn't conform to the facts in this case.

Finally, I had to tell him, "I'm in a bad position here. I told the lady I would help her, so I've got to sue you for malpractice."

"I know that. If you didn't do that, you'd be stupid because then she'll sue you for malpractice."

The lawyer told me to go ahead and sue him and he would refer it to his insurance company. So, I filed a lawsuit for malpractice.

The couple was living in Oakland at the time this happened, and I filed the case in Alameda County. We took depositions and started preparing the case. Then the insurance company's defense lawyer sent me a notice demanding the names of the experts I intended to use. There was a psychiatrist I had used in three other cases involving traumatic neurosis. I had his reports. All three of the cases had settled, but I still had the reports, and I knew the psychiatrist very well. So I put his name down on the notice.

But, before I called him, the lawyer on the other side called the psychiatrist to ask what dates he had open for a deposition.

The psychiatrist told my opponents I hadn't hired him for this case—so they hired him instead.

The next thing I knew, I got a notice from the defense saying that they had hired the psychiatrist that I had told them I was going to use. There was nothing I could do about it, because I hadn't talked to the man and made any arrangements, but I wasn't worried. I had also used a psychiatrist in Walnut Creek who was excellent.

I tried to settle the case. The lawyer for the insurance company offered $15,000, but my client, who knew something about law because she had been a reporter for a few years, would not take it. She was a very honest person, and I thought she would go over well with a jury. So, finally, we took the case to trial.

The defense attempted to show that she did not have traumatic neurosis, but that she was simply jealous because her ex-boyfriend married another woman and had deserted her. While she was on the stand, the defense attorney asked her a lot of embarrassing questions about her living with the ex-boyfriend and whether or not she was in love with him.

My doctors all testified that her injury had happened before the ex-boyfriend married someone else, so jealousy could have played no part.

I could see that the jurors liked my client. Even though she was asked some very embarrassing questions, she answered them honestly. I always advise my clients to do so, because if you answer a question which could prove detrimental to you truthfully, the jury will know that you are telling the truth in other matters.

The other side also brought in the psychiatrist that I had used in my previous traumatic neurosis cases. He was well-known in the field, and had been used as an expert in some big cases. By the time he finished telling about his background you'd think he was the greatest psychiatrist in the United States—maybe the world.

He also testified my client's injury couldn't have been caused by the blow she had received.

I let him continue talking. I didn't object to anything he said as he embellished his opinion further and further.

Finally, when I started to cross-examine him, I took the three written opinions he provided me about other clients. All three clients had had the same kind of injury. All three clients had had the same kind of symptoms. And the symptoms in all three cases he said, in each report, were caused by a blow to the face—as this was. It was as if he had written an opinion in this case, but one which was diametrically opposed to what he was testifying in court.

"Doctor, you've even handled three cases of traumatic neurosis for me, haven't you?"

"I think so."

I showed him the three reports on his letterhead and signed by him. In them he had written the exact opposite of everything he had just said on the stand under oath. He had testified that this kind of incident couldn't have caused this particular injury, and that this injury wasn't damaging in any way. In these three written reports, he wrote that this kind of incident could cause this kind of injury and that the damages in this kind of case were quite large.

When he realized what was happening, he slumped in the chair and began to shrink back. Everything I asked him, he confirmed. He completely changed his entire testimony. The jury could see that all he wanted to do was get out of the witness chair.

I had destroyed his testimony.

The defense attorney argued that the plaintiff's sufferings were simply a result of unrequited love. But the defense attorney took it too far when he started reading from *Romeo and Juliet*. I responded that I knew somewhere someone had written the fictional defense that he was attempting to make, but I hadn't realized it came from a book called *Romeo and Juliet*. The jury broke up.

When I argued the case to the jury, I suggested the figure of $400,000. It was much more than I expected, but when you give a figure to the jury and tell them they're entitled to bring in whatever they think is right, you're suggesting the figure as a possible gauge for what they bring in.

The jury returned a verdict for the full $400,000. Afterwards, they came over and congratulated me and my client.

The foreman of the jury said, "You know, Mr. Cohn, that psychiatrist who was on the witness stand? I was thinking to myself I never saw anybody who wanted to get out of a chair as bad as that man wanted to get out of that chair. You just destroyed him."

The psychiatrist had won my case for me by trying to win the case for the other side.

The jury had given me $400,000. I had been hoping to get $100,000 at the most. The defense made a motion for a new trial and we went before the judge.

"Mr. Cohn," the judge said, "$400,000 is ridiculous. Probably the healthiest person in the courtroom was your client. What I'm going to do is this. I'm going to reduce the amount to $200,000. If you accept that, then you get that. If the defense refuses to pay it, then I'll let the $400,000 stand and they'll have to appeal it if they want to change anything. I don't think if they appeal they'll come very close to a reversal. So if you'll take $200,000, they'll pay $200,000. That will be the end of it and I won't grant a new trial."

I accepted the $200,000.

It was twice amount of what I was looking for. The jury loved my client. And she was a very lovely lady.

The Case of the Burglar Who Told the Truth

33

In Perry Mason novels, Perry, by his fantastic cross-examination, is able to make the witness to realize that he is caught, and the witness stands up and says, "You got me," or words to that effect.

In real trials, this never happens. The closest I managed was in a civil fraud case. My client had been defrauded of substantial sums of money by the defendant, who, I had been informed, had been involved in a criminal matter previously. I had the defendant on the stand, but I didn't know the facts of his previous brush with the criminal justice system.

"Sir," I concluded my cross, "is it not true that you have been criminally charged with fraud?"

He leapt from the witness chair and faced the jury.

"That's a lie! Never in my life have I been charged with a crime! And besides, I got probation."

—◆—

The closest I came to Perry Mason in a criminal case, was one I shall call "The Case of the Burglar Who Told the Truth."

I was representing a man who had been convicted of burglary on several prior occasions. He was now working as a painter. He had married a very beautiful young woman and was trying to go straight. The police had searched his home with a warrant and found a make-up box in his basement, filled with jewelry.

The police asked him to explain it. He said a friend of his had brought the box over and asked him to keep it for him. He had told his friend that he could leave it there, but to pick it up when he was able.

Unfortunately, his friend was still in the burglary business, and was subsequently convicted on several charges of burglary.

The box contained sixteen pieces of valuable jewelry stolen from several stores in San Francisco, and the District Attorney charged my client with sixteen counts of burglary. The Assistant District Attorney, Janet Aiken, was very competent and later became a judge.

When the case came to trial, I subpoenaed the gentleman who had left the box. He was readily available, as he was serving time in prison. He was a good-looking young man with a pleasing personality, and he admitted being a professional burglar, amusing the jury with stories of how he operated. He would use a celluloid card as a lock-pick to enter an apartment while its occupants were away. On one occasion, he rang the bell of an apartment and received no response. Assuming the premises to be unoccupied, he picked the lock. As he entered, a very pretty young lady wrapped only a towel, just out of the bath, asked him what he was doing there.

He informed her he was an investigator for the owner of the building who had told him to go all the apartments and look through them to make sure that everything was in good working order. They held a pleasant conversation and he even dated her after the incident. The witness was one smooth character.

The District Attorney cross-examined him and asked him where he was on June 30 of the previous year.

"I don't remember."

The District Attorney refreshed his recollection by saying "Isn't it true that you were in San Francisco County Jail for thirty days?"

"Yes, I believe I was."

"When did you get out?"

"I think I got out on the 15th of July. I entered the 15th of June."

The District Attorney asked if the County Jail allowed him to leave the premises.

They didn't.

The District Attorney asked if he was in the County Jail the entire time.

He had been.

I didn't quite understand the reason for the cross-examination, but I assumed there was a reason.

Later, the District Attorney called as a rebuttal witness a very attractive young lady. The District Attorney took a ring from the exhibits that had been marked for identification.

"I'll show you this ring. Do you remember this ring?"

She examined it very thoroughly.

"Yes. This is my ring. I know it's my ring because I had just had it cleaned and the jeweler's tag from cleaning was still on it. I remember it had it when I left it."

"Do you remember when you got the ring back from the jeweler's?

"Yes , I got the ring back on June 27th."

"When was the last time you saw the ring?"

"I had the ring on the 27th. I didn't wear it because I wasn't going anywhere I would need a ring like that, and I put it in my jewelry box. On the evening of June 30th, I went out on a date. I went into my jewelry box to select some jewelry to wear with my dress that evening. I picked up the ring and looked at it and was going to tear off the jeweler's tag, but I changed my mind and put it back."

"Did anything happen to that ring?"

"Yes, when I returned home that evening, I went to put the ring that I had on back in the box and I noticed that quite a bit of my jewelry was missing, including that ring."

The ring was established to have been in the box the police had found in my client's basement, the contents of which the witness had admitted stealing. But the witness could not have stolen this ring because he was in jail on June 30. Or, so it seemed.

I felt my client was telling the truth. I also felt the burglar I had called as a witness had been telling the truth. I went over and looked at the ring, and I looked at the markings on the tag. They seemed to match the handwriting of the owner of one of the jewelry stores the witness had admitted burglarizing at a time he was not in the County Jail, the fruits of which he had placed in the box found in my client's basement.

My client's case now looked very, very tough.

I requested a recess for lunch, it being five minutes to twelve, and asked if I could have the Court's permission to take the ring and a police inspector with me.

Judge Levin informed me I could and I asked if the District Attorney would assign a police inspector to go with me.

"Yes, the two officers who have been handling this case would be happy to go with Mr. Cohn."

The officers had a police car. I asked them to drive me to Post Street, to the location of one of the jewelry stores the witness had claimed to have burglarized.

The officers were still parking their car when I jumped out and walked into the store well ahead of them. I saw the owner of the store standing at the counter and I walked over to her and showed her the ring.

"Is this one of your rings? One of the rings that was stolen from you in a burglary?"

She identified it by the handwriting on the tag. But how to get her in court?

By this time the officers had caught up with me. I told her the officers were from the Burglary Detail and asked her to be in court at 2:00.

"It's very important. I can have the police send a car to pick you up." She said there was no need.

"See you at 2:00." The conversation had gone so fast the officers had no chance to speak, and she was left with the impression that I was either a police officer or a District Attorney. I took the ring and left.

That afternoon I did not sit at the defense table, but took a seat at the prosecution table, instead. At 2:00 I would see if my plan worked.

Promptly at 2:00 the judge took the bench, the storeowner walked into the courtroom and I asked the judge if I could call a witness who could shed some light on the case.

Swiftly, I called the storeowner to the stand. Her testimony saved my client. She testified the ring had been stolen from her shop in May, not June (while my client's friend was still at liberty), and she identified the tag as a price tag in her handwriting.

The District Attorney was rattled. She recalled the woman who claimed the ring had been stolen from her.

"Well, the ring looks awfully like mine. I thought it was mine and mine did have a tag of some sort, but now that I look at it, it's probably not the same tag and not the same ring."

The jury brought in a verdict of not guilty on all sixteen counts. And so ended The Case of the Burglar Who Told the Truth.

Not only do witnesses not leap up and confess as they do for Perry Mason, cross-examination can go too far, as I learned in an early case where I thought I had caught an arresting officer in testimonial hubris.

My client was a young Hawaiian sailor who was charged with burglary.

By my client's account, he had joined several other sailors who took him out on the town and got him smashed. Then they disappeared. He was trying to find his way back to his hotel when he went by a grocery store. It had a glass door. As he went by, he lost his balance, fell into the door and the door broke open.

He looked around. He put several cartons of cigarettes in his pocket, and removed several dollars of change from the register, which was open, when a husky police officer appeared and arrested him for burglary.

The District Attorney had indicted my client to avoid a preliminary hearing, and the case came on for trial before Judge Wollenberg. It was Judge Wollenberg's first jury case.

My defense was that my client had not entered the premises with the intent to commit a crime. That would be burglary—a felony. My theory was that he had fallen against the door and the door had broken open and he had found himself in the store, and had picked up a couple of cartons of cigarettes and some small change, which would only be petty theft, a misdemeanor.

I had been tipped off that the cop who had arrested my client had just been on the force a couple of months. The officer's name was Barnaby O'Leary.

O'Leary took the stand and testified that he had arrested my client after seeing him go in the store and coming out with the cigarettes and the money.

I cross-examined him. "Did you smell his breath, Officer O'Leary?"

"Yes, I did."

"What did you smell?"

"I smelled alcohol."

"Did you watch how he walked?"

"Yes, I did."

"How did he walk?"

"Not very steady."

"Now, did you talk to him?"

"Yes, I did."

"Did he slur his speech?"

"A little bit."

"Did you smell alcohol on his breath?"

"Yes, I did. A little bit."

"How long have you been on the police force?"

"About ninety days."

I was in great shape. All I had to do was stop. But when you're young and you're just starting, you're going to want to bury the nail even better, so I went on.

"How many people have you arrested for being intoxicated since you've been on the police force?"

"This is the first one."

Again, I had him. But, I wanted to pound the nail in even further.

"This is the only fellow you ever arrested who was intoxicated?"

"Yes."

"He had liquor on his breath?"

"Yes."

"He staggered?"

"Yes."

"But you say he was sober, is that right?"

"Yes."

"You only had one arrest but you still say this man was sober?"

"Yes."

"Do you consider yourself an expert on intoxication?"

He looked me in the eye and he said "Yes."

Well, I could even have quit then, but you can't stop an eager young lawyer who wants to be Perry Mason.

"What qualifications do you have that caused you to believe that you are an expert in intoxication?"

"Before I got this job, I was a bartender for eight years."

All was not lost, however. The jury came back in after three hours and they gave Judge Wollenberg the verdict.

"Wait a minute, Mr. Foreman, is this your verdict?"

"Yes that's our verdict—all our verdict."

"I've explained to you how to fill this out. You haven't filled it out correctly."

"That's the way we want it to go to you."

"You've said on this verdict form that you find this young man guilty, but you don't want him found guilty unless he is going to get a suspended sentence. Is that what you have here?"

"Yes."

"You can't do that. You have to find him guilty or not guilty of the charges, but I decide what his punishment is going to be—not you."

The foreman asked if the jury could talk a minute, then he asked if they could have their verdict back.

Judge Wollenberg gave the foreman the verdict form, and the jury went out for another hour. Then they came back in with a verdict and gave it to the judge.

"Wait a minute. In this you say: 'We find the defendant guilty but we give him probation.' You can't give him probation."

"Then we can't find him guilty. If he's going to go to jail, we can't find him guilty. We figured the boy was intoxicated and he might have done something wrong, but none of us think he should be jailed."

"Well will you do this for me—will you strike the part where you give him probation? Just say you find him guilty. Then, trust me to carry out what I think are your wishes."

The foreman looked at all the people on the jury. "I think that's fair, Your Honor."

The judge directed the clerk to record the verdict, and the clerk recorded it, and he continued, "I want to thank the jury for your verdict, but stay there. I'm going to give this young man probation. He can leave the country on a ship—he's a seaman—I just don't want to see him back in this courtroom again on any charge. Is that understood?"

I replied "Yes, Your Honor."

My client thanked the jurors, returned to Hawaii and mailed me the remainder of my fee.

It wasn't Perry Mason, but the right thing was done.

What makes a jury come to its decision? Not always what you would think, as I learned in one case.

I had been practicing law for a few years when a gentleman came into my office who was an executive for a fairly large firm in the Bay

Area. He told me his firm had had a Christmas party at a restaurant.

After the party was over, about two or three o'clock in the afternoon, he was giving one of the executive secretaries a ride to her home in his car. He was going up a hill and to his left he saw a large sedan coming toward him at an excessive speed. The sedan passed him and he started to make a left turn. Unfortunately, a police officer on a motorcycle was chasing the sedan and my client's view was blocked by the sedan he was chasing. When my client turned left, the police officer hit his car and was killed.

My client was charged with vehicular manslaughter and asked if I would represent him.

I agreed to take the case. I went out to the scene and drove my car the same route. I could see that from where my client was when the sedan went past him he could not have seen the traffic officer on the motorcycle, because my client was at the bottom of an incline when he started to make the left turn, and the officer was coming up the incline.

At that time I was the attorney for the press photographers' association, so I had a friend of mine who was a good photographer make a short movie of my client going up the hill. The movie showed what my client could—and couldn't—see.

I selected a jury and I liked to select people who were a little like me if I could, and I wanted to get working people rather than those who were college-educated—people who could understand my approach.

We tried the case for a week. It carried with it at least a year in jail. The jury returned a verdict of not guilty in an hour and a half.

Afterward, one of the jurors—a tall longshoreman—came over to me and said, "You know, Mr. Cohn, I was for you the moment this trial started."

"Why?"

"Well," he said, "I've got a sister who lives in New York, and she's married to a man who's in the ladies dress business—he makes and sells dresses. His name is Cohn, C-o-h-n, like you. And he's the nicest man I ever met. I was for you from the first day."

Cop-killer Harold Miller today
a strange bit of remorse over hi
of Police Inspector Denis Bradl
Miller says he's sorry it wasn',
Ins_____ Max Gi____, instead.
The s___gy-hai_____x-convict s.
Gira____ at n__ u_ __d was alwa
me."
"_'m s___y that co_ (Bradley) wa
killed," he declared at City Prison.
"If it had to be anyone. I wish it
have been Girard.

Some Cameos

34

As attorney for the American Guild of Variety Artists, I came to represent top nightclubs in San Francisco and many of their performers, including Billie Holliday, Josephine Baker and Duke Ellington.

Duke Ellington was playing Facks Two when the Internal Revenue Service closed it for failure to pay back taxes; and George Andros, owner of Facks Two, called me in a panic.

"Duke Ellington is over here and he is out of his mind. His instruments are locked up!"

The government had a lock on the door of Facks Two.

Fortunately, I knew a reasonable gentleman at the Internal Revenue Service, and I called him and told him what the score was.

"You know, I can get the instruments by filing a third-party claim, but why go through all this trouble in court when I can't get Duke Ellington his instruments in time for him to make his gig in another town and he'll lose the money?"

He was, as I said, reasonable and we went down to Facks Two and Duke identified his instruments and we removed them. Duke couldn't believe it and thanked me profusely—and the IRS locked the door again.

I eventually worked out the entire matter with the IRS and they gave George Andros time to pay them off, which he did, and he was able to reopen the nightclub.

Several years later, Artie Samish invited me to watch the games of the World Series from his box at Candlestick Park, right behind first base. When I took my seat, Duke Ellington was there, also a guest of Artie's, and he insisted on telling everyone that I was the greatest lawyer in the United States. I explained all I had done was to convince the IRS to allow him to take his own instruments, but he would have none of it. To listen to him, you would think I had saved him from the gas chamber.

San Francisco had two beautiful nightclubs, both on Columbus Avenue in North Beach. One was Bimbo's 365 Club and the other was the Italian Village.

One day the owner of the Italian Village called me and asked me to come up and see him. He had a problem. He had booked Anna Maria Alberghetti into his club and she was only eighteen years old at the time. Don Marshall, head of the Alcoholic Beverage Control Division of Enforcement had heard about it, and told him she could not perform.

"I've got her booked and we spent money on advertising. Is there anything you can do?"

I called Don and made a suggestion.

"I know she's not twenty-one, but I've been there, Don. Miss Alberghetti can enter the nightclub through the door to the dressing rooms, go out on stage and perform, go back to her dressing room and leave through the door she entered."

"What's that got to do with it?"

"It's very simple. The law says that no minor can appear as an entertainer in any portion of a restaurant that serves liquor. The portion of the restaurant that she enters is the back, where the dressing rooms are, then the stage, and she never enters any portion of the restaurant where liquor is served."

"Nate, the whole place..."

"Wait a minute. Do you realize what you are saying? You're an enforcement agent, aren't you?"

"Yes."

"You enforce everything equally for all citizens, don't you?"

"Yes."

"Well, then, you've got a problem."

"What do you mean?"

"You go to a college football game and the players play on the field, they don't play in the stands. But in the stands, fans are served beer, an alcoholic beverage. You go to the racetrack. Some of the jockeys are not 21. Yet, there are bars in the turf club and the clubhouse. Go to high school football games and spectators are drinking beer in the stands. A lot of baseball players are under 21. Beer is served there—there are bars at the baseball stadium. You are going to have to close up all the bars selling liquor at sporting events if you insist on stopping Miss Alberghetti from performing, because I'm going to go into court and get an injunction requiring it."

Don agreed to come over to the Italian Village and look things over and I showed him how one could come in through the back door and come out on the stage.

"You see, liquor isn't served in this portion of the premises."

"Would you actually go to court over this?"

"Absolutely."

"Okay, tell your client he can book her in. And show her how to do this."

The owner was ectastic. "What are you doing tomorrow night? I want you to have dinner with the Alberghettis and me."

At that time, the law did not say that a minor could not eat on premises where liquor was sold, she just couldn't perform in that part of the premises.

The next night, I joined my client, Miss Alberghetti, her brother and her mother and father. Her brother was eleven, but he had just conducted a symphony orchestra.

While we were having dinner, a friend of mine, Johnny Martin, came by. Johnny sang at the 365 Club in practically all the shows, and he wanted me to introduce him to the Alberghettis.

Johnny started speaking Italian to the Alberghettis. They were very impressed. Then he turned to me.

"So that you won't feel left out in the cold..." and started speaking Yiddish. Then, he turned back to the Alberghettis and explained what he had done, in Italian.

Miss Alberghetti asked how his Yiddish was.

"Okay. I said, "it's just got a drop of Italian mixed in."

Anna Maria perfomed at the Italian Village for a week. Afterwards, I ran into the owner of the Italian Village again, on the street. I expected thanks for my brilliant work.

"How did it go?"

"I'm sorry I hired you."

"What do you mean?"

"She didn't draw anybody, and we lost money on her. If I hadn't hired you, I wouldn't have been able to have her perform and I wouldn't have lost money!"

Politics 101

35

I have also been involved in politics my entire career: in fact, since before I became a lawyer. When I came back to San Francisco from Texas and Los Angeles in 1937 to look for a job, I made the rounds of the newspapers looking for a job as a copy boy, hoping to get a foothold in journalism. Jobs were scarce, but, finally, a job came up on the *Chronicle*. At the same time, I was offered a position working for a small advertising agency, Walter Barusch Agency at 25 Taylor Street. The city editor of the *Chronicle* told me I'd be better off going with the advertising job because reporters didn't make very much money, so I started doing publicity for Walter Barusch.

I did publicity for theater clients and a dog show, and then after a few weeks, Walter came in to see me.

"Nate we've got a big one. I want you to handle it." I was 19 years old, and there were only three people in the agency: Walter who couldn't write anything, a young lady, and myself. Walter said we'd been hired by Culbert Olson to handle his campaign for Governor in Northern California and I was going to handle the campaign.

I told Walter I'd never handled anything like that before, that I knew nothing about politics and I wasn't even old enough to vote.

"You can do it. Just remember: we get 15% commission on ads and 25% on printing and 25% on posting, and please try and use as much money as we can where we get the best commission."

The first thing he wanted was for me to design a 24 sheet—a big billboard—then a half-card and quarter-card for posting. Walter told me that Culbert Olson was coming to San Francisco and would be at the Clift Hotel, a few blocks from the office. He wanted me to meet Olson and help him around in the Northern California area.

Walter said Olson would be speaking, and his secretary would give me a list of where he would be speaking, and I was to find out what the audience wanted to hear and prepare a card for him setting these things forth, so that Olson could make speeches telling his audience what they wanted to hear and how he was going to help them.

I met Olson at the Clift Hotel where he had a suite. He was a tall, good-looking, wavy-haired man. If you were casting the role of Governor in a movie, he would be perfect. He was running against Merriam. Merriam had become Governor when Governor Rolph had passed away.

I met Olson and his campaign chairman, who advised me if anyone wanted to give me a contribution to give it to him—not to Mr. Olson.

Olson was one of the most charming men you could ever want to meet. I would meet him when he was in San Francisco at the Clift Hotel and give him the cards that I had prepared, stating what each of his audiences wanted. We would go to the different places around the Bay Area where he was to speak, and I would have circus friends of mine go there early in the morning and park their cars in all the parking places. That way, when Culbert Olson and I arrived, my friends would pull out and Olson and I would be parked right in front, while, when Merriam arrived, he would have to look for parking.

We had a little band that I hired which would play everywhere Olson was slated to speak, and as he walked in, the band would play "Happy Days Are Here Again." Olson loved it.

During the whole campaign I had all the show people who were wintering in San Francisco working for Olson throughout Northern California.

Two other men I met when I met Olson were Stanley Mosk, who later became Attorney General and then California Supreme Court Justice, a wonderful young man at the time, who was Olson's secretary, and George T. Davis, who was an attorney. Davis loved publicity, and was representing Tom Mooney and Warren Billings who had been incarcerated for the Preparedness Day Parade bombing in 1916. Olson had declared that Mooney and Billings were innocent and that he would pardon them if he were elected Governor. George T. Davis traveled all over the State speaking for Mooney and Billings' release.

Olson won the election. Walter told me that he had talked to Olson, who told Walter that he liked me very much and that he really appreciated my work. Walter had the idea that because of my background in outdoor shows, carnivals and fairs he would ask Olson to appoint me to the State Fair Board for the State Fair in Sacramento. Then, Walter suggested, if I were appointed to the State Fair Board, I could hire Walter's agency to handle publicity for the State Fair.

I knew nothing about law at that time but it didn't seem to me legitimate thing. I was very nervous about it, and when Olson decided I could not be appointed to the State Fair Board because I was not 21, it brought me great relief.

That was my first experience with politics.

Years later, when Pat Brown was Governor, I was in Sacramento with a client having lunch at a hotel on the south side of the Capitol Park. The Governor's top secretary, Adrien Sausette—she had attended law school with me in my first year and left to go to work as secretary to Brown when he was District Attorney of San Francisco—came in and saw my client and me having lunch. She told me that Pat Brown wanted to talk to me.

After lunch, I went over to the Capitol with her. She had a key to an inside elevator which took us directly up to Pat Brown's office without going through the reception area. When I walked in, Pat saw me.

"I want to ask you something. You're very close to Jess Unruh—probably his best friend. I've been told by my people that Jess is thinking of running against me in the primaries for Governor. Is that true?"

"Of course not. Jess is too intelligent to have a primary fight with you which could destroy the Democratic Party in California."

He started telling me things he was going to do, asked my opinion on an appointment for judge and offered me a judgeship.

"You're one of my commissioners, aren't you?"

"No."

He told Adrien to remind him about it.

A week later, I received a letter from Pat saying that he was appointing me to the State Recreation Commission. I immediately researched the State Recreation Commission and from what I could gather they did very little except prepare a report to the Governor on recreation in California.

I attended two or three meetings and came to the conclusion that the State Recreation Commission was a waste of money for the

California taxpayers. I called Pat and told him so. Immediately after that, the State Recreation Commission was told that each county had the right to certain monies that were to be spent on recreation areas. There were certain regulations to be complied with in order to get this money, and they had assigned the State Recreation Commission to decide whether the counties met the requirements.

On the State Recreation Commission, in addition to myself, was a very nice lady by the name of Betty Forey, who was chairperson. Nicholas Roosevelt, who was related to the family of Theodore Roosevelt, was also a member. There was the Mayor of a small town in Modoc County, there was a Labor leader from Southern California, and there were a couple of other people who were politically strong in different counties.

We would have meetings around the state to listen to people from the different counties asking us for monies for their counties.

We had a lady we called "The Chief" who advised Betty. "The Chief" would find that many of the requests were not in keeping with the rules. There had to be a certain amount of acreage, and multiple uses. Some of the counties, espcially those north of San Francisco wanted money for boat launchings, for example, because they had all the parks and recreation areas they needed: the whole county was a recreation area. I would ask them if they could get the property across from the property they had presented in their diagram as empty property. They could. Could they put bike paths and picnic areas there? They could. That would meet the requirement that the areas be for multiple uses—boat launchings, bicycle paths and picnic areas—and I would move the Recreation Commission grant them the money. Everyone was happy.

Pat Brown called me and told me that the supervisors of a northern county had called him and told him I had really helped them and that they wanted to thank me for it. I told Pat I thought that was what I was supposed to do: represent the Governor to get the people what they wanted. I also told Pat again that the whole commission was a waste of government money and they should combine the Recreation Commission with Parks and Beaches.

Pat told me that, since I was a friend of Jess Unruh, Speaker of the Assembly, I should talk to Jess about changing the law and Pat said he would appoint me chairman of the new commission. I talked to Jess, and also told him it was a waste of state money. Jess had someone on his staff draw up a law that combined the two commissions and he passed it.

However, Ronald Reagan ran against Pat Brown for Governor in the next election, and beat Pat. Consequently, Ronald Reagan was able to appoint the new commission and, as you might expect, I was not on the new commission.

I had promoted myself out of my position in a commission: not too smart for a person supposedly knowledgeable about politics.

In 1965, Harold Dobbs ran for Mayor. Harold had been brought to me by an associate when he was running for Supervisor, and he asked me to help him. I was able to get quite a lot of support for Harold and, after he was elected Supervisor, he was friendly and appreciative.

My name came up for appointment to a position proposed by Mayor Elmer Robinson. I had been advised by Robinson that he was supporting me. Hank James and I went to a City Hall election-night vote count and I ran into Harold and another supervisor, and told them that my name was going to come up before the Board of Supervisors. They said they absolutely would support me. Later on, I found out that, although the Mayor had told me he was going to support me, he was, in fact, supporting someone else; and I was told I had no chance of getting the position.

My name was proposed before the Board of Supervisors and Harold and the other Supervisor voted against me. When Harold ran for Mayor, he was running against Jack Shelley and I thought I would do whatever I could to repay Harold for the broken promise. Shelley asked me to help him and I told him I would.

The Calamari Club is a private, all-male club which meets every Friday for lunch and to roast each other and our guests. Its membership is limited to 36, including five judges, five lawyers, five public officials and five union heads. The rest of the members are business and professional men.

At that time there was a whole group of people running for different offices in San Francisco, among them a member of the Calamari Club who was a Municipal Court judge, Clarence Linn. I

found Linn to be a pompous man and a very poor judge. Judge
Morris, who was the Kingfish of the Calamari Cub asked me if I
would do him a favor.

I told Judge Morris of course I would.

"I want you to handle the campaign for Clarence Linn for judge."

"No way, Judge. I don't like him, I don't think he's a good judge."

"You promised me you would do me a favor. You don't go back on
your word!"

"I guess I can't go back on my word. Tell Clarence to get in touch
with me and I'll try to help him."

In the meantime, a lawyer Clarence Linn had insulted in court
decided he would run someone else against Clarence, and he picked one
of the best criminal lawyers in the United States, Leo Friedman, to run
against Linn.

Leo was a close friend of mine, but I was stuck with helping Linn. I
went to see Leo and I explained the situation. Leo said he understood,
and told me not to worry, and to do what I had to do.

Clarence Linn came over to my office and I set up a campaign for
him. However, he made it very difficult. For some reason, he wanted to
show people how independent he was. If he was speaking before Labor,
he would speak in favor of Management, and if he was in front of group
of Management enthusiasts, he would speak against Management.

After three weeks of this campaign, I was at my wit's end. Then, my
secretary told me, "I have some good news. Clarence Linn called and
said he doesn't want you to handle his campaign, he's got somebody
else." I was relieved.

I thought back to Harold Dobbs and Jack Shelley and the Mayoral
race. I didn't want to just come out and support Shelley against Dobbs,
and it occurred to me I should put out a recommendation card for all
the offices.

At that time I had approximately 5,000 friends, acquaintances and
people I knew in San Francisco, and I went to a printer and had him print
50,000 yellow cards recommending an entire slate of candidates. For
example, there was a lawyer in North Beach I liked very much, George
Moscone, who was running for Supervisor, and the polls showed his
standing to be very low. Leo McCarthy was a young man I knew who was
also running for Supervisor. I included them in my recommendations.

The Calamari Club. Nate "bribes" Judge Lazarus at a meeting of the Calamari Club.

I sent out 5,000 letters to the people in my files asking them to sign five cards and mail them to five different friends and I mailed these cards out. The other 25,000 cards I took to the candidates I had endorsed and gave them the cards, suggesting they give them to their friends to be mailed to their friends.

At the time Dobbs was favored 8-5 to win the election for Mayor.

My home was right across the street from a polling place and before I went to work at about 9 a.m. the morning of the election, I went across the street to vote and noticed there were quite a few yellow cards on the sidewalk in front of the polling place, which seemed to have been thrown away by people leaving. I drove around San Francisco and saw that all the polling places had many of these yellow cards on the sidewalk.

That evening, Phil Burton, his wife and I sat in Orestes' restaurant and listened to the election results. Jack Shelley had won. Burton was going to go to Shelley's campaign headquarters a few blocks from

Orestes where we were watching the results upstairs. I told him I had to get to bed so I could get up and go to court in the morning.

Art Caylor, who had a political column in the *San Francisco Daily News,* wrote a column a short time later saying that it was the first time in his career he had ever seen anyone do what I had done. Every person I had recommended for the Board of Supervisors was elected. Nor were they all incumbents. Everyone on my card was elected with the exception of Judge Linn, and in the column Art said he understood that I had placed Linn on the card reluctantly and he was the only one in the entire card that lost.

Two days after the election, I received a letter in the mail from Phil Burton, who was a State Assemblyman. Phil was running for Jack Shelley's Congressional seat which had become vacant when Jack Shelley was elected Mayor.

The election was on a Tuesday. I received the letter on Thursday and I was amused to see how fast Burton had acted. The next day, Friday, I received a telephone call that three political heavyweights in San Francisco wanted to see me.

I agreed to see them late Friday afternoon. About 4 p.m. that Friday the three heavyweight political people walked into my office.

"What can I do for you?"

"Would you be interested in running for Congress on the Democratic ticket against Phil Burton?"

I was quite surprised and quite shocked. They said they would guarantee $50,000 for campaign contributions up front among them, and that they believed that they would be able to get at least one of the newspapers to support me against Burton. They said they thought that because of my career and background I was as popular with the minorities and Labor as Burton was, and they thought that I could possibly beat him in the primary election.

This caught me quite unprepared. I had never even thought of running for office in any way, and Phil was a close friend of mine and I had supported him in his election to the Assembly. I told them that I would like to have the weekend to think the matter over, and if they contacted me on Monday I would give them an answer.

The next day, Saturday, I was working on a case in the office and went over to Vanessi's for lunch—and who was at the bar but Phil Burton.

We had a drink together and I told him what had happened. I told him I also understood you have to spend four months in Washington, D.C. every year. He said "Nine months."

We talked about the elements of the job as we had lunch together, and I decided I would tell the three gentlemen that I would not run in the primaries, and that I was going to support Phil Burton.

As we were leaving, Phil turned to me. "Nate, if you did do it, I'd beat you in the primaries."

"That's something we will never know," I said. And we both laughed.

He Invented
Chicanery

36

One of the clients I had the privilege to represent was a man who was called by Earl Warren, when he was Governor, the most powerful man in the State of California—more powerful than the Governor when it came to his clients. That man was Artie Samish. But the title I suggested for his autobiography said it best: he was "the man who invented chicanery."

When Artie was a young man, he worked all over Sacramento. He worked in the Motor Vehicle Department, he worked for the legislators and learned how things worked. Then he put his knowledge to work as a lobbyist.

When the State had made it hard for the San Francisco-San Jose bus line, Artie went to a bank, got the bank to back him, and bought the bus line. He kept the line for two weeks and sold it for quite a bit of money.

Artie eventually became the lobbyist for some of the most powerful groups in California: he was lobbyist for the liquor industry, he was lobbyist for the sugar industry, he was lobbyist for the banks, he was lobbyist for the racetracks, he was lobbyist for sport franchises and he was even lobbyist for chemical corporations.

Artie's procedure was: "select and elect." He would select someone to run for office that he liked, and who he thought would be friendly to him, and, because he was the lobbyist for cigarettes and tobacco, beer and wine, during election time his clients would make billboards available and he would use the billboards to advertise for these candidates and for or against legislative bills and ballot propositions.

Artie was also lobbyist for the trucking industry. When someone in the legislature wanted to increase taxes on trucks, the trucking industry hired Artie to oppose it, and Artie put a picture of a big hog on billboards all over the state: "Oppose the road hogs. Vote No." It had nothing to do with the bill, but it worked.

Artie put a picture of an old, motherly lady with a broom on a billboard, "Make a clean sweep for the State. Vote No." And people voted "No."

Artie would selectively provide money to their campaigns, and keep the politicians he supported in office. But if one of them ran afoul of Artie, he would run someone new against him, and with the money he had and all the aid he could summon up from his clients, Artie's new candidate would defeat the old.

On many occasions, he "selected and elected" the majority of the legislature. In those days, assemblymen worked only part of the year and made around $200 a month. They had no real money to run for office, and Artie would take care of them, but he would never give any money directly to anyone.

With his knowledge, Artie became the most successful lobbyist in California history.

When Artie grew angry with the Senator from Los Angeles—at that time where was one State Senator for every county—Artie had potential opponents brought in to him for interviews.

Artie was not satisfied with any of the possibilities he had seen and asked if they had any among them who wasn't a lawyer. His aides brought in one man.

Artie asked: "What have you done?"

"I wrote a song."

"What song?"

"Mexicali Rose."

"Can you sing it?"

Artie had him retrieve his guitar from his car, and the aspiring candiate sang "Mexicali Rose" for Artie. Artie congratulated him: "Glad to have you aboard. You're going to be the next Senator from Los Angeles."

And Jack Tenney did became Senator from Los Angeles.

Once he became Senator, Tenney established an Un-American Activities Committee in the California Senate, modeled on the House Un-American Activities Committee in Washington, and installed himself as Chairman.

But when Tenney began calling Artie's friends from Hollywood to testify in front of his committee, Artie called another audience with Senator Tenney and explained he was not happy with Senator Tenney's committee. Senator Tenney replied he was a senator and that no one could tell him what to do. You

"I have some advice for you then, Senator," Artie warned. "Go write another song, because you're not going to be senator very long." In the next election, Tenney was defeated.

———•———

Artie was angry with another assemblyman who had not voted the way that Artie thought he should have and Artie decided to teach the man a lesson and run someone against him to remind the gentleman that it if it wasn't for Artie, he would not be in the Assembly.

Artie sent his aides down to Main Street in Los Angeles and found a man living in a little hotel trying to make enough money to pay his rent. Artie's aides asked him how he would like $200 a month, a new suit and nice work. They told him they would put on a campaign for him. They told him they were not going to get him elected, but he looked good and they would give him a few hundred dollars a month, and put him up in a hotel room. When the gentleman won the Republican nomination, one of Artie's top aides told Artie he wanted to run the man for the Assembly seat in November: he told Artie the candidate was one of the finest men he had ever met and that he could win the election. As long as he felt that way, Artie told him, he would provide him as much money as he needed for the campaign and Artie's man was elected to the Assembly. He was the only assemblyman in Sacramento who lived on the $200 a month salary and this man proved to be the most honest man in the Assembly.

———•———

Artie himself was six feet tall, at least one hundred pounds over-weight, and loved acting the clown. Artie's hobby was, in fact, to collect paintings of circus clowns.

Artie was also a sucker for mothers and kids.

When Artie learned about a young newsboy who was the sole support of his mother and worked day and night selling newspapers, Artie found an empty store, had his clients in the liquor industry stock the store, paid the rent for one year and gave the store to the newsboy so he could more adequately support his mother.

It was public knowledge that any athletic team for youngsters could always go to Artie and get funds for uniforms and equipment, and even, on occasion, for trips to participate in tournaments.

Artie also liked to maneuver public officials into bets which would make the them look silly.

Artie inveigled a very dignified and reserved public official into a bet. The loser would have to push a peanut across the lobby of the Senator Hotel in Sacramento with his nose. When Artie won, the loser found himself surrounded by news cameras, TV cameras, and many, many laughing public officials as he pushed a peanut across the lobby of the Senator Hotel with his nose.

To Artie, that was humor.

In addition to his feelings for mothers and children, Artie also supported the working man.

When Senator Knowland ran for Governor of California against Pat Brown, the top producers and movie studios in Los Angeles offered Artie a million dollars to pass Knowland's right-to-work bill. Artie turned down the million dollars, and, in fact, worked hard to defeat the right-to-work bill without a fee. He made billboards, radio time and other advertising available without charge because Artie felt the bill would injure the income of working people.

Artie always supported Labor and poor people without fee.

Artie became so powerful in the state that one of the national magazines sent a reporter to interview Artie. Artie, like a lot of people who have tremendous power, thought that he was invincible and clowned around with the reporter. The reporter had a picture taken of Artie with a puppet on his lap, representing the California Legislature, and Artie holding the strings.

The writer had told Artie he would not use any material Artie told him not to use, so Artie had told him a lot of stories, and, in the end, the writer did include some of the stories that Artie had told him not to.

As soon as the magazine article hit the newstands, the federal government determined get rid of Artie. Senator Kefauver was investigating influence in politics in California and called Artie before his committee.

Senator Kefauver asked Artie: "You receive millions from clients, what happens to it?"

"All the money I get I keep track of, and I write out checks to spend that money legitimately."

"What do you do with the checks when they come back from the bank?"

"I throw them in the wastepaper basket."

Kefauver threw Artie out of the committee hearing. The U.S. Attorney in Sacramento then subpoenaed Artie to come before the Grand Jury.

"Mr. Samish, you appeared before the Kefauver Committee?"

"Yes, I did."

"And you told Senator Kefauver that you would get money and you would write checks. Is that correct?"

"Yes."

"And then Senator Kefauver asked you, 'What did you do with the checks when you got them back from the bank?' And you told him you threw them in the wastepaper basket. Is that true?"

"Yes, I did."

"Well," he said. "Don't you know that it's a violation of law to destroy those checks?"

"I didn't destroy those checks."

"Well, you told Senator Kefauver you threw them in the wastepaper basket."

"Yes, but the Senator didn't ask me what I did with the wastepaper baskets."

"What did you do with the wastepaper baskets?"

"I kept them. If you want the checks, just say so… Tell the gentlemen outside to bring the checks in."

Artie had several people with wastepaper baskets full of the checks waiting outside the Grand Jury room, and they brought them in.

I was not his attorney at that time and really had nothing much to do with it, but a friend of Artie's had asked him to help a man with an advertising agency in New York who wanted to get a liquor company client, and Artie told the liquor company that he'd appreciate it if the liquor company gave their advertising to the agency.

In gratitude, the head of the agency came to Artie and gave him a check for $250,000.

Artie explained that he didn't want anything for it, he had done it as as favor, but the advertising man had gone to his partners and told them that he had had a hard time getting Artie to do it and that he had promised Artie $250,000, and didn't want to look like a fool, coming back with the $250,000.

Artie took the check, and Artie endorsed it back and asked the advertising man for a list of his employees. Artie wrote the names down and had him the money distributed to the agency's employees.

However, the Internal Revenue Service was looking for ways to get Artie and charged him with tax fraud for not paying tax on the check, and Artie was convicted of tax fraud.

The judge thought very seriously of giving Artie probation after he heard the case, but Artie refused probation because he didn't want probation officers bothering his wife and his family. Artie prefered to serve his term without probation and the judge sentenced Artie to twenty four months at McNeil Island federal prison.

When Artie arrived at McNeil Island, he had his friends bring fantastic food into the prison at his expense: steaks every night for himself and all of the prisoners. The warden figured it wasn't hurting anyone to feed his prisoners good food, and Artie became the pet of the whole place.

On his release, everyone at Mc Neil Island gave him what they called a graduation party—with all the prisoners and all the guards attending—and Artie left prison with a celebration.

When Artie came back to San Francisco, he was no longer a lobbyist, but he had made investments which gave him all the money he needed to live on the rest of his life.

I first met Artie Samish in 1948. Since my father had owned and managed circuses and carnivals, I knew personally the owners and operators of circuses and carnivals throughout the United States and I formed an organization called the Western Outdoor Showmen's Association to protect and promote circuses and carnivals on the West Coast.

One of the owners of an outdoor show informed me that a bill had been introduced in Sacramento taxing circuses and carnivals and requiring licensing information from everyone working on circuses and carnivals. The bill would have made it impossible for a circus or carnival owner to operate in California, and the Showmen's Association wanted me to go to Sacramento to find out about the bill and stop it, if possible.

I had supported some of the assemblymen and senators in Northern California, so I flew to Sacramento and took a cab to the Senator Hotel across the street from the Capitol, and talked to a close friend of mine who I had helped when he ran for assemblyman, Charlie Meyers. I told Charlie why I was there and I asked him what advice he had. Charlie said the first thing I should do was to see Artie Samish.

Charlie told me Artie kept his office in a suite of rooms in the Senator Hotel and he agreed to introduce me to Artie.

Artie said he had nothing to do with the bill—he was not for it or against it—but not to worry. Artie said he didn't know who was behind the bill, but there was a lobbyist for the movie theaters who might feel that the circuses and carnivals might be competition, and Artie sent me to speak with her, telling her that he had sent me.

Hulda McGuinn, the lobbyist for the movie theaters told me she had nothing to do it the bill.

I also went to see Jerry O'Gara, a State Senator, about the bill (I had assisted him in his unsuccessful campaign for City Attorney).

When I told Senator O'Gara my problem, he said, "Don't worry, it's a cinch bill. If it gets by the Assembly, we'll knock it out in the Senate."

"What's a cinch bill?"

"That's where somebody introduces something in the legislature which is outrageous and a lobbyist works out a deal to kill the bill."

I thanked Jerry, but I had the feeling I didn't want the bill to go to the Assembly and have to wait for the Senate to defeat it.

That afternoon I went back to the Senator Hotel and Charlie Meyers invited me to a cocktail party for legislators and their friends in a banquet room in the Senator Hotel. Mr. Sebastian, the manager of the hotel, greeted the guests as the host of the cocktail party. Charlie told me that the party was actually being thrown by Artie Samish, but Artie didn't want to be the host, so the manager was acting as the host. After the party, Charlie went back to the Capitol across the street and I went to the bar.

A gentleman came over to me at the bar.

"Are you Nate Cohn? You're down here on the bill regarding carnivals and circuses, right? Let me buy you a drink. Maybe I can help you."

I ordered a drink and he ordered a drink. He brought out a big roll of $100 bills, and threw it on the counter. "I can take care of this for you. I'm a lobbyist. That's my job."

"Are you connected with Artie Samish?"

"No."

"With Hulda McGuinn?"

No, he had his own office.

"Then why are you doing this?"

"Don't you understand? I need $15,000 from you. You get 15 from your client. You keep 5, I get 5 and my friend who kills the bill gets 5."

I said I hadn't been sent to Sacramento to give away money.

I also realized all he had to do was to lie, and I would have no way to prove it, so I kept quiet.

"Wait a minute..." He went to the phone and came back.

"$9,000—3 for me, 3 for you, 3 for my friend who kills the bill..."

I explained I had no authority to give away money, and wasn't going to provide any money to kill the bill.

"Okay, $6,000. 2 for you, 2 for me, 2 for my friend who kills the bill..."

"I'll explain it once more. I'm not going to pay you money. And I'm not going to do something that doesn't look kosher."

He warned me the bill would go through.

Charlie Meyers had told me that Tommy Maloney was chairman of the committee which was going to hear the bill. I was friends with Tommy, so I went to see him. Tommy told me the bill was on the calendar for the next day, and to just come there and make a pitch. The bill's author was also on the committee.

At the hearing, I made my pitch. Tommy looked at the assemblyman who had authored the bill and announced, "It's been moved and seconded. This matter will be put over for three weeks."

Tommy told me not to worry, the bill would be killed when I came back in three weeks.

I got in touch with the head of the association of county fairs and told him that if the bill passed they would have no carnivals at any of the fairs. Then I contacted the Shrine, the American Legion and several other organizations which use carnivals and circuses to raise money for charities, and asked them to be at the next meeting or there would be no carnivals or circuses to sponsor their charitable works.

When I went back three weeks later, representatives of all these organizations were there. When Tommy saw how many people had come, he told me I needn't have done that, because the timetable would make it impossible to pass the bill. I asked him what I should do. He said he would take care of it.

When the bill came before the committee, Tommy said the bill had been withdrawn.

That was my first encounter with the legislature, a bill and Artie Samish.

I got to know Artie Samish better playing poker.

Jack Goldberger, who was the president of the Joint Council of Teamsters, was a good friend of Artie's and had a group called the Laborites which met for dinner Friday nights in a flat. Afterwards, a group of us—mainly Labor leaders—played poker. Artie joined us for the weekly poker games and as we got to know each other better, he started using me as a lawyer. Fortunately, everything I did for him was successful—all civil cases, nothing criminal.

When Artie saw what I was doing in my criminal cases, he used to tell me, "Nate, if you'd been my lawyer, you'd have gotten me acquitted."

"Artie," I reminded him, "if I had been your lawyer, I'd have worked for you maybe a week! In those days you told everybody what to do, and when you told me that the first time, I would have explained to you that

I don't do that. And the second time, I would no longer have been your lawyer."

"Oh no, we'd have gotten along," Artie insisted.

Artie never did anything halfway. One day he called me up. "You want to go to the track on Saturday?"

When Saturday came, he picked me up in a big Chevrolet made especially for him, and we traveled down 101 on Bayshore. When I say traveled, Artie didn't really drive the car, he just aimed the car and pushed his foot all the way down on the accelerator. When we reached the turnoff at Bay Meadows, I asked, "Why are you speeding like this? We're going to get killed here."

"I've got a horse that I was given in the first race—Number Five. I want to get there in time to place a bet."

When he turned off 101, all the traffic was stopped, so Artie pulled out of the traffic, across the sidewalk, and drove across lawns all the way to the racetrack turnoff.

"Artie, look what you're doing!"

"Don't worry about it," Artie tried to assure me.

"I'm not worried about it. I just don't like what you're doing to people's lawns!"

When we arrived at the racetrack, an attendant tried to stop Artie, but Artie just waved at him and drove to the front gate of the racetrack, left his car there and told the attendant: "Park it for me." Artie walked through the gate without a ticket, telling the guard, "He's with me."

As we were walked in, all I could think was: "That Number Five horse must be important!"

I don't bet a lot of money, but in this case, I extended myself. I bet twenty dollars on Number Five, which was at 5 to 1. Artie went to the fifty-dollar window.

When I caught up with Artie, he had a table for us in the best section of the track. Number Five got out in front and stayed there. I was pleased, I had a hundred dollars coming back, but Artie had a chagrined look on his face.

"Artie, what's the score? You flew out here. You drove through people's lawns, you broke every law on the books and you don't look happy."

"When I got here, one of my close friends said Five was not going to win, so I bet Number Two."

"I can't believe that you almost killed to play that Number Five. Then you come out here, and you get talked into betting on Number Two!"

"That's the way life is..." Artie philosophized.

—— • ——

One day, Artie came to me and said, "They want me to write a book about about my life. Eugene Burdick, who teaches political science over at the University of California, is very anxious to do the book. I want you to represent me." Burdick had just written the bestseller, *The Ugly American*. The project was promising.

"There's only one thing, Artie. You must put into your contract that I have the right to cut anything that might be damaging. You don't want to injure some friend of yours by having something in a book that could embarrass them."

Artie agreed that was an excellent idea.

I met Burdick and his wife for dinner at Orestes Restaurant, which I had a half-interest in, along with Artie. Burdick was young, muscular and clean-cut. After dinner, we went to Candlestick Park to watch the Giants play the Dodgers.

Artie didn't act like the average person who goes to the stadium, either. He drove through the gate to the ticket box and parked there. Then he walked right past the gate, taking us with him. He just told the ticket-takers it was okay—and he told them to watch his car. He didn't want to have to walk too far to his car because he was very heavy.

After the game we took Burdick and his wife back to Orestes Restaurant, and Burdick told me he was going to go to Palm Springs for a two-week vacation. He was going to start the book after he returned and he wanted to get together with me then.

Burdick went to Palm Springs a healthy young man and calm as a cucumber. In Palm Springs he fell over with a heart attack while playing tennis and died.

Now Artie was without an author for his book, so Artie suggested a gentlemen named Thomas who had written the life story of Jimmy Durante, who was a good friend of Artie's. Artie insisted on the same contract, including my right to strike anything I considered to be objectionable from the book.

When I received the galleys, I found that the author had used more than a bit of imagination in the book, and I struck out quite a bit. The author rewrote the book and it came back to me three or four more times. Finally, I told Artie: "I don't want to have to read that whole book every time. Just show me where he's changed it."

"He changed everything."

When I struck out everything I didn't like, however, the book had no novelty and it never hit. The book was entitled, *The Secret Boss of California*. I had suggested: "He Invented Chicanery," but the publisher preferred their title.

I still think I was right.

The Most Honorable Politician

37

In my long years of association with politics and politicians, one politician stands out as the most honorable I ever knew: Jesse Unruh. Unruh was the Speaker of the Assembly of California and had been the campaign manager in California for John F. Kennedy when he ran for President in 1960. Throughout the 1960's he was probably the most powerful man in California other than the Governor, Pat Brown, and they were rivals. Jess's people disliked Brown and Brown's supporters were worried about Jess—who they thought might run for governor against Pat Brown and beat him—than they were about any Republican rival.

When I met Jesse he was already a national figure. When he was running the Kennedy for President campaign, the papers had started called him "Big Daddy," as he was heavyset, many pounds overweight at the time, and he decided to slim down.

Sy Farber, who later became Vice Chancellor of the University of California Medical School, was Jess' doctor. Sy was also doctor to Pat Brown and practically all the politicians. Sy was helping Jess slim down, and Sy's office was in my building. Jess stopped in to see me.

My secretary announced, "Speaker Unruh is here." I was a little surprised to have the Speaker of the Assembly just drop in.

Jess told me he had a problem and that Sy had told him I was in a unique position to help him with his problem.

"If I can, I'd be happy to."

"A lobbyist came to me with a bill. I told him that I did not want to put it through this session, I would put it through next session, because it wouldn't go through this session. Everything was wrong. The atmosphere was wrong, the timing was wrong. The man went to another assemblyman, who did put in the bill, and the bill failed. Then he went to the Teamsters and told them I killed the bill."

Jess said he loved the Teamsters and had always been close to them. However, there was no way he could go to the Teamster officials and tell them he hadn't killed the bill because if he did, they would think he was trying to cover something up.

"Sy said you could take care of it."

I told him I would see what I could do.

"Thank you, Nate."

I asked him when he was coming back to see Sy.

"Next week."

"Come up next week and I'll have an answer for you then."

When I called Jack Goldberger, Jack got back to me in thirty minutes: "Tell Jess we love him. Don't worry about it."

Next week, I told Jess it had all been taken care of.

"Really?"

"Yeah. You want to call Jack Goldberger?"

"No, I take your word for it."

"Is there something I can do for you?" Jess asked.

"Not really."

We got to talking and could see that we were on the same team. Finally, just as he was about to leave, I said, "Wait a minute, Speaker, there is something you can do for me."

He looked at me as if to say, "Oh boy, here it comes..."

"I'm not going to ask you to do something for me, but my friend Judge Walter Carpeneti is the chairman of a committee that is trying get raises for the judges..."

"Oh no, we went through that with them. We told them no raises for any judges this session. Besides, why would you want us to do that?"

"You said to ask you if there was something I would like you to do. I would like to help Judge Carpeneti and I also think it would be good for everybody."

"How do you mean?"

"There are a lot of lawyers who would love to be judges and would be great judges, but they can't take the judgeship because they would have to reduce their living condition to take it.

"I had a chance to become a judge under Governor Knight, and when I checked out how much money I would have made, I came to the conclusion that I would have to sell one of my cars, I could buy no more suits, I would have to take my lunch to work and I couldn't go on any more vacations.

(l-r): Nate, Jesse Unruh, Speaker of the California Assembly and future California Senate President John Burton.

"Who wants to give up everything that you're doing in order to be a judge?"

He laughed. "You're a good salesman. Tell Judge Carpeneti he's got his raise."

"Thank you very much."

I went to the Calamari Club and told Judge Carpeneti, who had become Kingfish of the club after Judge Morris died: "Judge, the judges are going to get your raise." I could read his mind: a schnook lawyer is going to tell me that I'm going to get a raise?

"I talked to Jess Unruh. I asked him to get you a raise and he said he would."

Walter was very courteous, but I could read his mind, and he thought I was dreaming.

But the judges did get the raise. Jess reversed the decision.

Jess and I became quite friendly. We would have lunch together and talk, and any time a legislator or state official would get in trouble, Jess would have them see me and I became expert in putting out the fires.

I was very fortunate that only one of the legislators who got in any trouble received any kind of publicity. I kept everything out of the papers. I stopped every accusation and everyone that I handled was cleared with no problems.

The one legislator that got the publicity had a man working for him who went before the Grand Jury and told a phony story there. I went on television the next day and explained to the television audience that the charges were all a fraud and told them to pay no attention. The District Attorney took umbrage, but I pointed out, "You can bring any nut in there and I can't cross-examine him. It's very unfair." The Grand Jury threw the whole thing out.

"I owe you one."

"Well, you can do something for me. Two friends of mine were elected to the Assembly and I would be happy if you could make sure they are taken care of."

"Who are they?"

"Willie Brown and John Burton."

"Those two? The first week they were up here they were looking at ways to get rid of me. I slapped them down and they'll never be heard about again. To get to their office you'll have to go through the ladies room. No bill will ever come out with their name on it."

"You said you owed me one, and I'm asking for it. I want you to take care of the two of them."

Later on, at the Chicago Convention in 1968, Jess told me, "I'm glad you did what you did. Willie Brown is one of the brightest guys we've ever had here and John Burton has got more common sense than anybody out there. He just takes everything nice and easy. I love both of them now."

Everybody was happy. Willie Brown went on to replace Jesse as Speaker of the Assembly and later became Mayor of San Francisco, while John Burton became President of the California Senate.

One of the things I did for Jess was to hold a luncheon at Orestes Restaurant in San Francisco in his honor. He had a strong reputation in Southern California, but was not as well-known in northern California and if he was going to run for a statewide office later it would be impor-

tant, so I invited one hundred top political personages in San Francisco
to a lunch with Jess.

At the lunch, I took him around the tables and introduced him to
the people individually. After it was over, guests had to walk out through
an entrance which was only six feet wide, and Jess and I stood in front
of that entrance; as people left I introduced them to Jess.

One of them was Walter Carpeneti, who stopped to thank Jess for
getting the judges a raise.

"Don't thank me," Jess said, pointing at me. "Thank him."

Walter couldn't believe it.

That was the kind of guy Jess was.

One time I called Jess in Sacramento and he answered: "Nate, be
careful. They're going crazy up here in Sacramento. Everybody's bugging
everybody's phones. You don't know who's listening. Don't talk on the
phone."

"I didn't say anything wrong."

"I know, but they bug the phones."

"Jess, stop it."

"What?"

"You're the Speaker! Pass a law. The law now says that as long as one
person knows that the call is being bugged it's legal. All you have to do
is pass a law saying that both parties to the conversation have to know.
You have to fix it so the Police Department, in emergency cases, can do
it, but you don't have to protect anybody else. You're not worried about
the Police Department, you're worried about politicians who are bugging one another."

A week later, he introduced the bill into the Legislature, which
became known as the Unruh Act.

Then Hal Lipset, a top private investigator, called me.

"Nate, Jess Unruh is your friend. He just put a bill through that puts
me out of business. You know I go to a bar and I put an olive in the mar-
tini with the toothpick sticking out and I can bug conversations. I can
have a witness talk to me and rebut things he said in the case, and we
can kill them. I can do it for you."

"I can't tell him to kill the bill."

"Why not?"

"I'm the one who told him to pass it."

———— · ————

One time, Jess called me at home at midnight. He was back east at a meeting of legislators. A U.S. Senator was in some kind of trouble.

"Jess, I'm in San Francisco. You're back east. There's no way I can do anything."

"I thought you might think of somebody."

"Wait a minute. I have a friend of mine who's a lawyer there. Let me give you his number."

On the east coast it was three o'clock in the morning.

"Call him and call me back."

Jess called me back forty-five minutes later.

"I got a hold of your friend. He said he'd get out of bed to take care of it right now."

Jess called me back again an hour later. It was about two o'clock in the morning, California time. "Thanks Nate, everything is clear out here. Thanks very much."

Of all the legislators I helped, only one man thanked me. That was the man who had been investigated by the Grand Jury. He'd done nothing wrong.

I think a lot of legislators don't want to thank you because if they thank you, they think that would imply that they had done something wrong. In any event, none of the rest ever thanked me.

———— · ————

Jess appointed me on the California delegation to the Chicago Democratic Convention in 1968.

It was a decisive position at a decisive time. Jess was head of the delegation and Robert Kennedy, who had won the California primary, had been murdered, so the delegation's votes were up for grabs. Jess was for McGovern who was a friend of Kennedy's, but Jess told the entire delegation we were free to vote whatever way we thought best, and we were under no obligation to do what Jess thought.

At the convention, I was in the elevator and Jess joined me in the elevator.

"Nate, they're playing games with your friend, Joe Alioto." Alioto was the Mayor of San Francisco and a presidential aspirant. "He thinks they're going to make him the Vice Presidential nominee with Humphrey."

"What do you mean? Who's it going to be?"

"It's going to be Muskie."

"Who's he?"

"I don't know. Some senator from up north. He's going to be the nominee, and they've got your guy convinced he's going to be the nominee."

"He's not my guy."

"You ought to go over to his hotel and tell him."

"Jess, you don't know Joe. Joe is a very egotistical. If I tell him something like that, he's going to get angry at me for telling him. I'm not going to say a word."

"Well, they've got him making him the nominating speech and we've got to place him on our delegation to do that, or he can't go on the podium."

I suggested he throw out another delegate.

"I can't throw him out. He's there because of the position he has with Governor Brown."

"If you want me off the delegation, I'll withdraw."

"No, that's okay. I'll get someone else."

Jess found someone else to resign from the delegation and Joe Alioto was appointed to it, and he made the nominating speech for Humphrey.

I'd known Joe Alioto for a long time. I listened to it, and his heart was not in it. He must have found out that they weren't going to make him Vice Presidential nominee. He was a beautiful orator, but his speech was way below his average.

The convention was held at the stockyard auditorium, and it was stuffy inside the convention—there were people all around, some of them reading papers, some of them talking—and, frankly, it was boring.

I went outside and looked around for some relief—and found it. Right outside our caucus room was a room that said "Gulf"—Gulf Oil

Company. There were men drinking and pretty waitresses waiting on them. I asked the first man who came out: "What's this all about?"

"This is a special room for Gulf Oil."

"I own an interest in a car wash in San Francisco. We use Gulf gas. Does that make me eligible?"

"Sure. If you want to, come in."

They had three television sets there and I would go in and have sandwiches and drinks. When a caucus was called, all I had to do was walk across the hall.

Dr. Farber was also a delegate, so the next time I had a chance, I invited Sy to join me.

The Gulf room was filled with tall Texas oilmen with big hats and who looked tough as hell. On the television, we could see the Chicago police beating kids on the street in front of the hotels where the delegates stayed.

"That's good for 'em! Get 'em with the club!" The oilmen were cheering the police on.

Sy was a doctor and couldn't stand it. "Wait a minute. Do you realize what's happening? If they hit this poor kid on the head they could ruin him for life? For what? For picketing?"

I was afraid we'd be thrown out bodily, but nobody paid any attention and the next day, I took Jess' administrative assistant and Sy over there. When they called a caucus for California, we walked across the hall, and sat down with all the other delegates.

All the big shots that were in the delegation would come out of the hotel at three or four o'clock in the afternoon and get into buses, which would take them down to the auditorium. They had to sit in hot buses, then they'd go to the stockyard auditorium and eat hot dogs for dinner.

Mo Bernstein was a San Francisco Fire Commissioner. The first day, he said, "Nate, don't get on the bus."

He had called the Fire Commissioner of Chicago, who had assigned him a fireman and a limousine. Mo and I drove out to the auditorium in a limousine while everyone else was baking in these hot buses.

Then I invited Sy and Jess' administrative assistant. There was a big steak restaurant near the stockyards, and we would drive up in a limousine on our way to the auditorium. As we got out, the *maitre d'* would say, "Oh, Mr. Bernstein, we have your table."

We would have a great steak dinner, get back in the limousine, ride a short distance to the convention and go in while all the big shots were wiping the sweat from their brows with a hot dog to look forward to.

The buses would drive down one main street in Chicago where the houses on each side were painted in front and all the yards were beautifully manicured, and people on the route waved at the delegates, cheering them on. The driver of our limousine took us on the next street. The backs of the houses were a shambles, and the street was filthy. That was Mayor Daley's Chicago.

No newspapers or literature were allowed into the auditorium during the convention, but the day of the nomination Humphrey signs showed up all over, and newspapers supporting Humphrey. That was Daley's way, too.

One night, I took two friends from San Francisco out about four o'clock in the morning—Johnny Monihan, who had a bar in San Francisco, and George Moscone, who later became Mayor of San Francisco. We also had an Italian lawyer from San Francisco with us, a classy guy, and at four o'clock in the morning with perhaps two other people in the restaurant, the Italian lawyer decided he was going to go over the wine list with the captain.

"Why are you doing that at four o'clock in the morning?"

"I've got to have good wine."

I had a good time in Chicago, but it was a terrible situation. Kids were protesting outside our hotels and the police started beating everyone in sight with clubs.

What had happened was that Eugene McCarthy wanted to get the nomination and had invited all the hippies to come to Chicago and parade around the auditorium with signs to make the delegates think the people wanted McCarthy.

All the delegates came before the California delegation to appeal for our uncommitted votes. Jess favored McGovern. I liked Humphrey. McCarthy came before us and said, "I want you ladies and gentlemen to know that, in the entire world, I am the second most experienced economist."

That had to be the biggest piece of bull I had ever heard, and it turned me off. I wouldn't have anything to do with him after that.

The funniest guy was a comedian, Pat Paulsen. He came before us and if he had actually been a candidate, he would have won the California delegation because he was funny. McGovern was the Kennedy candidate. Humphrey was with the President, but the President backed away. He didn't even support him.

A colonel, Daley's number one assistant, gave us a briefing when we arrived. He declared the City welcomed us and it was ours to do whatever we wanted to do and to enjoy ourselves—but not after two o'clock in the morning. After that, he couldn't be responsible for what the Chicago Police might do.

I found out what he meant a short while later.

Hugh Hefner called me at the hotel and invited me to come to lunch at his castle in Chicago. Mel Belli was a friend of Hefner's and had told him I was in town.

I brought nine other delegates with me over to Hugh Hefner's. Hefner sent a Mercedes limousine and we went to the Playboy Castle, and they took us down to the dining room, but his assistant apologised for him: "Mr. Hefner is very sorry he can't join you, but he was out last night until four o'clock in the morning and he had a battle with a policeman. That kept him tied up until six or seven this morning. He had just got in and he was too knocked out to join you. You're invited to the parties he has at night."

Even Hugh Hefner had his problems with the Chicago police.

We couldn't go at night because that was during the convention, but Hefner's assistant took us through the whole place.

When Jess decided to run for Governor, he came up from Los Angeles with his friend, Manning Post, to talk to me and Mo Bernstein. Manning was the Treasurer for all his campaigns and for several Presidential candidates. Manning and Jess wanted to know what we thought Jess' chances were against Reagan in the gubernatorial election.

As Speaker of the Assembly Jess was the second most important politician in California, and a close friend, but I didn't want to tell him something that was primarily for my benefit rather than his.

I told him, "Jess, I don't know if you can beat Reagan. He's a popular Governor, he's an actor. But if you want to run, I'll personally do anything I can to help, and I'm sure Sy Farber will say the same thing." Mo told Jess he would support him. He was not eager for Jess to run for Governor, but he didn't want to come out against him. On the other hand, he didn't want to come out for him. Then we all went over to Sy Farber's apartment on Pacific Avenue in San Francisco to discuss it with him.

Sy told Jess that Jess should think about what he wanted to do, but that whatever Jess decided, he would unconditionally support Jess. Manning Post said whatever Jess wanted, he'd do.

I called over to Joe Piccinini, my partner at Orestes and told them to put together dinner for all of us and send it over to us in a cab, which he did. Jess said he would let us know what his decision was.

Some weeks later I received a phone call from Jess: "I've made up my mind. I'm going to go for it."

"If you do, I'll go with you."

"I want you to meet me down in Los Angeles at my house at ten o'clock in the morning."

I got on a plane and went down there. I took a cab out to his house, and there were cameras everywhere: newsreel cameras, TV cameras. I went up to the house. The man at the door said, "Nate, come in. Jess wants to see you." The front room was loaded with Jess' friends and supporters.

"I'm going to announce my candidacy," Jess said, "I want you to be here."

Everybody went back out through the front door of the house.

"Hold it a minute, Nate, I want to talk to you about something else… I want you to stand with me. You're going to be on national television. It'll be good for you to be seen on television all over California. When I make my announcement, you'll be the only one standing with me."

We went up there and I stood next to him as he made the announcement that he was going to run for Governor of California in the next election.

He was a hell of guy, but he was too honest. He would not take money from any organization or group that he'd done anything for. He wouldn't take any money from any group that he thought he might do something for in the future. Consequently, he had no money for his campaign.

Worse, someone in Los Angeles came up with an idea for an "easel campaign."

He set up an easel up in front of a man's home in Beverly Hills who had given Reagan a large contribution. He was surrounded by newspapermen and cameras.

"Now, this house here only pays taxes of x number of dollars. This house over here pays double the taxes…"

The man who owned the house came running out. He had been playing tennis, and was wearing tennis shorts and had a tennis racket.

"What's going on on my property?"

"I'm Jesse Unruh and I'm running for Governor against Ronald Reagan and I'm showing …"

"Get off my property! Get off my property! Who do you think you are, trespassing on my property!? Get out of here!"

The newspapers took it all down, while Jess stood there. What could he do?

Then he came up to San Francisco, and went out to Bay Meadows Race Track with an easel. The horse players were running into the track to make bets. They weren't interested in listening to what Jess was saying about taxes. He looked foolish.

I said to myself: "This is ridiculous!"

Finally, Manning Post called me up.

"Nate, we understand you're unhappy."

"I've got things going up here for Jess. Jess will carry San Francisco, maybe a good part of Northern California. But, from what I understand, you guys are screwing it up down there."

"Well, come down and see us."

I went down there and Manning Post had an office in a big storefront. He was Treasurer for the whole Unruh campaign. They took me around and showed me the place.

I went up to Manning. He said, "Should we go have lunch?"

"Yes, let's do that."

Over lunch, I told him how serious it was. "There's no way we're going to win this election. What I wanted to do was to go on television and say, 'Jesse Unruh did this, Jesse Unruh did this, Jesse Unruh did this...' I don't like a negative campaign. He taught at one of the big colleges. He put together all the legislative programs for the different states. He helped all the assemblies in the United States form an organization. He did all kinds of things. They're talking about an easel campaign—what Mr. Reagan did or what he didn't do."

But it was too late; and things didn't get better with the campaign, and it wasn't just the easels.

One day, Jess' son was in a car with some idiots, and was stopped by the police. It turned out that someone in the car had marijuana on him, so Jess had to get him out of trouble.

Jess wanted to get the kid away from his idiot friends, and he called me because he wanted to have him shipped out with the Marine Cooks and Stewards Union as a waiter. I called Ed Turner who was a close friend and was head of the union, and Ed set it up. Jess came up to San Francisco and took a whole day off of his campaign to get the kid straightened out and get him shipped out. When we finished, it was close to dinner time. I said to Jess, "Let's go have dinner."

"Where do we go?"

"I have a favorite Italian restaurant, the greatest food around."

We went to a little restaurant in North Beach, La Pantera. The whole thing was family-style. You sat at a table with ten people. They heard who Jess was and the owner came over and joined us. They were having the greatest time, singing songs.

As I was driving Jess back to the airport, he turned to me and said, "You know, Nate, this has been the best day I've had in this whole damned campaign."

I had everything in San Francisco tied up for Jess. I had no loopholes. In fact, Sam Yorty who was a close friend of mine, had asked me to help in his campaign for the nomination. I told him I couldn't help him because I was campaigning for Jess. One day, Yorty's campaign manager came up to see me.

"I wanted to see who the hell you are. Everywhere I've gone in San

Francisco, you've got it all tied up. I can't get in!"

"I told Sam I couldn't support him."

"I know. He told me that, but I thought I'd get somebody, instead of nobody..."

We had big dinner for Jess at the Press Club. I was the chairman of the dinner. My wife Carolyn was sitting next to Jess' wife. We got through with the dinner. I had all these people enthused about Jess. My wife said to Jess, "Can I talk to you for a minute?"

"Of course."

"You're going to have to take your wife to a beauty parlor, and get her hair cut. You're to have to get her to lose about ten or fifteen pounds, and you're going to have to go to a clothing store and get her some clothes that look halfway decent."

She was talking about his wife who was only a several feet away from her!

Jess? I could hear him. "I understand, I understand. Thank you, Carolyn. Thank you, Carolyn."

Jess was the most honorable guy I ever saw in politics.

You Can Sue City Hall, But...

38

The old adage has it that you can't sue City Hall. You can. But whether you have what it takes to win is another matter entirely, as I found out when I represented the foreman of the San Francisco Grand Jury, Henry North, in suing Mayor George Christopher for defamation.

Henry North was the Executive Vice President of Metropolitan Life Insurance Company. Metropolitan had a building which took a whole block on California Street, a block below Powell Street. The Ritz Carlton Hotel occupies the building now.

North became very active in San Francisco and was a member of the exclusive San Francisco clubs and was also involved in many enterprises in San Francisco for the benefit of the city, and everyone knew Henry. He was accepted by the city and he became a San Franciscan immediately.

When North was out being entertained or when he was entertaining others, he drank. He would go to luncheons and have a drink or two. On many occasions you could see he had had a couple of drinks— maybe too much—when he went out in the evenings. But he never bothered anyone.

Henry North was in his sixties and was known as a swinger. He never did anything outlandish, but there was no argument that when he went out at night sometimes he had one too many. However, he always had a driver, so he didn't have to worry about driving under the influence.

When he was appointed to the San Francisco Grand Jury by one of the judges, the judge in recognition of his position and his importance made him the foreman of the Grand Jury. Henry was very proud of his position as foreman of the Grand Jury.

One day, one of the members of the Grand Jury suggested that they invite the Mayor of San Francisco, George Christopher, to tell the Grand Jury about Candlestick Park. There was a lot of talk about people making money off the building of Candlestick Park and they wanted to straighten things out as to what the truth was about the building of the ballpark. Some of the property where Candlestick Park was built was landfill. Originally, the property had sold for very little money, but it became quite valuable when the City decided to build the stadium on it. There were a lot of people who had had the foresight to buy property out there, even though it was in the worst part of San Francisco, at the end of Hunters Point, and there was talk whether the windfall for these investors had been arranged for intentionally.

Mayor Christopher, at the time Candlestick Park was built, was a Supervisor. He and another Supervisor, Francis McCarthy, who later became a Superior Court judge, saw that Big League baseball was going to move to the West Coast. The owner of the Brooklyn Dodgers wanted to move his team to Los Angeles because there were so many people in Los Angeles, and he wanted to move there fast. However, the other owners would not let him come out California by himself. The owners said if he could get somebody to move another team to San Francisco when he went to Los Angeles, that they would go along with his request.

He sold Horace Stoneham, who owned the New York Giants, on the idea that San Francisco was a great baseball town and that Stoneham should move his team to San Francisco while he went to Los Angeles. Stoneham went for it.

When it became known that it was possible that a Big League baseball team would come to San Francisco, Christopher and McCarthy contacted the baseball league and Stoneham and were told that if the city built a stadium in San Francisco, there would be a team. They had to either have a stadium, one under construction or one about to be constructed.

The San Francisco Seals had a stadium at 18th and Potrero. It was a beautiful stadium, but it only seated thirty thousand to forty thousand people. There were plans to add another twenty or twenty-five thousand people to the stadium by building the stadium up, but there would be no parking.

At that time, Ben Swig, who owned the Fairmont Hotel, suggested that the city build the stadium in downtown San Francisco so people could go to the baseball games on a streetcar or walk over from their offices, or take a short cab ride. However, there was this property out in the Candlestick Park area and a contractor, Harney, who wanted to build the stadium there. The city had a group work on building the stadium. They formed a nonprofit corporation and started buying property out in Hunter's Point, and hired Harney to build it. They hired an architect by the name of Bolles to design the stadium. Bolles was a well-known architect in San Francisco and had a fine reputation, but he had never built a stadium of any kind. Bolles obtained the plans for a Portuguese soccer stadium and used those plans to build Candlestick Park.

Harney wanted the stadium named Harney Stadium, but the Supervisors insisted on Candlestick Park. Harney became somewhat angry over that, but he had made quite a bit of money on the building of the stadium.

The City used funds that had been approved for the project by the voters, but they also used funds from other monies that had been appropriated for other matters, such as sewers, etc., and the five million dollar stadium—which had been more or less voted on by the people—cost a great deal more. And when it was built, there were certain sections where—if you sat on the left side, the third-base side—you couldn't see the left-field wall. If you sat on the first-base side, you couldn't see the end of the right-field wall. The wind was terrible. And the city ended up putting more money into the stadium.

All these stories were being tossed around in San Francisco when Mr. North's Grand Jury invited Mayor Christopher to answer their questions.

George Christopher was now the Mayor of San Francisco, a mayor well-liked and well-respected in San Francisco, and a very personable man. The Grand Jury asked him many questions, but Mr. North leaned over backwards to be courteous and polite to the Mayor, and then Christopher had the whole Grand Jury in the palm of his hands.

After the Mayor appeared before the Grand Jury, Henry North thought it would be a good idea to be open with the city. He had a court reporter put the proceeding into transcript form with all the questions and answers, and he paid for it out of his own pocket. He then distributed copies of the transcript to all of the Grand Jurors and to the press, and the press called on Mayor Christopher, telling him that they had a copy of what he had said before the Grand Jury.

Christopher became furious. He had believed that what that he said before the Grand Jury would not be released to the public, and feeling that way when he testified, it seems Mayor Christopher had taken some liberties and now was having second-thoughts about his testimony.

The reporters gave him a copy of the transcript, and before he really even had a chance to read it, they started asking him questions about the Grand Jury testimony. Mayor George Christopher, who could be intemperate, declared, "Well, Henry North was drunk and incoherent when I was in there!"

The reporters wrote it all down.

Mayor Christopher pounded it in more by saying, "...and I was told when he was named to the Grand Jury that he was fixable."

The reporters wrote that down, too.

Mayor Christopher's statements came out in all the papers, declaring that Henry North, the foreman of the Grand Jury and chairman of an insurance company, was fixable, drunk and incoherent.

There was quite a turmoil—after all, a mayor's word carries a lot more weight than that of the average person—and I received a phone call from Henry North about a week later saying he wanted to have lunch with me at the Fairmont Hotel. I knew Henry and we had been friendly, but I had never represented him. We were not close friends, and we had never been out together. We knew each other primarily from civic functions and dinners.

When we met, Henry was cold sober.

"You know what's happened," he said. "It's really hurt me quite a bit. It makes me look very bad. It makes the company look bad, and it isn't true. I was cold sober when I was there.

"I don't know where he got the idea that I'm 'fixable.' I've got all the money I want. I've got all the power I want. I've got all the prestige I want. Why would I take money, or be fixable? It's ridiculous. I want to sue the mayor."

The year was almost 60% over when we met. "If you sue him, you're going to fix it so the Grand Jury can't function for the rest of the year, because you'll be involved in a lawsuit and you're the foreman. I don't know how they could do it, but all the work that the Grand Jury is doing would be marked off for the end of the year. You could sue him, but what I would suggest is that you wait until December 31st—you have plenty of time because it's been only a short time since he made the statement. Wait until December 31st, and then file the lawsuit and

brought motions before Judge Devine. We started at 9 o'clock in the morning and I had to argue—with time off for lunch—until 4:30 in the afternoon against his motions. When he finished, however, every motion had been denied. I was still in the ballgame—as it were.

On one occasion, I received a telephone call from the editor of the *San Francisco Chronicle*. A reporter at the *Chronicle* had complained to the editor about my client. It seems he went over to the Metropolitan Life Insurance Company's headquarters to interview Henry North just before lunchtime. The reporter went to the secretary and wanted to see North, but North wouldn't see him because he was busy. The reporter kept bothering him, and finally, North sent for two security people who took the reporter and physically carried him all the way from North's office around the building and threw him on the lawn.

"What in the world is going on, Henry? We don't want the press to be antagonized by us. You take a good reporter and your security people pick him up and throw him out on your front lawn like that?"

"He kept bugging me."

"Henry, you could have just said a word to him."

"I was busy. I had to go somewhere."

"Where did you have to go?"

"I had to go to a luncheon given by the San Francisco Advertising Club. I was the main speaker—on good public relations."

"Henry, I hope you told them how you got good public relations with the *Chronicle*!"

I also took the deposition of Mayor Christopher. In taking his deposition, I tried to be as gentlemanly as possible. My office was filled with reporters and they were waiting for something to happen, or for me to attack him or do something wrong, but nothing like that was going to happen. I got all the information I wanted and I got down the name of the person who allegedly told him that Henry was fixable, and Christopher said it was Johnny Shannon.

I knew that I had a declaration in my pocket that said this wasn't true, and I had a few other things that I could impeach Christopher with. As I was finishing up, I asked, "Now, Mayor Christopher, you know you have a reputation for once in a while blowing up a little bit. Isn't that true?"

"Yes, but you do, too—like the time you asked me to make you police commissioner and I turned you down."

That was too much. "That's a damned lie! At no time did I ever ask you for any appointments to anything, especially as police commissioner.

"You want to play that way?"

I pulled out a file I had obtained from the Attorney General's office concerning Christopher's conviction for price-fixing on milk during World War II and I started asking him some embarrassing questions. As soon as I asked him the questions his lawyer objected to them and told him not to answer. I asked him two questions and then said to myself, this is silly, and said to Christopher and to his lawyer, "My reputation as a gentleman is more important than my getting back at this gentleman for lying about me. So, I have no further questions."

The press thought they were going to have some excitement and I had let it die.

Christopher stood up and one of the reporters asked him for a picture shaking hands with me. He had his right hand out, but I stood behind my desk with my two hands at my sides.

Eventually, I relented. "I'm only doing this for you," I replied, and as I went to put out my hand, Christopher dropped his hand, saying, "I'm not going to shake hands, either!" And he stormed out.

The whole city was talking about the lawsuit. There was a streetcar that went by City Hall and one of the motormen on the line would yell out to the passengers "On your right is the City Hall, occupied by Mayor George Christopher. After the lawsuit is over, Mr. Cohn will own that whole building," and everyone would laugh.

One morning I was sitting in my office and a reporter for the *News* by the name of Joe Murphy came by. Murphy was a great reporter. He was the kind of reporter that you see in the old movies, getting tremendous stories out of nothing. Joe drank a little—well, he drank a lot, and he came over to my office one morning on a Thursday at about 9 o'clock.

"What's up?"

"I want to talk to you. I was down this way anyway and I wanted to ask you something."

"What's that?"

"What's happening in the Christopher case?"

"Nothing. We're waiting to get a date to go to trial."

"Is there anything happening?

"No."

"Did you talk to anybody?"

"No.

"Do you want to go downstairs to the place next door and have a cup of coffee?"

"Sure."

We went downstairs for a cup of coffee and we talked generally. Then he said, "Let me ask you a question, Nate."

"Sure."

"Would you settle this case?"

"Any lawyer will settle a case."

"Well, what would you settle it for?"

"I don't know. We're suing for a couple of million and if we got half of that we'd probably settle it." That's all I said to him.

"Okay."

We talked some more and he left.

That was on a Thursday. Thursdays an organization called Saints and Sinners met for lunch at the Mark Hopkins Hotel. Jake Ehrlich was the Ringmaster of the Saints and Sinners, but he cut the name down to "Master." Jake loved that, because when people called Jake "the Master," other people didn't realize they were talking about him as Ringmaster of the Saints and Sinners. They thought it meant he was a master lawyer, which he was, too.

I got to the hotel a little after lunch. The *maitre d'* in the room where we were having the meeting of the Saints and Sinners came over to me. "Will you call the editor of the *Call-Bulletin*?"

I did.

"I thought we were friends!"

"I thought we were friends, too."

"Well, why did you have a press conference and not invite us?"

"What press conference?"

"On the front page of the *News* is a headline: 'Christopher-North Case Might Be Settled.' Then there's a two-column story going from the headline to the bottom of the page saying there might be a settlement, that you're willing to settle for a million dollars."

"Joe Murphy came over and had a cup of coffee. He asked me the question, 'Will you settle?' I said, 'Sure.' He said, 'What would you settle for?' I said, 'I don't know—a million bucks.' That's all I said."

"God damn that Murphy! You know, there's only one thing I'm happy with."

"What?"

"That the *News* doesn't have two Murphys!"

We were only a month away from trial when I received a phone call one morning from another reporter, "Nate, I don't know if you know what's happening, but North is getting ready to dismiss the case."

"I've never heard anything like that. He hasn't talked to me."

"Check it out."

I tried to get a hold of Henry North, but I couldn't get a hold of him. Then another reporter called me. "You know what happened?"

"What happened?"

"This is the story I got: Henry North was in Las Vegas and J. Joseph Sullivan"—a close friend of Christopher's—"was in Vegas and saw Henry there. Henry was having a good time and drinking quite a bit. Sullivan kept feeding him drinks and got on the plane with North. They flew to Los Angeles from Vegas late at night and then took a plane from Los Angeles to San Francisco. In Los Angeles, Sullivan called Christopher. Sullivan kept buying North drinks and North was smashed. They got into San Francisco early in the morning and Sullivan told North he was going to drive him home.

"He put North in his car and drove out to Christopher's home and then stopped the car. By this time it was 5 or 6 o'clock in the morning, and Sullivan told North he had to make a stop. North asked him who he was going to see. North told Sullivan he couldn't see Christopher because he had a lawsuit against him, and he was going to go to trial but Sullivan assured North, 'Henry, you're a bigger man than that. That's all foolishness. You don't have to hide from anyone. Come on in. It will just take a minute.'

"So, they went in," the reporter told me, "and they gave North almost a bottle of Scotch and Sullivan told North how if he went to trial, the lawyers were going to cross-examine him and he was going to look terrible, he was going to embarrass his family and they were going to take him apart, and he was not going to get anything out of it because he'd already said he's giving the money to charity. The next thing you know, they got North to sign a paper saying that he was going to dismiss the case. Then they took him home and they all agreed to meet in Christopher's office later that morning."

The reporter said they met in Christopher's office, where they announced to the press that North was filing a dismissal with prejudice in his lawsuit against George Christopher and then was going out to the ballgame with Christopher.

In the meantime, one of the supervisors, another friend of Christopher's, came to my office and told me that North had dismissed the case.

I was astonished. He never called me. He never said a word to me.

There was nothing I could do. I tried to call North, but I couldn't reach him. He was in the Mayor's office and then they were going out to the baseball game. The headlines read: "North's Suit Against Christopher Dismissed."

The next day, North went back to his office. None of his friends could fathom what had happened and one of the reporters at the *Chronicle* printed a story about what had happened that made North look terrible. He was made to look like a loser and most of North's friends dropped him like a hot potato. He ended up moving out of his house into the Press Club for awhile. North went down the drain. It was really something.

That ball game was the last time Christopher ever talked to North.

I never held what happened against George Christopher. I did hold it against J. Joseph Sullivan. When Sullivan ran for City Attorney, I did everything I could to defeat him—and he was defeated.

I understood what Christopher's position was. When someone is facing a two-million-dollar lawsuit, he is under tremendous pressure to do anything to get out of it. Christopher didn't do anything illegal. Sullivan, who was a lawyer, was wrong in what he did, but he lost out on being City Attorney as a result, and he soon drifted out of sight and passed away.

George Christopher became a good friend of mine and I still have great respect for him as a man and as Mayor of the City of San Francisco.

Playing Poker with Jimmy Hoffa... and the True Story of Jack Ruby

39

I was the attorney for the American Guild of Variety Artists on the West Coast, and, in addition, I represented quite a few people in show business. Being the attorney for a labor union, I was also invited by Jack Goldberger to become a member of an organization called the Laborites.

Jack Goldberger was one of the top Teamster officials and head of the San Francisco Labor Council. When the Teamsters withdrew from the Labor Council, Jack formed little group across the street from the Labor Council, and called it the Laborites. On Friday nights we would have dinner at the Laborites, prepared by some of the members, and we would play poker afterwards, and I got to be steady up there. The food was excellent and I liked to play poker.

One night, there was an AFL-CIO convention in town, and the Teamsters held a joint convention with the AFL-CIO. Jack Goldberger brought some of the top Labor leaders from all over the United States up to the Laborites to have dinner, and a couple of them would play cards.

We were playing poker, and there was one fellow at the end of the table to my left who was a labor official from New York City. He was a lousy poker player, but a nice guy, and I was concentrating on him and paying no attention to the man on my right. After a couple of hours of playing, there was a pot I split with the player to my right and I looked at him said, "Darn it, you look familiar. I just can't place you."

"I'm Jimmy Hoffa."

"That shows you how bright I am!" He laughed and became quite friendly. Hoffa was a very close friend of Jack's.

Several years later, Jimmy Hoffa was incarcerated in a Midwestern penitentiary. One Friday night, Jack Goldberger saw me at the

Laborites, and told me, "You know, Jimmy Hoffa's wife is in a hospital here in San Francisco, and she has a very bad heart. Can you recommend someone to check her out?"

Sy Farber was Vice Chancellor of the University of California Medical School and one of the top internists in the country.

"Can you call Dr. Farber and have him check her out?"

I called Dr. Farber and I told him what had happened. He said he would take care of it.

One hour later, Dr. Farber called me and said he had had Mrs. Hoffa transferred to the University of California hospital. Jack told me he wanted to thank me.

I told him I was happy to do it and asked him to thank Sy, because he was the one responsible.

A week later, I received a telephone call from Jimmy Hoffa's lawyer.

"Nate, Jimmy is in San Francisco at the Hilton Hotel, and he wants you to come by so he can thank you for everything you've done for him. Can you drop by this evening after work?"

"Sure."

At the Hilton Hotel, Jimmy Hoffa, who was supposed to be in federal prison, was in a two-floor suite with his lawyer. Henry Lewin, who was running the hotel, was also there.

Hoffa's lawyer explained to me that Dr. Farber had called President Nixon and told him that Mrs. Hoffa was in dire circumstances, and that she needed to see her husband. He had asked the President to make arrangements so Jimmy could visit his wife. President Nixon had Jimmy Hoffa released from the penitentiary into the custody of his lawyer, and Jimmy had flown out to San Francisco with his lawyer on a commercial airline, without any marshals or deputies, and to the Hilton Hotel, where they took rooms.

Jimmy said he wanted to thank me. He had been up to see his wife and was spending time with her.

He was in the hotel without handcuffs or any restraints of any kind. I couldn't believe it, but Hoffa was busy talking to some people, and I was in a hurry to go somewhere, so I told the lawyer to give him my regards, and that I appreciated his thanks, and I left.

The lawyer called me back several times over the next few days—Jimmy wanted me to join him for dinner. Jimmy was there for about a week until his wife was better. Then he returned to prison.

I can't ever recall hearing of a person in a federal penitentiary being released to his lawyer to go visit his wife, especially a highly publicized person such as Jimmy Hoffa, and the person doing it being the President of the United States, but I saw it with my own eyes.

Since the day he shot President Kennedy's accused assassin, Lee Harvey Oswald on national television, I have been reading stories about Jack Ruby which are unbelievable. Everyone who seems to want to write a book or get their name in the paper, writes a story about the Kennedy assassination or Jack Ruby in order to get attention or sell books. I knew something about Jack Ruby through a friend of mine, Benny Barrish.

Benny was very well-known in San Francisco. He was a prizefighter, then he sold liquor, and then he had a bail bonds office. I had represented him in the Tarantino matter.

Everybody liked Benny and he ingratiated himself with all of the policemen. He liked the idea of doing things for people and having people like him and respect him. He used to come up to the Laborites because he was very close to Jack Goldberger.

Jack would do anything for anybody. If he could do you a favor he'd do it, regardless. He was also very legitimate, and Jack was good at settling strikes and the public officials in San Francisco used Jack to settle many strikes, not just Teamster strikes.

Jack liked Benny and Benny would come up and have dinner with us at the Laborites. Benny wouldn't play cards, but he would hang out there and have dinner and then he would leave.

One evening I was having dinner and Benny came over and asked me for a favor.

"If I can do it, Benny, I'll try. What is it?"

"I've got a friend of mine who has a little strip club in Dallas, Texas. He used to run a strip club in the Tenderloin District with his sister, but he couldn't make a buck here. He's a nice guy, but he's having trouble making money. He just can't seem to get off the goose egg."

"What do you mean?"

"Well, he was here and he tried everything he could to make the club go. His club was one of the few clubs in San Francisco that couldn't make a dime. Someone suggested that they didn't have many clubs like that in Dallas, Texas, and he and his sister sold their club and moved to Dallas, Texas. They didn't get much for their club in San Francisco so they opened a club with everything they had in Dallas."

"So?"

"Well, he's been trying to get it off the ground. He's inviting the cops to come there as his guests every night. He's doing everything he can but he can't get it off the ground. He's having problems."

"Well, what can I do?"

"He has to pay AGVA, the entertainer's union, a certain amount of money that goes in their retirement plan and their health and welfare. He hasn't been able to pay that. Now the union is threatening to close his club if he doesn't pay it."

"Well, how much does he owe?"

"I think he owes about $500."

"Benny, you mean the man can't dig up $500?"

"No way. He can't dig up five hundred cents. He's got no connections that will help him. He's got no places where he can borrow money. He's got no people there that really want to help him financially.

"You're the attorney for AGVA on the west coast. Dallas is included in the American Guild of Variety Artists' west coast office. If you could call Irv Mazzei who is the head of the AGVA on the west coast and ask him to give this guy some slack, give him two or three more months to pay the $500; he wants to pay it as fast as he can, but Mazzei is going to close him."

"I'll see what I can do."

Monday morning I called Irv Mazzei in Los Angeles and told him the story.

Irv understood. "The guy's broke. He's telling the truth. He's just not making a dime in there. He's got nobody that he knows that he can go to for money. He's got no way to get any money except through the place. If you ask me to, I'll extend it for three months. He won't pay anything for three months and tell him to save whatever he can save and at the end of the three months, see if he can pay me the $500. If he can't, don't tell him, but I'll give him another extension. The guy really has no connections. He has nobody at all to help him and I know he's not making any money."

The next Friday, I told Benny Barrish about the extension. Benny thanked me profusely and he called the fellow—his name was Jack Ruby—and told him that I had fixed it for him and he had some extra time.

"Thanks, Nate. If I had any money I'd loan it to Jack, but I'm short of money too. The poor guy doesn't have dollar one. He's got no connections."

"Doesn't he know anybody in Dallas that could help him?"

"He doesn't have any connections with anybody that could help him."

"Okay, if you have any more problems let me know."

Some time later, I was at home and I was watching television. The President of the United States had been shot and killed, and I saw Jack Ruby in the downstairs area of the police department walking around. In fact, he struck me because he reminded me very much of Benny Barrish. I saw him walk up and shoot Oswald, the man who was accused of killing President Kennedy. I realized that that was the same man that Benny asked me to talk to American Guild of Variety Artists about. I was very surprised and shocked.

Several days later, Benny called and wanted to talk to me again. I asked Benny to come on down to the office and Benny told me more about Ruby.

Benny told me about the strip joint that Jack Ruby and his sister owned in the Tenderloin and how he had bought the club in Dallas. Because the club was doing so poorly,, Ruby became very friendly with the cops in Dallas. He would invite the cops to come to his show and see his show and have drinks free. He was cultivating policemen and politicians in Dallas, but he still couldn't make any money.

I had the idea, and I told Benny, that I felt that Ruby believed that Oswald had killed the President and Ruby wanted to be a hero and he shot him.

Benny asked me if I would be interested in defending Jack Ruby in the criminal case for killing Oswald.

"Of course I would. It is one of the biggest cases I ever have seen. It is a worldwide interest case, but, let me tell you something, I have an obligation not only to do a job for clients when I get them, but also to advise people in their best interest. I'd love to do the case. I'm not worried about the money, I'd do it for free. But, for Ruby's own interest, Ruby should hire a white Baptist criminal lawyer from Dallas. He should get the best criminal lawyer in Dallas who is a Baptist.

"If you bring in a Jewish lawyer like me from San Francisco to defend a Jewish guy who's charged with a crime in Dallas, Texas, he is going to lose points with juries and with judges.

"If you have a local lawyer who is a white Baptist, a top criminal lawyer in Dallas who is respected by the judges and by the people, they'll give Ruby a medal rather than send him to jail."

Benny said he would tell Ruby's sister what I had advised.

Benny called me back. "Nate, I talked to Jack's sister and they've been talking to people and they feel that they have to plead Ruby not guilty by reason of insanity. The case will be a psychiatric defense.

"Somebody told her that the best lawyer in the United States in that type of a case is Mel Belli because Mel has tried a lot of cases where they sued for mental damage and for mental incapacity. They think that he knows more about medicine than a lot of doctors and that the traumatic stress syndrome and the traumatic stress of his mind at that time is the way to defend him."

I didn't want to say anything. Mel Belli was as good as a lawyer as you could get, but I did say that, with all due respect, I still thought she should get a Baptist lawyer from Dallas.

I explained that the Dallas jury were going to look at Mel as an Italian lawyer from San Francisco. I didn't know whether that would play. I knew damn well that if they had me, they'd think, "A Jewish lawyer from San Francisco to defend a Jewish guy from Dallas," and I would have points against me with the jurors even though I thought it was a defensible case."

That's how Ruby got Mel. The media pictured Mel as kind of a colorful, loud, flamboyant lawyer. For a case like that in Dallas, Texas, that meant that Mel was swimming with a hundred pound sack on his back.

Mel was an excellent lawyer, but in that one case I don't think Ruby did as well as he could have.

I kept reading about Ruby and seeing movies about Ruby and from what Benny told me they're not 99, they're 105% wrong. Ruby was not a mobster, he had no connections and he never went to Cuba to kill Castro. 101% of all of the fiction that came out of the studios and the books really was foolishness.

A Bit
About Belli

40

Many years before, when I was first starting to practice law, a tall, good-looking black man came into my office. He had been working for a general contractor building San Francisco Airport and the general contractor for the job had loaned him to a sub-contractor. The sub-contractor had hired workers to plant bricks of dynamite in the ground and blow them up, then another crew would drill with jackhammers into the ground around the holes. On this occasion, my client was operating a jackhammer which hit some unexploded dynamite. The explosion threw the jack-hammer into his left shoulder and broke it.

My client had gone to several lawyers, but when they examined the case, they had come to the conclusion that it was a workmen's compensation case, and my client could not sue for damages. Somehow, he had heard of a case or two that I had tried, even though I was young at the time, and thought I might be able to help him.

Since I was not besieged with prospective, lucrative clients I took the case. I had plenty of time for research, and I came up with the theory that my client was a special employee of the sub-contractor. When the general contractor had loaned him to the sub-contractor, the sub-contractor had control over him, and the sub-contractor was responsible for any damages done to my client and my client was not covered by the sub-contractor's workmen's compensation coverage since he was an employee. Under that theory, I sued the sub-contractor for general negligence and took depositions. My theory survived demurrers and I ended up on trial in Redwood City.

About three weeks before the trial date, I took the file and called Ingmar Holberg, who was at that time, one of the top personal injury lawyers in California. Holberg took many cases from other lawyers to try for them.

I left the file with him and he told me to come back a week later.

When I went back, he told me there was no way he could work this case into his calendar. I got the message Holberg didn't think much of the case, so on that note, I would have to try it for what it was worth.

The case was assigned for trial to Judge Edmund Scott. I had never met Judge Scott, but I was told by the lawyers in San Mateo County that he was a very tough judge, but he knew his law. I was opposed by the law office of Alexander, Bacon and Mundhenk. Mundhenk was known to be a crafty and exceptionally well-qualified defense attorney, and juries found his personality pleasing. Mr. Bacon would argue points of law with the judge, and was a master writer of briefs. It seemed I was thoroughly outclassed.

I had been warned by other lawyers to prepare to try the case very quickly. If another judge had tried the case, the case might go three weeks, but Judge Scott, they advised me, would try the same case in a week. Still, they assured me, Judge Scott knew his law.

Mr. Mundhenk offered me some advice the first day: "I can see you are going to be a fine lawyer, but let me tell you something. What you should do is have the court reporter prepare the transcript of the previous day's testimony overnight. They get it to you about 5:00 in the morning, and then you can go over it, to make sure that you know what the testimony was."

I smiled and said, "Thank you very much, Mr. Mundhenk, that's very good advice, except there's one thing wrong with your advice. I have a total recall memory and I can remember all the testimony that was given in the case word for word."

He walked away.

During the trial, Mr. Mudhank's office brought in several expert orthopedists who testified that the injury to my client's shoulder was not actually causing him any trouble because, instead of taking the shoulder blade and putting it together, then waiting for it to heal, they overlapped one part of the shoulder blade on top of the other, and the two orthopedists said that this made the shoulder strong, because instead of one bone, my client had two bones sealed together.

I asked the doctors where they went to school. One of them said he went for school to a top university in the area, and I asked him if he went to the school's football games.

"Yes, I do."

"You'd do anything to help the football team win, wouldn't you."

"Yes."

"Did you ever think of going to the coach and suggesting that he break the collarbones of the linemen so the bones of their collarbone would be stronger?"

Before Mr. Mundhenk, or even Judge Scott, could realize where I was going, the jury broke up. The doctor became embarrassed, and I let him go.

My doctor was a general practitioner. He had a little office out on Ocean Avenue, and didn't specialize in anything, but he was the only doctor I could afford to bring into court. I examined my client's chart with him in his office before his testimony, and I went over his report. I noticed at the bottom of the report he put down that my client had athlete's foot. When we went over it, he said, "I shouldn't have mentoned athlete's foot, because this is an injury to the shoulder."

"No, you mention athele's foot, too."

"Why?"

"What happens when a person gets nervous? They perspire."

"That's true."

"I once had athlete's foot when I was playing basketball in high school, and the doctor told me that the reason I had it was because after I took a shower I didn't completely dry my toes, or, when I was playing my feet would perspire, and the perspiration would cause the athlete's foot. When a person has a pain in the shoulder, and they're nervous about their body, they perspire."

He caught on quickly. "That's right. Good."

When I put him on the stand, I had him read the whole report, and Mr. Mundhenk went straight to its bottom.

"You have an injury to the shoulder, an injury to the arm, an injury to the face, and you have athlete's foot. That has nothing to do with the injuries sustained in this instance!"

"It could."

"How could it?"

"When a person has tremendous pain in their shoulder they become nervous, they perspire and that could cause athlete's foot. We don't really think this is an injury that he should be paid for, but it could happen."

The jury broke up again.

My colleagues all told me that in the San Mateo County courts, if a plaintiff lost a leg or an arm, they could expect between $5,000 and $10,000, at the most. Several judges in San Mateo County had told me the same. One settlement judge even told me that in San Mateo County a black man would receive much less for their injuries than a caucasian, and I should keep that in mind.

We tried the case for ten days, and in my closing argument I asked for $100,000 for damages. Bacon and Mundhenk looked stunned, as if I had asked for the resignation of the President of the United States. Even the judge turned his back to the jury and looked out the window.

The jury was out for several hours. When they returned, they gave their verdict to the bailiff and the bailiff gave the verdict to Judge Scott. Judge Scott looked at the verdict, turned his back to the jury, gave the

12—SAN·MATEO TIMES
SATURDAY, APR. 21, 1951

$40,000 Award To S.F. Worker

(Times Redwood City Bureau)

REDWOOD CITY, April 21.—A jury yesterday awarded a $40,000 judgement to Amos Watkins, San Francisco jackhammer operator, who received injuries on a Mills field earth-moving project two years ago.

Defendants in the action were George Lewis and Paul C. Queen of the Lewis and Queen construction company.

While working on the drainage project, Watkins struck dynamite that exploded and tore away a portion of his shoulder. The four-day trial was heard by Superior Judge Edmund Scott.

———O———

verdict to the clerk, told her, "Record the verdict," and turned his face to the window again.

The clerk read the verdict in a low tone of voice. I couldn't hear exactly what she said, and I asked my client what the verdict was. He said he didn't know, he thought it was $4,000, so I went up to the clerk and asked her what the verdict was.

"$40,000."

The foreman of the jury came over.

"Mr. Cohn, I want to congratulate you. I think you did an excellent job in this case. I was trying to get you the $100,000, but, just between you and me, some of the jurors said, 'What is a black man going to do with $100,000? $40,000 is plenty.' And that's what we came in with."

I thanked him profusely for the verdict.

I was in amazement. Mundhenk looked stricken, and Bacon looked as if he had been hit in the head with a sledgehammer.

The judge excused the jury.

"I expect there will be some motions in this case."

Mr. Mundhenk assured them there would be.

When the news came out that there had been a verdict of $40,000 for a broken collarbone for a black man in San Mateo, I received a phone call.

"Nate, this is Mel."

"Mel?"

"Mel Belli."

"Oh, how are you Mr. Belli."

"I want to congratulate you. You're doing what lawyers should be doing, you're getting what we call adequate verdicts. I've been speaking for years about what I call the 'adequate verdict.' You have achieved an adequate verdict. I want to take you to lunch. You did a great thing for lawyers in Northern California.

The next week he did take me to lunch and invited me to become a member of the San Francisco Trial Lawyers Association, which he had organized. At that time the organization was by invitation only.

The next week, I received a motion for new trial on the grounds of excessive verdict from Bacon and Mundhenk and I received a motion for new trial on the grounds the evidence was insufficient to support the verdict.

When we appeared before Judge Scott he asked us to come into chambers.

"Gentlemen, I've given great thought to this. I'm going to reduce the verdict to $25,000, which I think is very high anyway. If the defendant agrees to pay it and the plaintiff agrees to accept it, the case is over. If the defendants do not agree to pay it, I'm going to let the $40,000 verdict stand, and I think the law and Mr. Cohn's presentation of the case indicate the verdict will not be overturned. If Mr. Cohn does not accept the $25,000 at this point, I'm going to grant a new trial and try it all over again."

They paid the $25,000, which was still, unfortunately, a record for such an injury in San Mateo County.

Belli and I became great friends as his reputation increased. In 1954, *Life* magazine dubbed him "The King of Torts."

Later, I became involved in a messy divorce case Mel had against one of his wives. He was first represented by another attorney in his office, Vasilios Choulos, but after a hearing in Judge Clayton Horn's courtroom erupted into name-calling, Judge Horn advised Belli to hire another lawyer and to come back.

A couple of days later, Mel called me and asked me if I would have lunch with him. I suggested we meet at Vanessi's.

There, Mel told me about the commotion at the hearing before Judge Horn, who wanted another lawyer who did not work for Mel, and he asked me if I would represent him. I said that there was only one way I would represent him.

"You're a friend of mine. I like you very much, but, if I represent you, you have to understand that I run the case."

"Do you mind if I give you suggestions?"

"No, but, remember, I will make all decisions and I will do everything exactly as I feel it should be done, and if we get to the point that you do not agree with me, I will withdraw and you will have to hire another lawyer."

"I want you to represent me. That will be acceptable."

We next had to appear in court before Judge Horn on an order to

Three or four months later, I ran into Joe in City Hall in San Francisco. He was a defense lawyer and was defending cases for the city. The members of NACCA were plaintiff's lawyers. In fact, I didn't know of any other defense lawyers who were members of NACCA, so I thought I'd ask him.

"Joe, how long have you been a member of NACCA?"

"I've never been a member of NACCA."

⊢——·——⊣

During the convention I was attending the main dinner one night, and sitting next to me was a very pretty young lady, Dacia. I asked her if it would bother her if I smoked a cigar.

"No, I like cigars. I smoke them myself."

She told me that her husband was a young lawyer who had come to the convention because he had just become a lawyer and wanted to participate.

"Would you like a cigar?"

"I would love a cigar. Can we smoke?"

"Of course you can. You're with me and you're at our table."

I gave her the cigar, and she put it in her purse.

"No, no, no. You've got to smoke the cigar here or give it back."

"Can I?"

"Absolutely."

We lit our cigars and enjoyed them together.

The next morning, I had to appear at a seminar in our hotel in Miami Beach. Everyone was happy with my speech. When I left the stage, I wanted to get out of the hall but it was early in the morning. I couldn't walk out because other people would be speaking after me and it would be impolite. I spied a section where there were only a few people, and I sat down there, pulled out a cigar and started smoking.

Within three minutes, the very beautiful lady I had met the previous evening came and sat next to me. I gave her a cigar, she unwrapped the cigar, clipped the end and sat there, smoking the cigar. Within five minutes practically every eye was on this corner of the room, rather than on the speaker on the stage, watching us smoking cigars.

She was a sweet girl and had a fine husband. I'm sure he turned out to be an excellent lawyer.

—·—

Before the convention, NACCA had advertised that there would be a tour to Havana, Cuba after the convention. We all thought of going to Cuba, but I had been to Cuba a year or so before when Batista was in charge. I was so upset by the way people were practically slaves that I did not want to go back.

Then we read in the newspapers that there was fighting in the streets of Havana and that Fidel Castro had taken over.

There was a booth in the hotel where we were staying that had a sign up: "Tour to Havana." That raised my interest because no one was planning to go. Everyone felt the same way. They had read that there was fighting going on. Who was going to take a chance of going down to Cuba when there was a war going on?

I went over to the booth and saw a well-dressed gentleman behind the counter wearing a Masonic pin.

"Let me ask you a question. What are you doing here?"

"We're setting up a tour."

"Anybody going?

"Nobody wants to go. I don't understand it."

"Well, you understand, we read in the paper that it isn't safe to go over there."

"You are safer there than you are in Miami. I guarantee you!"

"Look, you're a Mason and I'm a Mason. You can't lie to me. Tell me the truth."

"I guarantee you. I am the manager of a hotel in Havana. Fidel Castro is a close friend of mine. The top three floors of my hotel are his head-quarters. You come to Havana and you will be as safe as you can be. You will be treated as you have never been treated before. I will guarantee it."

I talked to some fifty or sixty lawyers, I told them this story, and we all decided to go to Havana.

We went to this gentleman's hotel in Havana and were assigned excellent rooms. In the lobby of the hotel were soldiers of the sort we saw in the cartoons, with green outfits, beards and scarves, and rifles.

The hotel manager explained to me what was going on. He told me that Castro had been to law school and had become a lawyer, but he saw the conditions for poor people in Cuba: they weren't getting medical attention, they weren't getting food, they weren't making any money. They were all being used. And he returned to Cuba to help them, and he did help them: he got rid of Batista.

He told me that Castro was trying to help the people of Cuba. Some of the people of Cuba worked in the fields and lived in adobe houses with no heat, no windows, no running water and no toilets. They ate poor food, just what they received from the company store—mostly rice—and were living in abject poverty.

He explained that what was happening down there was that many Americans and wealthy Cubans owned properties in Cuba and, rather than paying the government taxes on the value of what they owned, they signed declarations that the property was worth thirty, forty, fifty thousand dollars when it was worth millions. They paid taxes on tens of thousands when their property was worth millions and paid Batista some under the table, and the owners saved money.

Another group bought a bank with two million dollars, then loaned themselves three million dollars with no interest. They used that bank any way they wanted. He explained Castro took the banks over for the government so that the money that came into the banks for profit could be distributed to the people for medical attention.

Castro went to the Cubans who had property and had been cheating the government for years and told them he was taking over their property for the people. Castro was going to pay them the value of the property and determine the value of the property from the affidavits they had filed under penalty of perjury. They had kept all the money that they should have been paying in taxes.

The manager informed us he would give us a big cocktail party downstairs in the hotel, so I suggested to him: "Castro's a lawyer. There are some top lawyers here. This is an excellent opportunity for him to come down here and meet these lawyers and tell his side of the case, because, from what you are saying the United States is trying to protect a bunch of thieves, while refusing to do business with Castro because he's being harsh on thieves."

He explained: "Castro is going to need some income from big countries—either Russia or the United States. He wants to do business with the United States, but the people of the United States have been supporting these people who have been raping this country and using the people of this country and not paying them for their work.

"They are claiming that Castro is a communist because his brother went to Russia. Nixon went to Russia. No one said that he was a communist. The Mayor of San Francisco, George Christopher, went to Russia. No one said that he was a communist. But, if Castro's brother goes over there to see what they will offer us if we're not going to get anything from the United States, he's a communist. Castro wants to feed the people. He wants to provide the people with medical attention, to take care of them if they are sick, to give them enough to eat. He wants to do good for the country."

We went down to the cocktail party. There, I saw a lady there who worked for the hotel who was taking pictures. I asked her how many exposures she had left.

"Seven."

"What do you charge for a picture?"

"Five dollars, American."

"Here's fifty dollars. I'll tell you whose picture to take and I will buy all the pictures."

When I had been in Cuba before I had hired a driver with a limousine. His son was a doctor in Texas. I found him again and hired him to take me around. The manager arranged reservations for me, Fitzgerald Ames and Jack Werchick and our wives for dinner and to see a Vegas-type show outdoors on a big stage, with stadium-type seating.

At the cocktail party, the manager of the hotel supplied beautiful *hors d'oeuvres* and drinks. I kept waiting for Castro to come down, because we were going to take pictures with him, but Fitzgerald Ames became upset. "We've got reservations. I want to get my dinner. What the heck! We're going." I went over to a lawyer from Los Angeles who was a good friend, Ben Cohen—he looked like Adolph Menjou, with a little waxed mustache—and I took the girl with the camera over to him and explained to her I was giving my pictures to him.

"Take whatever pictures he wants," I instructed her. "He'll tell you what pictures to take." I explained to Ben she had already been paid, and that I had to go and did not want the pictures to go to waste.

When we arrived at the outdoor show, the manager had called over in advance, and we had excellent seats—they were back far enough that you could see the entire stage—and we had a great dinner.

Halfway through the show, all of a sudden the lights went on and the show stopped. We looked up the stadium side and from the top coming down was a man with a cigar in a green uniform, with a green cap. It was Fidel Castro. He had two aides with him, no gun, no pistol. No one had anything but cigars.

The entire audience stood up and applauded Castro. They went wild for him. When he sat down, they brought him brandy and he lit his cigar. Castro saw the show, and people were around him as their hero.

The next day we went to a cigar factory because I liked cigars. In this great factory there were many men and women sitting at little tables rolling cigars. On every table—there were hundreds of them— were two pictures. One was a picture of Jesus Christ and the other was a picture of Fidel Castro.

The guide who took us around told us that every day at lunch time all the employees in the whole country received an hour and a half to two hours off, and they have lunch and sit down and hear Fidel talk to all of them over the radio. He would explain to them what he was doing and why he was doing it. They loved him.

The driver of the limousine was also very helpful and he knew what was going on. I wanted to see the courthouse, so he went there, and a guide showed us the beautiful, brand new courthouse, the judges' chambers, the judges' bathrooms. When we were through, many Cuban lawyers who spoke English tried to tell us what was going on and we asked them questions.

Fitzgerald Ames asked, "How long is a judge in office?"

"He is in office for life."

"Has Castro appointed any judges?"

"Yes."

"If they are in office for life, how can you appoint any judges?"

"Fitz, he told you, they are only appointed for life."

Fitz started to catch on. He started to explain it to Jack Werchick and all the Cubans started listening to us. Everyone was breaking up.

I asked, "Do you have any female judges?"

"No."

"In every judge's bathroom there is a bidet. I thought a bidet was used by women."

All the Cuban lawyers looked at each other and started to laugh. One of the chuckled, "Never noticed it. Never paid any attention."

Finally, one of them explained, "When we put in a bathroom, a bidet is part of the bathroom. A bidet goes in automatically. No one paid any attention to the fact that we don't have any women judges."

That night we went to one of the nightclubs and we had a few drinks. I suggested to the rest of the lawyers with me, "Look, why don't we walk back to the hotel? It's not that far, only seven or eight blocks."

It was a beautiful night, and it was one o'clock in the morning. We walked down the south side of the street. On the north side of the street was a group of soldiers with an officer.

I had had a few drinks and became a little incensed that they seemed to be following us. I crossed the street and confronted the officer: "Why are you following us? We are just a group of Americans visiting Cuba. We thought Cuba was friendly."

"We have orders to protect you and to make sure that nothing happens to you. We're not watching you. We just wanted to make sure no one bothers you until you get back to your hotel."

Several days later, I was in a souvenir shop looking at souvenirs and in came a Cuban soldier, who seemed to be watching what I was doing.

"Why are you in here watching me?"

"I'm not watching you. We have orders to make sure that you're not cheated by any of the stores here."

I felt that was a good explanation.

While we were down there, we found that Castro's people were not antagonistic or angry toward the American people. In fact, they were very friendly.

I never met Castro and I never had my picture taken with Castro. Castro had joined the cocktail party at the hotel after I left and Ben Cohen got the pictures.

After I heard about the Bay of Pigs I was amazed how anyone could expect the Cubans to help the United States. In fact, it caused me to feel that the U.S. leaders needed help.

Lunches, Landsmen and Lawyers

42

As the reader may have noted, organizations have played a key role in my career and my life, and I have, as a result, founded several. One of those organizations is the American Board of Criminal Lawyers, which is now the premier organization for criminal trial lawyers.

The idea of the organization came to me in 1954. It occurred to me that there were many associations for trial attorneys, but none of them required actual trial experience in criminal jury cases and a specialty board was needed in the criminal field.

I used my own career as a gauge. I had been admitted to the bar for seven years and I had tried over fifty criminal jury cases and seven capital cases, so I decided those would be beginning requirements for membership, and I invited several distinguished criminal trial lawyers to lunch in a private room at Jack's Restaurant in San Francisco to propose the idea; among them Jake Ehrlich, Leo Friedman, Leslie Gillen, Jim MacInnis, Ben Davis, Andy Bodisco, Joe McNamara, Sol Abrams, Herman Mintz, Abe Dresow, William Ferdon and Joe Kennedy. There was unanimous support for the idea and Jake Ehrlich, Leo Friedman and Jim MacInnis proposed I proceed to form the organization and they would join and support the new Board of Criminal Lawyers.

However, my trial calendar did not permit it and the idea remained just an idea until a day some twenty years later. I was in a courtroom and a young lawyer asked me how to arraign his client. I explained the process to him. When I asked him what his client was charged with, I was shocked. He was representing a man on a murder charge and did not even know how to conduct an arraignment!

I recalled that in the past I had observed several other murder trials where the defendants were represented by attorneys with little or no criminal trial experience.

It was time to pick up where I had left off in 1954, and in 1978 I wrote to criminal attorneys throughout the United States whom I knew

The Three I's (l-r) San Francisco Mayor Joseph Alioto, Sailor's Union of the Pacific President, Morris Weisberger, Louis Lurie, Nate, Jack Goldberger, District Council President, International Brotherhood of Teamsters and George Reilly, President, California Board of Equalization, at a meeting of the Irish-Israeli-Italian Society in 1971.

to be competent, experienced criminal trial lawyers and invited them to a meeting at the Jack Tar Hotel in San Francisco.

Most of those I invited attended and at the meeting, all agreed that the organization was a great idea and those who qualified joined, officers were elected and I was selected the first president of the American Board of Criminal Lawyers.

The founding members of the American Board of Criminal Lawyers were Melvin Belli, Jack Berman, George T. Davis, James C. Hooley, Jerrold M. Ladar, James Lassart, James Martin MacInnis, Lincoln Mintz, Thomas F. Norman, Harriet Ross, George Walker, Daniel H. Weinstein, Dennis L. Woodman, Grant Cooper, Walter L. Gerash and William Raggio.

The conditions of membership were: ten years of practice as a criminal defense trial lawyer; fifty jury trials, of which 35 have been felony trials, including a minimum of five major felony trials wherein the penalty could have been death or life imprisonment tried to a judgment of acquittal or a verdict substantially less than charged; and the recommendation of three judges, at least one of whom shall have presided over one of those felony trials within the three years preceding the application, or by a unanimous vote of the Executive Committee of the organization.

We held our first convention in San Francisco and the organization continued to grow until it became a national bar association which certifies expert criminal trial lawyers, with over three hundred members.

$$\vdash\!\!-\!\!\cdot\!\!-\!\!\dashv$$

Another organization is the Irish-Israeli-Italian Society, a luncheon club that meets in San Francisco on the Wednesdays nearest Columbus Day, St. Patrick's Day and Israeli Independence Day. It all began when George Reilly of the California Board of Equalization was chosen Grand Marshal of the St. Patrick's Day Parade in San Francisco and asked me to serve with him as Deputy Grand Marshal.

George was also the most continuously elected man in the history of California and President of the California Board of Equalization. He was also perhaps the number one Irishman in the United States and he was president, at one time or another, of many Irish organizations, and a member of the Calamari Club.

The driver of our convertible Cadillac was none other than the alleged victim in the Cash or Clobber Collection Caper—Walter Barkett, who was not Irish, but Assyrian! Nowhere else but San Francisco would the Grand Marshal of the St. Patrick's Day parade be riding with a Jewish Deputy Grand Marshal and an Assyrian at the wheel.

There were no hard feelings between us over our earlier dust-up in court, and, as we started out, Walter took the opportunity to bend my ear again over his own personal dream. Walter wanted to rebuild King Solomon's Temple in Israel and wanted my help in raising funds for it.

As we drove up Montgomery Street toward Market Street, we heard cries of "Hey, George!" and "Hello, George!" I suggested to George that

Saint Patrick's Day. Grand Marshal of the San Francisco Saint Patrick's Day Parade, George Reilly, and Deputy Grand Marshal, Nathan Cohn, with Walter Barkett at the wheel.

perhaps he should run for Mayor of San Francisco again: people still seemed to love him.

But as we turned onto Market Street, the cries turned to "Hey, Nate!" and "Hello, Nate!" George suggested perhaps I should consider a mayoral bid instead.

Then Walter, who had been silent, piped up.

"George, Nate! It doesn't matter how many people like you. One person who doesn't like you can do you more damage than a thousand who like you do you good!"

An idea had begun to form in my mind. I noted to George the affinity of the Irish for the Jews and suggested that if the Irish and the Jews were to get together they could take over the world. I proposed that we form an organization of Irish and Israelis. I would invite my friends and George would invite his friends and we would all have lunch together at different restaurants in San Francisco. The organization would have two presidents, an Irish president and an Israeli president, and John Shimmon, George's administrative assistant, would be the Secretary. We held the first luncheon of the Irish-Israeli Society at Orestes Restaurant.

It was so successful that, not long after, Sam Yorty, Mayor of Los Angeles called me: "Can I come?" Thus, Sam was the guest speaker at the second Irish-Israeli Society luncheon, which we held at the Hilton Hotel.

Soon, we had to expand the society. Our Italian friends wanted to make it the "3 I's," and we became the Irish-Israeli-Italian Society, and chose as the Italian President, Charles Barca, Chief Inspector of the San Francisco Police.

Sam Yorty called to ask for a charter for a Los Angeles chapter of our organization. George and I flew down to Los Angeles to inaugurate the Los Angeles chapter. A man named Cohen, who was head of Grey Line, provided us a limousine to the Biltmore Hotel from the airport.

I brought with me Thad Spencer, a boxer I co-managed, who was a contender for the heavyweight crown and Steve Allen was the emcee.

When George Reilly retired, Mary Callanan, who had been San Francisco City Treasurer, replaced George and when Charles Barca retired, we selected Leonard Stefanelli to replace him.

The "3 I's" still meets three times a year, filling the dining room of the San Francisco Italian-American Athletic Club on Washington Square. If you are running for office, it is an obligatory appearance. It is open to men and women of all races and creeds, uniting them all in a drinking song.

———— • ————

Another organization that some people believe I started is the Landsmen, but in fact, although I was a founding member, the organization was not my idea, although the name was mine.

Over thirty years ago, Jeremy Ets-Hokin, Art Commissioner of the City of San Francisco and CEO of Ets-Hokin Construction invited me to a dinner at the World Trade Center where he had invited a group of men to meet, dine and socialize. Jerry would host the first dinner, and each invitee would, thereafter, host a dinner. Dress would be black tie, and I bought a tux.

The guests at that first dinner included Goodwin Knight, former

Governor of California; Jesse Unruh, Speaker of the Assembly; Ben
Swig, owner of the Fairmont Hotel; Louis Lurie; Jerry; Ed Zelinsky;
Mr. Murphy of Murphy Steel; Jake Ehrlich and Melvin Belli. We enjoyed
excellent food and unlimited potables and several of the guests spoke off
the record: a memorable evening.

At our second dinner, Mel bestowed upon us the name "Clansmen,"
intended as a take-off on Frank Sinatra and his "clan." However, after several dinners, I had the feeling that some of our minority guests and members were uncomfortable with the name "Clansmen" and I changed
"Clansmen" to "Landsmen"—a Jewish word meaning people from the
same vicinity. Our vicinity is now very large. Members travel from
Honolulu, Reno, Las Vegas, Los Angeles, Seattle, Chicago, Omaha, Miami,
New York, Atlanta, Newport Beach to attend the Landsmen dinners.

I threw the third dinner at Orestes and invited the original guests
and many of my friends. Jerry was so pleased with the event that he
asked me to take over scheduling of the dinners and their operation.
Dinners were then hosted by Ben Swig, Lou Lurie, Sy Farber, Mo
Bernstein, Hank James, Bob Nicholson, General Andrew Lolli, Judge
Fitzgerald Ames, Tommy Harris, Mayor John Shelley, Henri and Werner
Lewin, Jerry Flamm, Ivor Morris and many others, including a fabulous
trip, rooms and dinner at the Mapes Hotel in Reno hosted by Bill
Raggio and Hal Lipset.

New members were added each time a member hosted a dinner and
invited guests. Many of the guests also wished to host dinners, and, after
a few years, I realized that the dinners were becoming too expensive for
one person, so some of the dinners were hosted by two or three members. Finally, we converted the dinners to no-host affairs, with each
member paying for his guests and himself.

Hotels and restaurants provided fantastic dinners with drinks, *hors
d'oeuvres* and excellent food. Among the unforgettable dinners was a
"Tom Jones" dinner Don De Porter produced at the Hyatt Regency. The
dining room was set in an old English motif and the waiters and waitresses were costumed in old English dress. The tables were formed in a
"U" shape, and live sheep were penned in the center while live chickens
clucked in cages at the far end of the room. Everyone was given an
apron and a Bota bag filled with wine and we watched some of our most
distinguished guests eat with their fingers as an orchestra played through

dinner.

Joe Betz and his lovely wife who had just purchased a replica of a French mansion invited us to hold a dinner at their mansion. Judges Ira Brown, Daniel Hanlon and Phil Moscone became chefs and prepared a gourmet dinner to the delight of everyone who attended, from the fantastic *hors d'oeuvres* to the triumphant dessert.

Henri Lewin invited us to be his guests at the Sands in Las Vegas and provided beautiful rooms where we enjoyed a three-hour show and forty-two courses of food and unlimited drinks.

The Landsmen honor outstanding men at each dinner, including Supreme Court justices, Mayors, newsmen, Labor leaders, business leaders, political office holders, justices of the appellate courts, doctors, lawyers, educators and others who have made a contribution to our state and our county, but speeches have traditionally been restricted and take little time from our nutriment.

———•———

In recent years, one other organization has occupied my interest and earned my support, the National Coalition of Concerned Legal Professionals (CCLP).

I first ran into CCLP when a CCLP volunteer organizer contacted me asking for referrals for a case they were assisting in in New York. I am now a member of its National Board of Directors.

CCLP is an all-volunteer, non-government-funded association of attorneys, paralegals, court reporters and other legal professionals, as well as concerned community members, who have committed to fight for legal recourse for those who cannot afford it.

CCLP pays no salaries and has no big administrative budget. It does not seek publicity but has been doing a quiet job of addressing the needs of low-income people, who often cannot afford access to redress for their grievances. CCLP is dedicated to addressing the conditions of poverty at the root of so many problems we as lawyers meet in different forms as criminal or civil legal problems. CCLP works together with other voluntary, non-government-funded community-based organizations through independent chapters in Sacramento, Los Angeles and New York as well as San Francisco.

Leaving a Mark
on the Road

43

nother impact I had on California and the nation was that I found a way for the state to raise substantial sums of money in a manner that would not generate yet another state bureaucracy and which people would voluntarily pay. Many states have followed California's example.

It all began with Al Williams' Cadillac. Al Williams ran the Papagallo Room at the Fairmont Hotel, and was a client of mine. Al did a make-over on his Cadillac. Al also had his name inscribed on the side with raised metal lettering.

Al sold the car to Dean Jennings, who was a top magazine writer. The *Call-Bulletin* had hired him to write a column similar to Herb Caen's in the *Chronicle*. But after Dean had a disagreement with the *Call-Bulletin*, he left the paper and offered me the Cadillac for the same price he had paid Al.

I set about putting the car into first-class condition.

I removed Al Williams' name and had my name added in metal letters. Hank James recommended a painter and I told the painter to make it like new. However, after checking it over the painter called me and told me the car had 17 coats of paint on it already, and asked me for permission to sand-blast the car.

Finally, the job was done and Hank James and I drove it to the Civic Auditorium, but when we got out of the car we found our laps were covered with sand, as was the dashboard.

I called the painter the next day and he confessed that sand had gotten into the car—he didn't know how—but it had.

That spelled the end for Al's Cadillac. I took it to the Cadillac dealership at Stonestown to trade it in for a new Cadillac. I didn't think it was right to sell the Cadillac to anyone in its present condition.

I thought that was the end of Al's Caddy—until three weeks later, when a policeman in Richmond, California called me. He said he had seen a car with my name on it being driven by a another man, had my car been stolen? I laughed and told him it was okay.

But the incident gave me an idea. I wrote to Governor Pat Brown and sent a copy of the letter to the newspapers. In it, I argued as follows: the state issues license plates to drivers and charges them for the plates. The state could charge an extra fee for personalized license plates and people would not feel taxed to pay an extra charge if they wished to do so. The *Call-Bulletin* felt it was an excellent idea and published an editorial endorsing my idea. I called Milton Marks who introduced a bill to this effect in the Assembly, but it did not pass. I was puzzled and called Jesse Unruh.

"We don't pay much attention to Milton," Jesse laughed, "and we don't want to set up another state bureaucracy."

I explained that my proposal did not create any new bureau.

"You can just put lines on a sheet of paper. Someone who wants the personalized license plate can put the name they choose down and several other names they would like. If the first name is taken, the Department of Motor Vehicles can go down the list to the next name until they find one unclaimed. They state can charge $25 for printing the plate, and $10 a year to keep the name. That way, it costs the state nothing, and no bureaucracy is created."

Jess told me to have Milton submit the bill again and it would pass.

At the time, Pat Brown was running for reelection and Ronald Reagan was running against him. By the time the bill passed and Milton called me to let me know, Ronald Reagan was Governor of California. Milton asked me what I wanted on my license plate. "Nate," of course. And for my wife, I asked for her name, "Carolyn." Milton told me that had one too may letters—a license plate could only have six letters—so I settled for "C Cohn." These were the first two license plates issued under the bill that I inspired and Governor Reagan signed into law, and we have retained those license plates to this day.

When Nate Thurmond, the basketball star, wanted "Nate," and found I had already taken it, his became "Nate 42" (his number), which he placed on a Rolls-Royce Silver Cloud identical to mine. When I would go to events at hotels, I would leave my Rolls with the doorman, but when I returned, I would find napkins under the windshield wiper reading: "Nate, call me, Cheryl" and the like. I put them together in an envelope and mailed them to Nate Thurmond. It seemed the right thing to do.

At last count, I was informed that the State of California had made over $300 million from specialty license plates. I made nothing for myself and purchased my own plates. The program paid for itself handsomely, and no one has ever objected to the cost of having their own personalized mark on their car—like Al Williams and his unfortunate Cadillac—or maybe not so unfortunate in its second life in Richmond.

Nate's 1965 Rolls-Royce Silver Cloud 3 with the license plate, "Nate."

Epilogue

In my career I also learned several important lessons. The most important was the importance of luck—and timing. I decided I wanted to become an attorney when as a boy I saw another boy quickly exonerated by a skillful attorney exposing the lies of his accusers. I thought I could help people and enjoy myself, too, but the advice of a high school counselor discouraged me from becoming an attorney. It was many years before, by chance, I met a young District Attorney who encouraged me to do so. By circumstance, I ended up on the front page of the newspapers with one of my very first cases and I began winning cases, without even knowing what I was doing.

My father used to say, "You only live life once, but if you do it right, that's enough." I was lucky, and I wouldn't have had it any other way.

Nate, Jake Ehrlich and Melvin Belli, masters of the trial.

Nate's co-counsel, Bella.